$15.95

The UCSD Pascal Handbook

A Reference
and Guidebook
for Programmers

Randy Clark
Stephen Koehler

The UCSD Pascal Handbook

PRENTICE-HALL SOFTWARE SERIES
BRIAN W. KERNIGHAN, ADVISOR

The UCSD Pascal Handbook
A Reference and Guidebook
for Programmers

RANDY CLARK
STEPHEN KOEHLER

PRENTICE-HALL, INC., Englewood Cliffs, New Jersey 07632 .

Library of Congress Cataloging in Publication Data

Clark, Randy.
  The UCSD Pascal handbook.

  (Prentice-Hall software series)
  Bibliography: p.343
  Includes index.
    1. PASCAL (Computer program language)
  2. UCSD Pascal Software System (Computer
  system) I. Koehler, Stephen. II. Title.
  III. Title: U.C.S.D. Pascal handbook.
  IV. Series.
  QA76.73.P2C56   001.64'24   81-17795
  ISBN 0-13-935544-8   AACR2
  ISBN 0-13-935536-7 (pbk.)

Editorial/production supervision by *Linda Paskiet*
Cover design by Jorge Hernandez
Manufacturing buyer: *Gordon Osbourne*

UCSD PASCAL and UCSD p-System are all trademarks of the regents of the University of California. Use thereof in conjunction with any goods or services is authorized by specific license only and any unauthorized use is contrary to the laws of the State of California.

© 1982 by PRENTICE-HALL, INC.,
Englewood Cliffs, New Jersey 07632

Printed in the United States of America

10 9 8 7 6 5 4 3 2

ISBN 0-13-935544-8

ISBN 0-13-935536-7 {PBK}

PRENTICE-HALL INTERNATIONAL, INC., *London*
PRENTICE-HALL OF AUSTRALIA PTY. LIMITED, *Sydney*
PRENTICE-HALL OF CANADA, LTD., *Toronto*
PRENTICE-HALL OF INDIA PRIVATE LIMITED, *New Delhi*
PRENTICE-HALL OF JAPAN, INC., *Tokyo*
PRENTICE-HALL OF SOUTHEAST ASIA PTE. LTD., *Singapore*
WHITEHALL BOOKS LIMITED, *Wellington, New Zealand*

2179534

for Dick and Joan Conn

Table of Contents

Preface xiii

Introduction 1

   A Thumbnail History of Pascal 1
   Pascal at UCSD 2
   This Handbook 5

PART I   UCSD Pascal/A Definition

I.   A Synopsis 9
   1.   The Form of a Program 9
   2.   Declaration 10
   3.   Evaluation 11
   4.   Action 12
   5.   Communication 15
   6.   Modularity 15
   7.   Miscellany 16
   8.   Execution 17

II.   Lexical Conventions 19
   0.   Conventions of this Handbook 20
   0.1   EBNF 21
   1.   The Character Set 22
   2.   Symbols 23
   2.1   Special Symbols 23
   2.2   Reserved Words 24
   3.   Identifiers 25
   3.1   Definition 25
   3.2   Uniqueness 25
   3.3   Predeclared Identifiers 27
   4.   Comments 29
   5.   Token Boundaries 31
   6.   Indentation and Legibility 32

III.   Data Types and Operations 35
   1.   Introduction 36
   1.1   Constants, Variables, and Expressions 36
   1.2   Assignment 37
   1.3   Evaluating Expressions 38
   1.4   The Use of Data Types 39

2. Simple Data Types 40
2.1 Integer 41
2.1.1 Format 41
2.1.2 Comparisons 41
2.1.3 Operations 42
2.1.4 Routines 44
        abs 44
        sqr 45
2.2 Real 46
2.2.1 Format 46
2.2.2 Comparisons 47
2.2.3 Operations 47
2.2.4 Routines 48
        abs 49
        sqr 49
        sqrt 49
        sin 49
        cos 49
        arctan 49
        exp 50
        ln 50
        log 50
        pwroften 50
2.3 Long Integer 51
2.3.1 Format 51
2.3.2 Comparisons 51
2.3.3 Operations 51
2.3.4 Routines 52
2.4 Boolean 54
2.4.1 Format 54
2.4.2 Comparisons 54
2.4.3 Operations 54
2.4.4 Routines 55
2.5 Characters 56
2.5.1 Format 56
2.5.2 Comparisons 56
2.5.3 Operations 57
2.5.4 Routines 57
2.6 Special-Purpose Types 58

2.7	Type Conversions	59
2.7.1	Compatibility	59
2.7.2	Conversion Routines	59
	trunc	59
	round	60
	odd	60
	ord	60
	chr	60
	str	60
3.	Scalars and Subranges	61
3.1	Scalars	61
3.2	Subranges	62
3.3	Predeclared Scalar Types	63
3.4	Scalar and Subrange Routines	63
	ord	63
	pred	64
	succ	64
4.	Structured Types	65
4.1	Arrays	65
4.1.1	Format	66
4.1.2	Comparisons	67
4.1.3	Operations	67
4.1.4	Routines	68
	fillchar	68
	moveleft	69
	moveright	70
	scan	70
4.2	Strings	71
4.2.1	Format	71
4.2.2	Comparisons	72
4.2.3	Operations	72
4.2.4	Routines	72
	concat	72
	copy	73
	delete	74
	insert	74
	length	75
	pos	75
4.3	Sets	76
4.3.1	Format	76
4.3.2	Comparisons	77
4.3.3	Operations	77
4.3.4	Routines	78

4.4	Records	79
4.4.1	Format	79
4.4.2	Comparisons and Operations	81
4.4.3	Variant Records	81
4.4.4	The With Statement	82
5.	Dynamic Types	84
5.1	Files	84
5.1.1	Format	84
5.1.2	Standard File Handling	86
	eof	87
	eoln	87
	put	87
	get	88
	reset	88
	rewrite	89
5.2	Pointers	90
5.2.1	Format	90
5.2.2	Building Data Structures	91
5.2.3	Standard Memory Management	93
	new	93
	dispose	94
6.	Space Allocation for Data Types	95
6.1	Packed Data	95
6.2	Simple Types	97
6.2.1	Integer	97
6.2.2	Real	97
6.2.3	Long Integer	98
6.2.4	Boolean	98
6.2.5	Character	98
6.3	Scalars and Subranges	99
6.4	Structured Types	99
6.4.1	Arrays	99
6.4.2	Strings	99
6.4.3	Sets	99
6.4.4	Records	100
6.5	Dynamic Types	100
6.5.1	Files	100
6.5.2	Pointers	101
6.6	The Sizeof Intrinsic	101

IV. Overall Program Syntax 103

1. The Outline of a Program 103
1.1 Program Heading 104
1.2 Label Declarations 104
1.3 Constant Declarations 104
1.4 Type Declarations 105
1.5 Variable Declarations 106
1.6 Routine Declarations 106
1.7 The Main Body 107
2. Structure and Scope 107
2.1 Scope 107
3. Restrictions 109
3.1 Forward Declarations 109
3.2 Size Limits 110
3.3 Segment Routines 110
4. Units and Separate Compilation 111
4.1 The Uses Declaration 111
4.2 The Format of a Unit 112
4.2.1 Restrictions 113
4.2.2 Initialization and Termination Code 114
4.3 The Implementation of Units 115
4.3.1 Previous Versions 115

V. Procedures and Functions 117

1. Procedure and Function Declarations 117
1.1 Value Parameters 119
1.2 Variable Parameters 119
1.3 Procedures and Functions as Parameters 120
2. Calling Procedures and Functions 120

VI. Control Statements 123

1. Compound Statements 123
2. Conditional Statements 124
2.1 The If Statement 124
2.2 The Case Statement 125
3. Repetition 127
3.1 The While Statement 128
3.2 The Repeat Statement 129
3.3 The For Statement 130
4. Branching 131
4.1 The Goto Statement 131
4.2 The Procedure Exit 132
4.3 The Procedure Halt 133

VII. Input and Output 135
1. Standard Pascal I/O 135
1.1 Read and Readln 135
1.2 Write and Writeln 137
1.2.1 Field Specifications 138
1.3 Eof and Eoln 139
1.4 Page 139
2. Handling External Files 140
2.1 Opening and Closing Files 140
        reset 140
        rewrite 141
        close 142
2.2 Random Access to Files 142
        seek 143
2.3 Untyped Files 143
        blockread 143
        blockwrite 144
3. The UCSD p-System Environment 146
3.1 Keyboard 146
3.2 Device I/O 146
        unitbusy 147
        unitclear 147
        unitread 147
        unitstatus 148
        unitwait 149
        unitwrite 149
3.3 The Time Procedure 150
3.4 Ioresult 151
3.5 Screen I/O 152
        gotoxy 152

VIII. Memory Management 153
1. The p-System Runtime Environment 153
2. Segmentation 154
2.1 Code Segments 154
2.2 Controlling Segment Residence 155
        memlock 155
        memswap 155
3. Free Space 156
        memavail 156
        varavail 156
4. Free Space on the Heap 157
        varnew 157
        vardispose 158
        mark 158
        release 158

IX. **Concurrency** 159
   1. Concurrent Execution 159
   2. Processes 159
   3. Initiating a Process 161
        start 161
   4. Process Synchronization 162
   4.1 Semaphores 162
        seminit 163
   4.2 Signal and Wait 163
   4.3 Interrupts 163
        attach 163

X. **Compilation** 165
   1. Compiler Options 165
   1.1 Stack Options 165
   1.2 Switch Options 166
   1.3 String Options 168
   1.4 Conditional Compilation 170
   2. External Routines 172

PART II   **UCSD Pascal/A Guide for Programmers**

0. **Introduction** 175

1. **Bootstrapping the Programmer** 177
   Program 1: Factorials 177
   Program 2: Prime Factors 184
   Program 3: Pascal's Triangle 189
   Program 4: Palindromes (procedure) 195
   Program 5: Palindromes (function) 198
   Program 6: Roman Numerals 204

2. **Data and Expressions** 209
   Program 7: Long Integer Factorials 215
   Program 8: Quadratic Equation 217
   Program 9: Uppercase Translation 220
   Program 10: Matrix Multiplication 224
   Program 11: Integer/String Conversion 227
   Program 12: Pos Function 229
   Program 13: Uppercase (with sets) 231
   Program 14: Command Prompts 232
   Program 15: Date Increment 235
   Program 16: Symbol Table Routines 239

3. Flow of Control 243
   Program 17: Error Condition 244
   Program 18: Group Parser 245
   Program 19: Adaptive Quadrature 251

4. Input and Output 255
   Program 20: Lowercase Filter 257
   Program 21: Linear Regression 260
   Program 22: Print Queue 262
   Program 23: File Compare 278
   Program 24: Booter 280

5. Concurrency 283
   Program 25: Nim (coroutines) 286
   Program 26: Clock Interrupts 291

6. Units and Separate Compilation 293
   Program 27: Stack Operators 294

7. Memory Management 297
   Program 28: Variable-size Data Buffer 299

8. Advanced Techniques 301
   Program 29: Decimal to Hex Conversion 303
   Program 30: Memory-mapped Screen Unit 304

Appendices
   A. Lexical Standards 309
   B. Pascal Syntax 315
      1. Comparisons 315
      2. Operations 316
      3. Statements 317
      4. Railroad Diagrams 318
   C. Intrinsics 333
   D. Syntax Errors 337
   E. ASCII 341

Bibliography 343

Index 347

Preface

Before adding another book to the plethora of books about Pascal, we had to convince ourselves that it was worth the effort, that we were not reinventing the wheel. In our own work, for a long time, both of us have needed a complete and unified description of UCSD Pascal. Until now, there has been none.

This book addresses virtually all users of UCSD Pascal -- from the programmer who would learn Pascal, and the beginner who needs a reference, to the expert.

We have not tried to teach programming. That would require a radically different organization. The motivations to write a UCSD Pascal reference were, to us at least, more immediate.

UCSD Pascal is a language we have enjoyed using. Its embodiment of the concepts of structured programming makes it simple and useful. We believe in well-structured program development, and our comments and advice will make that clear. But we have no interest in being doctrinaire; we don't want programmers to follow dogma; we want them to write correct and viable programs. Neither Pascal nor structured programming is a culmination of the programmer's art; in time we expect to see still more powerful developments. But it will be a very long time before the full potential of Pascal is explored, and the techniques of its use fully mastered.

With those attitudes in mind, we hope that the present volume will be a useful tool for many users, for many years.

We are glad to be able to offer our thanks to a large number of people:

Al Irvine, for instigating the project and providing the environment for its completion;

All those who reviewed the manuscript, or portions of it: Gail and Paul Anderson, Winsor Brown, Rich Gleaves, Rick Grunsky, Sharon Koehler, Tom Marrs, Mark Overgaard, David Reisner, and Dale Sevier;

Niklaus Wirth, for starting it all; Roger Sumner, for his contributions to UCSD Pascal; and the community of Pascal users "without whom all of this would not have been necessary;"

Finally, all of those people who have offered friendship and encouragement. Most will be as pleased to see this book in print as the authors themselves!

DAUGHTER: Daddy, why do things get in a muddle?
FATHER: What do you mean? Things? Muddle?
DAUGHTER: Well, people spend a lot of time tidying things, but they never seem to spend time muddling them. Things just seem to get in a muddle by themselves. And then people have to tidy them up again.

Gregory Bateson
in Steps to an Ecology of Mind

The UCSD Pascal Handbook

Introduction

A Thumbnail History of Pascal

What is now called "structured programming" is a rather loose working philosophy, or set of principles, that concern the art of writing computer programs, particularly large computer programs. It grew out of academic discussions that took place for the most part in Europe in the late nineteen-sixties, and has become increasingly popular over the years, first in the universities, and now in the business world as well.

One of the tangible fruits of this debate is the book Structured Programming by Ole-Johan Dahl, Edsger W. Dijkstra, and C.A.R. Hoare (6). It is the original statement of this philosophy. Another tangible result is the programming language Pascal.

Pascal was designed by Professor Niklaus Wirth in the late sixties, finally implemented in 1970, and first described in his monograph, The Programming Language PASCAL (16), which appeared in 1971.

Structured programming has two major principles. The first is that a computer program is best conceptualized as a set of actions upon a set of data; the structure of the data determines the structure of the program. The second is that the programmer should use only those algorithmic constructs that are easily understood and easily analyzed.

A further tenet was introduced by Wirth in his 1971 article, "Program Development by Stepwise Refinement" (17). Stepwise refinement is a scheme for writing an algorithm by broadly sketching its outline, then filling in successive levels of detail in independent steps. In current computer jargon, stepwise refinement is a top-down approach.

In the view of structured programming, the larger the program, the more important it is that these principles be followed.

The language Pascal was intended to embody these principles. A Pascal programmer can write structured code easily: far more easily than by using the other languages that were current when Pascal was first introduced.

1

The algorithmic portion of Pascal is essentially a clean dialect of ALGOL 60. The data-description portion of the language is especially rich, and implements the ideas about data structuring expounded by C.A.R. Hoare.

Pascal was also intended as a teaching tool. In its cleanness, it was meant to make life easier for teacher and student alike. It was also meant to cultivate structured programming habits in beginning programmers.

Finally, Pascal was meant to be implemented as soon as possible, on as many different processors as possible. That is one of the reasons that it followed the model of ALGOL.

With what is now a ten-year perspective, it is apparent that Pascal became popular, and continues to grow in popularity, because it was so successful in combining all of its goals. Pascal has helped spread structured programming, and visa versa.

Pascal's significance for the future is essentially its significance in the past: an alternative to inconvenient and unsystematic programming languages.

Pascal at UCSD

In 1973 and 1974, at the University of California, San Diego, a growing interest in Pascal resulted in some early implementation work. Pascal appeared as a very natural step, since structured programming was already a popular concept on the campus (where Burroughs' ALGOL was the predominant language for systems work), and since a revision of the computer science curriculum was being planned.

In particular, the introductory programming class was to be changed. This class was the one beginning course in programming, regardless of the student's long-term intentions. The students were therefore an assemblage of (in roughly decreasing order of quantity): various engineering majors, psychology majors, computer science majors, majors in physical, biological, and social sciences.

2

As taught before the '75-'76 school year, this course followed the traditional lecture format. Structured programming was touched on, but the programs which students were required to learn and write were relatively short and simple. Many were numeric, and many more were pedantic examples with little or no relation to larger problems. In short, the course prepared students to write fairly short applications programs for problems which they were familiar with, or had been specifically taught about.

This approach was deemed undesirable in two major ways. The numerical problems presented an additional (and irrelevant) stumbling block for students with insufficient preparation in mathematics. The lack of preparation for building larger, more complicated programs was a loss to all students, and especially unfair to computer science majors.

Because of these considerations, the course was changed. The lecture format was dropped in favor of a self-paced ("Keller plan") format to accommodate the growing number of students. The introductory examples and assignments completely avoided numerical problems. The course emphasized program structure, the hierarchy of stepwise refinement, and the building-block approach to constructing large programs. Finally, the language used was Pascal.

At UCSD, Pascal was first implemented on the school's Burroughs B6700 computer. The batch environment of this machine was less than ideal, especially for students never before exposed to computers, and so Pascal was implemented again, this time on a PDP-11. After a term using the Burroughs, the introductory course began to employ ten PDP-11/10's. This was the start of a succession of implementations on dedicated computers, most of them small microprocessor systems.

The move to independent small systems caused the development of the "UCSD Pascal System," with its operating system, screen editor, filehandler, and other support programs.

This brief history motivates many of the aspects of UCSD Pascal that differ from the original definition by Niklaus Wirth. The type string and its associated intrinsic routines were introduced in order to avoid using numerical examples. Some of the variants in input/output handling were introduced to better suit the single-user, interactive environment. Later,

segments were introduced to adapt to the severe memory constraints of these mini and microcomputers. **units** provided a means of packaging code in a modular fashion, so that application libraries could be built. Last of all, but possibly most far-reaching in importance, the implementation of Pascal and its system was geared to portability, so the same software could run on machines with different processors and different peripherals.

The first compiler at UCSD was modeled after the compiler by Urs Ammann of the Eidgenossische Technische Hochshule in Zurich. This compiler generates code for an abstract machine. That machine can be either physically constructed, or (more frequently) emulated by an interpreter running on some other host processor. This strategy, coupled with standardized input/output in the Pascal System, is what made the system so easily transportable (p-System portability is described in Mark Overgaard's paper, "UCSD Pascal: A Portable Software Environment for Small Computers" (13)). The "P-code" generated by the UCSD compilers was substantially different from the original Zurich implementation.

Professor Kenneth Bowles sponsored the development of Pascal at UCSD, designed and taught the introductory computing course, and directed the Pascal Project for as long as it remained at the University.

UCSD Pascal is still popular as a teaching tool. It is used around the world, in a variety of versions, and it has been adopted for many applications that were not even envisioned when Pascal was first written.

This Handbook

We have attempted to describe UCSD Pascal in the greatest feasible detail. Our base language is the CURRENT state of UCSD Pascal (SofTech Microsystems' Version IV.0), but we have also tried to cover previous versions. On occasion, we describe aspects of the language that are specific to a particular processor.

The first part of this book is written as a definition of the language. After an overview of UCSD Pascal for those not already familiar with it, we take a bottom-up approach, starting with lexical details, then data types, then syntax and statements and more advanced topics. This seems the most straightforward way to describe any language. It follows, in very broad outline, the descriptions of Pascal written by Niklaus Wirth: we have found no reason to alter his approach. The wealth of data types is Pascal's most salient feature, also its most subtle; it should be presented as soon as possible.

The definition is intended to be a reference for programmers, and not a tool for compiler writers. There are already more rigorous sources for more technically oriented readers; please refer to the Bibliography.

The second part of this book is less formal. With the aid of examples, we have attempted to teach UCSD Pascal to a reader with programming experience, but no knowledge of any Pascal dialect. It should be useful to any readers with MORE knowledge than this minimum, but by no means is it intended as a course for beginning programmers. It takes a rather conversational, problem-solving approach to the presentation of the language. Since we have assumed a variety of readers, and tried to cover as much of the language as we could, our examples include both numerical and non-numerical problems. Not all of our examples are immediately practical programs, but all of them attempt to illustrate practical techniques.

The sample programs in the second part of the book are printed from program source that was actually run and tested, so to the best of our knowledge, they are correct.

UCSD Pascal, in virtually all of its incarnations, is embedded in the Pascal System (now also called the "p-System"), and some of its features (such as separate compilation and concurrency) depend on that operating environment. We have described these features as they must be used, and so to some extent have described the p-System, but this book remains focused on the language itself. The UCSD p-System Users' Manual (3), published by SofTech Microsystems, remains the source and reference for information on aspects of the system other than the UCSD Pascal language.

Tutorials on the Filer, Editor, and UCSD Pascal itself may be found in Bowles' Beginner's Guide for the UCSD Pascal System (2). Despite its title, more experienced users may also find it useful.

PART I

UCSD Pascal
A Definition

Chapter I
A Synopsis

This chapter is an overview of Pascal for readers who are not already familiar with the language. Those who have used UCSD Pascal before may skip it. Those who have used only other languages, or other dialects of Pascal, should read it in order to get a feel for the language and the UCSD implementation.

A Pascal program is relatively formal, when compared with such other languages as BASIC, FORTRAN, or PL/I. Pascal's restrictions require the programmer to be more disciplined, but the advantages include:

syntax that is easily understood,

implicit error-checking during compilation and runtime,

freedom to concentrate on the algorithm
rather than tricks of the language,

modularity of the program's structure,

readability.

All of these things tend to make a program less error-prone and easier to maintain. Correctness and maintainability are the goals of structured programming, and Pascal was designed to promote such a style.

This chapter is informal, and is meant to convey the "flavor" of a Pascal program without going into details. What we describe here should give you an idea of what to expect in the chapters that follow.

I.1   The Form of a Program

The text of a Pascal program begins with a heading, which is followed by an optional sequence of declarations, then by a list of statements enclosed in the words **begin** and **end,** and ends with a period.

Here is a trivially simple program:

9

```pascal
program FirstOne;

begin
    writeln('Hello, out there!');
end.
```

I.2   Declaration

All data in a Pascal program has a given 'type'.

Some types are part of the language (they are said to be "predeclared"). There are the numeric types integer, real, and long integer. There is the logical type Boolean, and the character type char. Sequences of characters may be represented by the type string.

These are constants of various types:

1523	{integer}
3.14159	{real}
'G'	{char}
'Hello, out there!'	{string}

Constants may be given symbolic names ('identifiers'):

```pascal
const
    year = 1523;
    pi = 3.14159;
    initial = 'G';
    message = 'Hello, out there!';
```

In a Pascal program, all variables must be declared. The type of a variable never changes:

```pascal
var
    yr_date: integer;
    factor: real;
    letter: char;
    greeting: string;
```

(The type of a variable in Pascal is much stricter than in some other languages (e.g., FORTRAN, PL/I). For a program to compile successfully, variables must be treated according to the rules for their type.)

The programmer may define new scalar types. A scalar is a finite sequence of values with symbolic names:

var   WeekDay: (Sun, Mon, Tue, Wed, Thu, Fri, Sat);

Subranges of scalars are also available:

WorkDay: Mon .. Fri;   {subrange of WeekDay}
rating: 1..10;   {subrange of <u>integer</u>}

In addition to the simple types, scalars, and subranges, Pascal provides the structured types **array, record,** and **set.** An **array** is a table of values (all of one type) grouped under a single name. A **record** is a group of values, possibly of different types. A **set** is a collection of values taken from a single base type.

Dynamic structures such as linked lists and search trees can be created using 'pointers'. A pointer is a variable that points to another variable of a given type. The variable pointed to has no name: it is allocated or de-allocated as needed.

Finally, long sequences of values can be contained in a **file.** In UCSD Pascal, a **file** is associated with a physical entity such as a disk file or a peripheral device.

I.3   Evaluation

New values can be calculated by combining existing values in 'expressions'. The result of an expression is of a particular type. Various operands are defined for different types.

Numeric expressions and numeric operators follow common algebraic conventions:

```
a + b + c
1.5 * ((i-1) * 2)
1 + 2 - 3 * 4
```

Relational operators may be used. Expressions with relational operators return a result of type <u>Boolean</u>:

```
date = today
date <> yesterday   {<> means "not equals"}
profit > 10000
```

Pascal also provides some intrinsic functions, which may appear in expressions:

pi * sqr(radius)
sqrt(sqr(b) - 4*a*c)

odd(factor)   {a Boolean function}

Functions may also be defined by the user.

To initialize a variable or change its value, an assignment may be used. The symbol for assignment is ':='. For example,

is_odd:= odd(factor);
area:= width * height;
round_area := pi*sqr(radius);

Each of these lines is called an 'assignment statement'. The semicolon (';') is used to separate statements, as shown.

I.4   Action

In general, statements in Pascal are executed starting with the first statement in the main program, and proceeding through until the end. Flow-of-control statements may be used to vary the order in which statements are executed by providing for decisions and repetition. Functions and procedures may be used to break the program into intelligible portions and improve its organization.

The **if** statement is used for a simple two-way (true/false) decision:

if profit > 10000 **then**
    plan_party;

if profit > 10000 **then**
    plan_party
else
    call_meeting;

The **case** statement is used for multiple-way decisions:

```
case month of
    Apr, Jun, Sep, Nov: days:= 30;
    Jan, Mar, May, Jul, Aug, Oct, Dec: days:= 31;
    Feb: if leapyear then
            days:= 28
        else
            days:= 29;
end;
```

There are three loop constructs in Pascal. The **while** statement is the most general form:

```
while not_done do
    fix_it;
```

The **repeat** statement is like a **while,** but always executes at least once:

```
repeat
    fix_it
until fixed;
```

The **for** statement uses a control variable, and repeats a given number of times:

```
for i:= 1 to 10 do
    clear;
```

Pascal also includes ways to do branching as in BASIC or FORTRAN, but these are typically used only in emergency situations, if at all.

A **procedure** is a self-contained portion of code. The form of a procedure is much like the form of a program:

```
procedure greet;

begin
    writeln('Hello, out there!');
end;
```

... and it is called by a statement that simply consists of the procedure's name:

    greet;

Parameters may be passed to a procedure when it is called:

    procedure area (height, width: <u>integer</u>; **var** result: <u>integer</u>);
        begin
            result:= height * width;
        end;

This could be called by a statement such as:

    area(12, 5, rectangle);

In this example, width and height are 'value' parameters, while result is a 'variable' parameter. In the code that calls the procedure, value parameters are unaffected, while variable parameters may be changed by the procedure (in the example, 'rectangle' will be set to the area that the procedure calculates).

A **function** is much like a procedure, except that it returns a result:

    function area(height, width: <u>integer</u>): <u>integer</u>;
        begin
            area:= height * width;
        end;

As we have seen, a function is called by using it in an expression:

    rectangle:= area(12, 5);

... or:

    if area(new_height, new_width) <> 0 **then** print_result;

Pascal allows recursion. A procedure or function may call itself. Some algorithms are much more elegant when expressed recursively; Pascal can implement them directly.

I.5 Communication

Simple (character) I/O is accomplished with the intrinsic procedures read, readln, write, and writeln. The intrinsic Boolean functions eof (end of file) and eoln (end of line) are provided for control.

If no other file is specified, these I/O intrinsics refer to the standard files input and output. In UCSD Pascal, input and output are both equivalent to the System's console.

File (record) I/O uses read, write, eof, put, and get. In UCSD Pascal, a file used within a program may refer to a System disk file or a peripheral I/O device. Random access is available with the intrinsic seek.

UCSD Pascal allows devices to be controlled directly (and swiftly) by a number of intrinsics including unitread and unitwrite.

Also in UCSD Pascal, a file may be declared without a type and manipulated by the intrinsics blockread and blockwrite. These are mainly used to transfer large portions of data swiftly.

I.6 Modularity

Code which is to be used by more than one program may be separately compiled. Such a code package is called a **unit**. A **unit** consists of an **interface** part, an **implementation** part, and optional initialization/termination code (**unit**s are a UCSD Pascal extension).

An **interface** part contains declarations, and procedure or function headings. These may be used by the program (or other unit) that **uses** the unit.

An **implementation** part contains other declarations, and the code for the procedures and functions that were declared in the **interface** part. All of this information is strictly private to the unit.

It is possible to change the **implementation** part of a **unit** (to improve an algorithm, for example) and recompile it. If the **interface** part has NOT been changed, programs and units that use the unit may continue to do so: there is no need for them to be recompiled as well.

More than one unit may be grouped together in a single codefile (often called a library). This can be useful, but is outside the scope of this book. Library handling is discussed in the UCSD p-System Users' Manual(3).

Units can also be useful for "breaking up" a program that is too long to compile in one piece.

I.7 Miscellany

This section describes some capabilities that pertain only to UCSD Pascal.

A procedure or function can be declared a **segment** procedure or function, in which case the System can swap it independently of the main program. This can be useful when running large programs that occupy a lot of space at execution time.

Concurrency is available in later versions of the p-System. A portion of code that runs concurrently is called a **process**. A **process** looks like a procedure. It is not called, but an instance of it is set into execution by a call to the intrinsic start. Processes may be co-ordinated by the intrinsics signal and wait. They are especially useful for I/O and interrupt handling.

It is possible to write a procedure or function in assembly language, and call it from a Pascal program. This is done by declaring it **external**. The assembly language ("native code") routine is responsible for conforming to Pascal's calling conventions. Such internal information is outside the scope of this Handbook.

Finally, there are a number of "compiler options" that allow:

control of the compiled listing,
control of the Compiler's output,
insertion of a copyright notice,
conditional compilation,
turning I/O checking off/on,
turning range checking off/on,
specifying a library,
control of include files

I.8   Execution

After a UCSD Pascal program has been compiled, it is run on the p-System by using the R(un or eX(ecute commands.

While a program is running, a number of things may cause what is called a "runtime error."   A runtime error may be caused by a bug in the program, or by a mistake made by the person operating the program.   When a runtime error occurs, the System aborts the program and displays a message on the console that looks something like this:

Divide by zero
Segment TEST   Proc# 1   Offset# 6
Type <space> to continue

If the program is at fault, it must be fixed.   If the program's operator is at fault, the program can (usually) be started again by the U(ser-restart command.

Descriptions of the p-System commands and the full list of possible runtime errors may be found in the UCSD p-System Users' Manual(3).   In this Handbook we indicate situations that will cause runtime errors, but the reader should be aware that the text and format of such messages are subject to change.

Chapter II
Lexical Conventions

A UCSD Pascal source program is essentially a stream of characters contained in a text file. For the program to compile successfully, it must conform to both the lexical standards of the language, and the syntactic (grammatical) rules. This chapter describes lexical standards. These cover the legal character set, the formation of identifiers, the set of symbols and reserved words, the formation of comments, and a few other topics.

The term "token" is a compiler-writer's term that refers to a single symbol or name in the source program: a special-character symbol, a reserved word, a constant, or an identifier. Since it is a useful general-purpose word, it appears here and there in this chapter.

For a description of textfiles as they are maintained in the UCSD p-System, please refer to the UCSD p-System Users' Manual(3).

II.0 Conventions of this Handbook

We have used few conventions throughout this book. The intent has been to clarify our topics, not obscure them. In some cases, we use a form of EBNF (Extended Backus-Naur Form). This will already be familiar to many readers. A description of EBNF appears at the end of this section.

A concise description of Pascal syntax in the form of railroad diagrams may be found in Appendix B.4.

In our examples of Pascal source (and elsewhere), reserved words are printed in **boldface,** and predeclared identifiers are underlined. This is to stress the difference between reserved, predeclared, and user-created identifiers; we realize that few users are capable of creating listings with more than one typeface.

Since UCSD Pascal is a particular dialect of the language, we have attempted to indicate where it differs from standard Pascal. When we say "standard Pascal," we are referring to those features of Pascal that are common to both the Jensen & Wirth definition (10), and the current American National Standards Institute (ANSI) draft standard (1). Where these two sources differ from each other, we have attempted to state that explicitly. As of this writing, the International Standards Organization (ISO) has a draft standard that is very similar to the ANSI draft.

When we describe a subrange, we shorten the conventional ellipsis (...) to '..', as in the Pascal language itself. In other words, 1..6 represents the digits (or integers) one through six, as 1...6 would indicate in common mathematical notation. The reason the book uses this notation is that Pascal does.

We have tried to keep the use of quote marks to a minimum. The usage in the book in general is illustrated by the usage in the preceding paragraph.

In informal descriptions of syntax (and NOT in Pascal programs themselves), words enclosed in angle brackets (< >) are names of things; usually they represent non-printing characters such as <return> and <esc>.

On some machines (such as the IBM Personal Computer) the return key is called <enter>.

II.0.1   EBNF

As we use it in this book, an EBNF expression is a description of some portion of Pascal syntax.   Here is an example:

```
assignment-statement =
    variable-name ":=" expression
```

The expression consists of the name of some syntactic object, followed by an equals sign, followed by a description of the object.

Within the description, anything in quotes must appear literally in the Pascal program.   A name that is NOT in quotes is the name of a syntactic object that is described elsewhere.   Square brackets ([ ]) surround portions of syntax that are optional, and curly brackets ({ }) surround portions of syntax that may appear zero or more times.   A vertical bar (|) separates different options, for example:

```
digit = "0" | "1" | "2" | "3" | "4" | "5" | "6" | "7" | "8" | "9"
```

Here is a slightly more complicated example:

```
repeat-statement =
    "repeat"
        [ statement {";" statement} ]
    "until" Boolean-expression
```

This EBNF expression tells us that a repeat statement consists of the reserved word **repeat,** followed by an optional statement list, followed by the reserved word **until,** followed by a Boolean expression.   The statement list itself consists of a single statement followed by zero or more instances of a semicolon preceding another statement.

Note that this expression does not define the terms 'statement' or 'Boolean-expression': they are defined elsewhere.

In this Handbook, we use EBNF to clarify the more confusing parts of Pascal syntax, especially those that involve recursive structures.   Since we have not attempted to construct a full axiomatic description of Pascal, we do not provide EBNF descriptions of those objects that appear in our EBNF descriptions but are self-explanatory.

II.1 The Character Set

UCSD Pascal source files may contain the letters A..Z, a..z, the digits 0..9, and the following special characters:

( ) [ ] { } + - * / < = > : ; . , ' ^

The underscore (_) may appear in identifiers.

The following characters may appear (along with all other printable characters) in comments or strings, but have no particular meaning:

! @ # $ % & ? | ` ~ \ "

Blanks (' ') and carriage returns (<return>) may also be present. They serve to delimit identifiers, and format the file in a legible way.

Virtually all current implementations of UCSD Pascal use ASCII (the American Standard Code for Information Interchange) to represent these characters.   The ASCII code is shown in Appendix E.

II.2   Symbols

A source program may contain symbols that are part of the Pascal language (special symbols and "reserved words"), identifiers that have been declared within the System ("predeclared identifiers"), identifers that the user has defined, and literal text (contained within comments or strings).

Symbols that are already part of the Pascal language may be divided into special symbols of one or two characters, and reserved words.

II.2.1   Special Symbols

These are the one-character symbols:

. , ; : ´ ( ) [ ] { } + - * / = < > ^

These are the two-character symbols:

:=   ..   <=   <>   >=   (*   *)

The symbol *** may appear within the code portion of a **unit**. This is not part of standard Pascal.

II.2.2 Reserved Words

Reserved words, like special symbols, are used in Pascal to represent syntactic constructs such as particular kinds of declarations, particular forms of statements, and groupings of statements.

These are the reserved words in UCSD Pascal (an asterisk indicates reserved words that are NOT part of standard Pascal):

and	goto	record
array		repeat
	if	
begin	*implementation	*segment
	in	*separate
case	*interface	set
const		
	label	then
div		to
do	mod	type
downto		
	not	*unit
else		until
end	of	*uses
*external	or	
		var
file	packed	
for	procedure	while
forward	*process	with
function	program	

Note the absence of **nil.** In UCSD Pascal it is predeclared rather than reserved.

II.3 Identifiers

Identifiers are used to represent constants, types, variables, and routines (procedures, functions, and processes). Some identifiers are predeclared, that is, they represent constants, types, or routines (but never variables) that the System has already defined.

II.3.1 Definition

An identifier consists of a letter, followed by an indefinite number of letters or digits. Single-letter identifiers are legal, and either upper or lower case, or a mixture of both, may be used.

Identifiers may also contain the underscore character ( ), but it is not significant (the purpose of allowing it is to make an identifier more legible).

An identifier may not be the same as a reserved word. An identifier MAY be the same as another predeclared identifier (this can lead to problems; see Chapter IV, Section 2.1 on the scope of identifiers).

These are legal identifiers:

    i   Parity   try13   c2unit78   c2_unit_78

These are NOT legal identifiers:

    4tran   {begins with a number}
    c2.unit.78   {contains special characters}
    try 13   {contains a space}
    _Parity   {begins with an underscore}

II.3.2 Uniqueness

Upper and lower case are not distinct.

These identifiers are equivalent:

    moss   MOSS   Moss   MosS

Only the first EIGHT characters of an identifier determine its uniqueness.

These two identifiers are equivalent:

  lostinspace   lostinspectionitem

Embedded and trailing underscores (_) are ignored.

These identifiers are equivalent:

find_disk   finddisk   Find_Disk   f_ind_d_isk   finddisk_

The Jensen & Wirth definition of identifiers does not include the underscore character, but does specify 8-character uniqueness. Both the underscore and the 8-character stipulation conflict with the ANSI draft standard, which states that all characters of an identifier shall be significant.

II.3.3 Predeclared Identifiers

These are the predeclared identifiers in UCSD Pascal (an asterisk indicates identifiers not in standard Pascal):

abs	*halt	page
arctan		*pmachine
*atan	*idsearch	*pos
*attach	input	pred
	*insert	*processid
*blockread	integer	put
*blockwrite	*interactive	*pwroften
Boolean	*ioresult	
		read
char	*keyboard	readln
chr		real
*close	*length	*release
*concat	ln	reset
*copy	*log	rewrite
cos		round
	*mark	
*delete	maxint	*scan
dispose	*memavail	*seek
	*memlock	*semaphore
eof	*memswap	*seminit
eoln	*moveleft	*signal
*exit	*moveright	sin
exp		*sizeof
	new	sqr
false	nil	sqrt
*fillchar		*start
	odd	*str
get	ord	*string
*gotoxy	output	succ

```
 text
*time
*treesearch
 true
 trunc

*unitbusy
*unitclear
*unitread
*unitstatus
*unitwait
*unitwrite

*varavail
*vardispose
*varnew

*wait
 write
 writeln
```

Note the absence of the standard predeclared identifiers pack and unpack.

The routines idsearch, pmachine, and treesearch are for the System's use, and are not described in this Handbook. pmachine is described in the UCSD p-System Internal Architecture Guide(5).

II.4 Comments

A comment is a passage of text that is ignored by the Pascal compiler. The purpose is to allow the programmer to explain the actions of the program in a language other than Pascal.

Comments may appear virtually anywhere in a source program. Like spaces or carriage returns, they delimit tokens, and so must appear BETWEEN them: a comment cannot appear in the middle of an identifier, constant, reserved word, or two-character symbol.

A comment is any text enclosed by the delimiters { and }, or (* and *).

These are comments:

    { A comment with fancy delimiters! }
    (*Another sort of comment, with less exuberance.*)

The delimiters may not be mixed.

These are not comments:

    (* two kinds of delimiters here }
    { the same problem, in reverse *)

Comments with the same kind of delimiter may not be nested.

This is not a legal comment:

{ This is an unsuccessful attempt {to create nested} comments. }

... the compiler would read this as a comment ending with 'nested}'.

A comment MAY contain a comment that uses the other type of delimiters.

These are legal comments:

(* This is a comment {that contains another}*)
{and so (*is this*)}

This construct is NOT legal in standard Pascal.

Comments may be longer than one line of source. If the compiler finds a comment that contains a semicolon (;), it will issue a warning in the program's listing file. This is because it is a common error to begin a comment, then forget to close it with a matching delimiter. The result is a comment that may "swallow" many lines of Pascal code (possibly the entire remainder of a program!). Since Pascal statements typically end with a semicolon, flagging semicolons within comments is a good way for the Compiler to notify the programmer of this potential error.

Comments that contain a dollar sign ($) IMMEDIATELY after the first bracket are treated as instructions to the Compiler. These must conform to a special format. A comment should not begin with a dollar sign unless the programmer wishes to invoke a specific compiler option. See Chapter X, on compilation.

These are compiler option comments:

(*$I-*)   {$L list.5.text}

These are NOT compiler option comments:

{ $I-}   space before the $
{$M+}   no M option at this time

II.5 Token Boundaries

Special-character symbols are tokens in themselves, but reserved words, constants, and identifiers, must be clearly delimited. Except for special-character tokens, one token must be separated from the next by a special character, space, comment, or <return>.

No reserved word, constant, or identifier may CONTAIN a special character, space, comment, or <return>. This means, in particular, that tokens may not cross the end of a line of source code. (A comment is not a token, and MAY cross a <return>.)

II.6   Indentation and Legibility

Aside from those mentioned in the previous section, there are no restrictions on the way a program may be laid out in the source file.   However, there are some traditions concerning the visual format of a structured program, especially a Pascal program.

In general, a line of source code contains a single statement, or in the case of large compound statements, a single phrase or reserved word.

The hierarchy of statements that is implicit in a structured program is indicated in the source by indentation.   Two or three spaces per level is usually favored.   **begin end, then else, case end, record end,** and **repeat until** pairs are typically indented so that they line up vertically.

The last line of a program, or a relatively long routine, is usually a single **end** -- this is often augmented with a comment that simply contains the name of the program or routine that is being ended.

This would not be considered a legible routine:

```
procedure decide;
var i: integer; sortof: real;
begin
for i:= 1 to 81 do
if choose(i) then move:= 0 else begin
traverse(move,sortof);
respond(sortof)
end end;
```

This is the same routine, and would look acceptable to most programmers:

```
procedure decide;

    var i: integer;
        sortof: real;

    begin
        for i := 1 to 81 do
            if choose(i) then
                move := 0
            else
                begin
                    traverse (move, sortof);
                    respond (sortof)
                end;
    end {decide};
```

... but we do know programmers who would prefer to write it this way:

```
procedure decide;

    var i: integer;
        sortof: real;

    begin
        for i := 1 to 81 do
            if choose(i) then
                move:= 0
            else begin
                traverse(move,sortof);
                respond(sortof)
            end
    end {decide};
```

... tastes vary! The important thing is that the programmer consider future readers of the program. Even the person who writes a program may be confused upon reading it some days (or hours!) later.

Chapter III
Data Types and Operations

UCSD Pascal provides a large number of data types, each appropriate to certain applications. This chapter is therefore the longest in the handbook. Each data type is described in terms of its intended use, representation in the source program, limitations, legal comparisons and operations, and the intrinsic routines that operate on it. Section III.6 discusses the internal representation of data types. Input and output of data is described in Chapter VII.

This chapter describes a number of intrinsic routines, but does not group them together. Appendix C contains a list of all UCSD Pascal intrinsics, and tells where their descriptions may be found.

III.1   Introduction

A Pascal program specifies a set of data, and a set of statements that operate on that data. The format of data, the variables which contain it, and the algorithms that use and modify it must all be specified explicitly.

III.1.1   Constants, Variables, and Expressions

In Pascal, the format of data is specified by its 'type'. Pascal offers a variety of predeclared types. Unlike many languages, it also allows the user to define new types. Identifiers are used as names of types.

A 'constant' is an object in a Pascal program that is a specific value of a specific type. As the name implies, it cannot be changed while the program is running. A constant may be a literal representation of the value, or an identifier that is declared as a constant.

A 'variable' is an object in a Pascal program that is of a specific data type, and contains a value. A variable can contain only one value at any given time, but that value may be modified (by an assignment statement, a procedure call, and so forth). Variables are represented by identifiers.

Both constants and variables may appear in 'expressions'. An expression consists of constants, variables, and operators that yield new values. Operators are defined in certain ways for certain types, and the result of an expression is either a value of a specific type, or is undefined.

These are numeric expressions:

```
height+1
(width * height)/2
1+1+1-3+14/7
```

These are Boolean expressions:

```
glass = house
(edge_test and emergency) <> finished
```

The identifiers in all these examples might have been declared as either constants or variables. All identifiers must be declared prior to the body of the program, unit, or routine that uses them (see Chapter IV).

A function is a kind of routine that returns a value of a specific type. This value may be used in an expression, and hence the function call may be embedded in the expression itself:

    a + 5*b + sqr(c)
    not eof(link_file)
    not eof
    findpos(oper)/findpos(op_sum)

... functions are described in Chapter V.

When a program runs, an expression may be evaluated, yielding some value. This value may be inspected on the spot and then forgotten, or it may be saved by assigning it to a variable (or printing it out, etc.).

III.1.2   Assignment

An assignment statement consists of a variable, followed by the symbol ´:=´, followed by an expression.

These are assignment statements:

    x:= 6
    graph := picturefile
    dog := eat(dog)
    i := i+1
    muffle:= seeknoise(pipe,5)*2.137

The action of an assignment is to change the value of the variable on the left of the := to the value of the evaluated expression. If the value of the expression is undefined, or of an incompatible type, then an error results.

The full semantics of expressions and assignments will become clearer when specific data types have been discussed.

III.1.3   Evaluating Expressions

Two rules govern the order in which operators are evaluated within an expression.

The first rule is operator precedence: certain operations "take precedence" over other operations, which is to say they are evaluated first.   For example, multiplication and division precede addition and subtraction.   Thus, the following expression would be <u>true</u>:

    5*3+4*6-2 = 37

... because the multiplications would be evaluated first, followed by the addition and subtraction.

The second rule is that subexpressions may be grouped together by the use of parentheses.   Subexpressions within parentheses are evaluated before the rest of the expression, and they may be nested.   Thus, by modifying the previous expression, we can produce the following <u>true</u> expression:

    5*(3+4)*6-2 = 208

And if we use nested parentheses:

    5*((3+4)*6-2) = 200

Other than these two rules, the order in which operations are evaluated is undefined.   The actual order is determined by the Compiler.

If the result of an expression depends on the order in which it is evaluated, parentheses should be used.   Sometimes the result of an expression will be known before the entire expression has been evaluated (for example, when a subexpression is multiplied by zero).   When this is the case, it is possible that part of the expression will not be evaluated.   The programmer should never assume that all operations in an expression will be carried out. This is especially important when a function call appears in an expression: since it will not necessarily be called, the program should not depend on any "side-effects" of its call.

The precedence rules for the operators on a given data type are described below with the description of each type.

III.1.4   The Use of Data Types

There are two ways in which a program may be seen as a model of the real world.   In one respect, a program may literally be an implementation of a model, and be used to manipulate that model: store and retrieve data, calculate results from that data, and generate new data for other uses.   In another respect, programs are used to control the machines on which they run: monitor input and output, issue instructions to the user, and accept instructions from the user.

In both these cases, the data structures that the program uses should mirror the real-world situation.   The more naturally data structures reflect the problem at hand, the easier it is to code the program, and the easier it is to use the program when it becomes a finished product.

Pascal presents a wide variety of data types for just this purpose.   Simple quantities, integers or floating point numbers, may be represented by values of types <u>integer</u> or <u>real</u>.   Yes/no states may be represented by <u>Boolean</u> values, and characters by values of type <u>char</u>.   The user may define new types ('scalars'), and simple types may be combined into more complex structured types that are richer and more useful representations of the real-world data that the program must deal with.

A full description of a set of data, of course, includes not only the data itself, but the possible actions that may be performed upon it (i.e., the interrelation of data items).   It is often the case that a single set of data-plus-algorithms can be useful to more than one program.   The UCSD Pascal construct of the **unit** allows the programmer to define such a set: any number of programs (or other units) may **use** a unit, and a unit may be compiled separately from these "clients."

III.2 Simple Data Types

This section describes the simple data types that are predeclared in UCSD Pascal. It ends with a section that describes the routines which perform conversions from one data type to another.

A variable or constant that is of a simple data type has only one element. It is not a collection of values, either of the same simple data type (see **array**, Section III.4.1) or of different data types (see **record**, Section III.4.4).

III.2.1   Integer

The type _integer_ is used to represent integral values (whole numbers and their negatives).

III.2.1.1   Integer Format

An integer value is represented by a sequence of digits. It may be preceded by a '-' or '+'. If no plus sign is present, the integer is assumed to be positive.

These are integers:

```
12345
51
+51
-51
-232
```

These are not integers:

```
1234.0      {contains a decimal point}
/51         {contains a special character}
89i5        {contains a letter}
```

Integers are defined over the range -maxint .. maxint. maxint is a predeclared constant in each Pascal implementation; in UCSD Pascal it is equal to 32767.

III.2.1.2   Integer Comparisons

These are the legal comparisons on integers:

```
=       ... means ... equal to
<>                  not equal to
>                   greater than
>=                  greater than or equal to
<                   less than
<=                  less than or equal to
```

Thus, the following comparisons are all <u>true</u>:

```
17 = 17
32767 > -32767
32767 >= 0
13 <> 43
0 <= 0
```

III.2.1.3   Integer Operations

These operations yield results of type <u>integer</u>.   The operands may be of type <u>integer</u> or a subrange <u>of integer</u> (see Section III.3).   Integers may also appear in expressions that yield results of type <u>real</u>: these operations are described below in Section III.2.2.

These are the legal operations on a single integer:

+	... means ...	unary plus (identity)
-		unary minus (change sign)

These are the legal operations on two integers:

+	plus (addition)
-	minus (subtraction)
*	times (multiplication)
div	integer divide (divide and truncate)
mod	modulo (remainder of integer division)

Thus, the following expressions are all <u>true</u>:

```
+2 = 2
-2 = -2
5+6 = 11
5-6 = -1
5*6 = 30
33 div 5 = 6
33 mod 5 = 3
```

The second operand of a **div** cannot be a zero: this causes a runtime error.

The operation **div** first performs the division, then truncates the result toward zero.

The operation i **mod** j is defined by:

    for i >= 0:   i - ((i **div** j) * j)
    for i < 0:   i - (((i+1) **div** j) * j) + j

j may not be less than or equal to zero.

This is the current ANSI standard for **mod** and **div,** which UCSD Pascal conforms to as of later IV.0 releases.   On earlier versions of the p-System, **div** and **mod** give implementation-specific results for operands that are less than zero.   Before relying on the results of **div** and **mod** for negative operands, the programmer would do well to test them on her own machine to discover how they are implemented.

When an expression is evaluated, the multiplicative operators *, **div,** and **mod** take precedence over the additive operators + and -.

The following expressions are all <u>true:</u>

    345 + 10 **div** 5 = 347   {the **div** is performed first}
    23*24*3+6 = 1662   {the *'s are performed first}
    6+3*23*24 = 1662   {ditto}

A unary operator may NOT be strung together with a binary operator; the following expression is illegal:

    5*-4

... whereas the following expression is legal and <u>true:</u>

    5*(-4) = -20

To override operator precedence, subexpressions may be grouped together with parentheses.   If there is any doubt about the order of evaluation of an expression, parentheses should be used to ensure that the program states what the programmer intended.

The following expressions are all <u>true</u>:

```
5 + 4 + 3 + 2 div 7 = 12      {the div is performed first}
(5 + 4 + 3 + 2) div 7 = 2     {the portion in parentheses
                                      is evaluated first}

5+4 - 3+17 = 23
(5+4) - (3+17) = -11


2 + 3 * 4 * 5 + 6 = 68
2 + 3 * 4 * (5 + 6) = 134
2 + 3 * ((4 * 5) + 6) = 80    {nesting parentheses can
                                      be useful}

(2 + 3) * ((4 * 5) + 6) = 130  {... and so forth!}
```

III.2.1.4   Integer Routines

This section describes the two functions, <u>abs</u> and <u>sqr</u>, that may take an integer value as an argument and return an integer value.   The function <u>odd</u> takes an integer value and returns a Boolean; the procedure <u>str</u> converts an integer (or long integer) into a string; these are described in Section III.2.7.   The function <u>ord</u> takes a scalar value and returns an integer, as described in Section III.3.4.   The function <u>sqrt</u> takes either an integer or real value, and returns a real value; it is described in Section III.2.2.

For information on the input and output of integer values, see Section VII.1.

<u>abs</u>(I), where I is an integer value (either a constant, variable, or expression), returns the absolute value of I.

The following expressions are <u>true</u>:

```
abs(15) = 15
abs(-15) = 15
abs(12-45) = 33
abs(-maxint) = maxint {= 32767}
96 = 12 * abs(-13+5)
```

44

sqr(I), where I is an integer value, returns the square of I.

The following expressions are true:

sqr(15) = 225
sqr(1) = 1
sqr(-6) = 36
sqr(sqr(3)) = 81

sqr and abs also work on real values: see Section III.2.2.4.

III.2.2 Real

The type <u>real</u> is used to represent fractional numbers and numbers of very large or very small magnitude.

Real numbers are represented by a numerical portion (the 'mantissa'), and an 'exponent' which determines the position of the decimal point. This representation is called a "floating point" representation, and is similar to conventional "scientific notation." More information on the internal representation of real numbers appears in Section III.6.2.2.

Because the mantissa of a real number (as stored in the computer) contains a limited number of digits, real values must not be considered precise values: they are accurate only to a certain level of precision. Some advice on the use of real values in calculations and comparisons appears in the Programmer's Guide, Chapter 2.

III.2.2.1   Real Format

A real value is represented by:

a sequence of digits that contains a decimal
point (.) (the decimal point must be preceded by
and followed by at least one digit), or

an integer value followed by an exponent
(the letter 'e' or 'E' followed by an integer), or

a real value with a decimal point followed by
an exponent.

A real value may be preceded by a '+' or '-'. In the absence of a sign, the value is assumed to be positive.

The exponent stands for "times ten to the power of" the integer that follows the letter 'e' or 'E'.

These are real numbers:

        12345.0
        1.2345
        +12.4
        -12.4

```
12e4
12.12e4
12.12e-4
12.12E-4
```

The range over which real numbers are defined depends on the particular implementation; see Section III.6.2.2.

III.2.2.2 Real Comparisons

The comparisons on real numbers are the same as the comparisons on integers. The operands may be real, integer, or a subrange of integer (see Section III.3).

=	... means ...	equal to
<>		not equal to
>		greater than
>=		greater than or equal to
<		less than
<=		less than or equal to

It is recommended that the = comparison NOT be used, since representations of real numbers can be very close in value without being identical. Calculations and comparisons using real numbers are discussed in the Programmer's Guide, Chapter 2.

III.2.2.3 Real Operations

These operations yield results of type real. The operands may be of type real, integer, or a subrange of integer (see Section III.3).

These are the legal operations on a single real value:

+	... means ...	unary plus (identity)
-		unary minus (change sign)

These are the legal operations on two real values:

+	plus (addition)
-	minus (subtraction)
*	times (multiplication)
/	divide (division)

The second operand of a division ('/') cannot be an expression whose result is zero: this causes a runtime error.

When an expression using real values is evaluated, * and / take precedence over + and -. As with integers, two real operations may not appear in a row. For example:

3.0 * - 5.6

... is illegal, while:

3.0 * (-5.6)

... is legal.

III.2.2.4   Real Routines

This section describes the functions that return a real value: abs, sqr, sqrt, sin, cos, arctan (or atan), exp, ln, and pwroften. The functions trunc and round are available to convert a real value to an integer; they are described in Section III.2.7.

For information on the input and output of real values, see Section VII.1.

In the examples, the = should be read as "approximately equals," since values are shown only to three decimal places. Within memory, they would be stored with greater precision.

abs(X), where X is a real value (either a constant, variable, or expression), returns the absolute value of X.

$$abs(1.5) = 1.5$$
$$abs(-1.5) = 1.5$$
$$abs(-1.2*45) = 54.0$$

sqr(X), where X is a real value, returns the square of X.

$$sqr(1.5) = 2.25$$
$$sqr(1.0) = 1.0$$
$$sqr(-6.0) = 36.0$$

(abs and sqr may also return integer values: see Section III.2.1.4.)

sqrt(X), where X is a real or integer value, returns the square root of X.

$$sqrt(4.0) = 2.000$$
$$sqrt(7.0) = 2.646$$

sin(X), where X is a real value or an integer value (in radians), returns the trigonometric sine of X.

$$sin(1) = 0.841$$
$$sin(3.14) = 0.002$$

cos(X), where X is a real value or an integer value (in radians), returns the trigonometric cosine of X.

$$cos(1) = 0.540$$
$$cos(3.14) = -1.000$$

arctan(X), where X is a real value or an integer value (in radians), returns the trigonometric arctangent of X. This function may also be called by atan(X) (this is a UCSD extension).

$$arctan(0.3) = 0.291 \quad \{= atan(0.3)\}$$

$$\underline{\text{arctan}}(0) = 0.000$$

$\underline{\text{exp}}(X)$, where X is a real value or an integer value, returns the constant e to the power of X.

$$\underline{\text{exp}}(1) = 2.718$$
$$\underline{\text{exp}}(6) = 403.429$$

$\underline{\text{ln}}(X)$, where X is a real value or an integer value, returns the natural logarithm of X (the logarithm with base e).

$$\underline{\text{ln}}(3) = 1.099$$
$$\underline{\text{ln}}(13) = 2.565$$

$\underline{\text{log}}(X)$, where X is a real value or an integer value, returns the logarithm base 10 of X. This function is a UCSD extension.

$$\underline{\text{log}}(3) = 0.477$$
$$\underline{\text{log}}(13) = 1.114$$

$\underline{\text{pwroften}}(I)$, where I is an integer value, returns a real value equal to 10 to the power of I. This function is a UCSD extension.

$$\underline{\text{pwroften}}(0) = 1.000$$
$$\underline{\text{pwroften}}(5) = 100000.0$$

III.2.3   Long Integer

Long integers are a UCSD extension to the type integer.   They
are used to represent integers with a magnitude that may be
greater than maxint or less than -maxint (they can represent
integers within -maxint..maxint as well).

III.2.3.1   Long Integer Format

A long integer constant is declared by simply defining an
integer constant with a magnitude outside the range -maxint ..
maxint, for example:

    const Rydberg = 10973731;

A long integer variable is declared by integer[n], where n, the
'length attribute', is an unsigned integer <= 36.   n represents
the maximum number of decimal digits that the long integer
may contain.   For example:

    var Big_Count: integer[10];

... specifies that Big_Count contains not more than 10 decimal
digits.

III.2.3.2   Long Integer Comparisons

The comparisons on long integers are the same as the
comparisons on integers.   The operands may be either integer
or long integer values.

=	... means ... equal to
<>	not equal to
>	greater than
>=	greater than or equal to
<	less than
<=	less than or equal to

III.2.3.3   Long Integer Operations

The operations defined on long integers are the same as for
integers, except that the **mod** operation is undefined:

+	... means ...	unary plus (identity)
-		unary minus (change sign)
+		plus (addition)
-		minus (subtraction)
*		times (multiplication)
div		integer divide (divide and truncate)

When expressions using long integers are evaluated, intermediate results are allocated the necessary amount of space.

When a long integer is assigned the result of an expression that uses long integers, it must have been declared with enough digits to contain the resulting value, otherwise an overflow error occurs.

The representation of long integers is machine-dependent. Some care must be taken, since different allocation schemes affect the overflow conditions of long integer operations; see Section III.6.2.3.

The compatibility of assignments using long integers is described in Section III.2.7.1.

III.2.3.4   Long Integer Routines

There are no long integer routines per se. The function <u>trunc</u> may be used to convert a long integer to an integer, and the procedure <u>str</u> may be used to convert a long integer to a string; see Section III.2.7.

Because Pascal requires that a parameter type be declared by a type identifier, the following declaration would cause a syntax error:

> **procedure** Large (Big_Sum: <u>integer</u>[10]);

... to declare a parameter of type long integer, an appropriate type identifier must be declared, as follows:

> **type** Digit10 = <u>integer</u>[10];
> ...
> **procedure** Large (Big_Sum: Digit10);

Long integers may NOT be returned as function results. In terms of standard Pascal, this means that they are not a true simple type, although they are used in a manner similar to the types integer and real.

For more information about procedures and functions, refer to Chapter V.

III.2.4 Boolean

The type Boolean is used to represent logical truth values.

III.2.4.1 Boolean Format

A Boolean value may equal either <u>true</u> or <u>false</u> (these values are predeclared). <u>false</u> is defined to be less than <u>true</u>.

III.2.4.2 Boolean Comparisons

The following comparisons may be used with Boolean operands.

=	... means ...	equals
<>		not equals (or XOR)
<=		implies
>=		is implied by
>		does not imply
<		is not implied by

III.2.4.3 Boolean Operations

The comparison operations that have already been described for <u>integer</u>, <u>real</u>, and long <u>integer</u> yield results of type <u>Boolean</u>. The operands may be of any compatible ordered type (see Section III.7.1):

The following are operations on Boolean values only, and yield results of type <u>Boolean</u>:

not	logical negation (a unary operator)
and	logical conjunction
or	logical union

In expressions, **not** has the highest precedence of any Boolean operator, followed by **and** (at the same level as the multipliers *, /, **div**, and **mod**), followed by **or** (at the same level as + and -), followed by all of the relational operators (=, <>, >, <, >=, <=, and **in**, which is described in Section III.4.3).

Since the value of a Boolean expression may be known before the entire expression has been evaluated, the Pascal language does not require full evaluatibn of Boolean expressions. For example:

flag1 **and** flag2 **and** flag3

... if flag1 is <u>false</u>, there is no need to check the values of flag2 or flag3.

The order in which Boolean expressions are evaluated depends on the Compiler, and may vary from implementation to implementation. The programmer should be aware of this situation, and not write code that depends on an entire Boolean expression being evaluated. In particular, a function call that must be made (because of its side effects) for the program to work should NEVER be embedded in a Boolean expression. (Conversely, the programmer should never assume that part of an expression will NOT be evaluated.)

III.2.4.4   Boolean Routines

The function <u>odd</u> takes an integer value and returns a Boolean; it is described in Section III.2.7. The functions <u>eof</u> and <u>eoln</u> each return a Boolean value based on file operations; see Section III.5.1. The function <u>unitbusy</u> also returns a Boolean value; see Chapter VII.

Boolean values cannot be written by any UCSD Pascal intrinsic; this is contrary to standard Pascal.

III.2.5   Characters

The type <u>char</u> is used to represent individual characters. Character values are ordered. The digits '0'..'9' and the alphabets 'a'..'z' and 'A'..'Z' are contiguous within the character set.

Characters are often used as elements of sets and strings; the reader should also refer to sections III.4.2 and III.4.3.

III.2.5.1   Character Format

A printable character value is represented by a single character, surrounded by single quotes (apostrophes).

These are characters:

'a'   'B'   '/'   '7'   '['

An apostrophe is represented by typing it twice: ''''.

Virtually all current implementations use the ASCII character set (<u>A</u>merican <u>S</u>tandard <u>C</u>ode for <u>I</u>nformation <u>I</u>nterchange). This is shown in Appendix E.

ASCII contains many nonprintable characters. Within the body of a program, a nonprintable character may be represented by using the intrinsic function <u>chr</u>. See Section III.2.7.2.

III.2.5.2   Character Comparisons

Character values have the same order as their underlying representation (usually the ASCII set).

Because the character set is ordered, the numeric comparisons (=, <>, >, >=, <, <=) may be used on values of type <u>char.</u>

III.2.5.3   Character Operations

Character values may be assigned to variables of type char, and parameters of type char may be passed, but there are no operations on characters.

III.2.5.4   Character Routines

There are no character routines per se.   Character values may be read or written using read and write: see Chapter VII, Section 1.   An integer may be converted to a character with chr, and a character to an integer with ord: see Section III.2.7.2.

The intrinsics pred and succ may be used with character values. These are described in Section III.3.4.

For examples of converting characters to numeric values, or lower-case to upper-case and visa versa, see the Programmer's Guide, Chapter 2.

III.2.6 Special-Purpose Types

UCSD Pascal defines two types that are used in the handling of concurrent processes. They do not appear in the standard language.

processid is used by the System to distinguish concurrent processes. Every process that is start'ed is assigned a unique processid. The programmer may examine this value, but may not alter it.

semaphore is used to synchronize concurrent processes. The intrinsic procedures signal and wait each depend on a parameter of type semaphore. Semaphores are initialized by the procedure seminit, and may be associated with a hardware interrupt vector by the procedure attach.

Concurrent processes are described in Chapter IX.

III.2.7 Type Conversions

III.2.7.1 Compatibility

An integer variable may be assigned an integer value, or the result of an expression that contains (legal) operations on integers.

A real variable may be assigned a real value, an integer value, or the result of an expression that contains operations on real values or integers.

A long integer variable may be assigned an integer value, a long integer value, or the result of an expression that contains operations on integers or long integers.

A Boolean variable may be assigned the result of a comparison, or the result of an expression that contains operations on Boolean values.

Variables of type char, processid, and semaphore, may be assigned a value of the same type, but are never operated on.

Subranges of the type integer may be used wherever it is legal to use integers, but the overflow conditions of an expression will depend on the subrange bounds.   See Section III.3.

III.2.7.2 Conversion Routines

trunc(X), where X is a real value, returns an integer value equal to the whole part of X; the fractional part is discarded.

The following expressions are true:

$$\text{trunc}(12.3) = 12$$
$$\text{trunc}(-12.3) = -12$$
$$\text{trunc}(67.0) = 67$$

trunc(L), where L is a long integer value, returns an integer value equal to L. If L is not in the range -maxint .. maxint, an overflow results.

<u>round</u>(X), where X is a real value, returns the integer value nearest X.

The following expressions are <u>true</u>:

$$\begin{aligned}
\underline{round}(12.3) &= 12 \\
\underline{round}(12.7) &= 13 \\
\underline{round}(4.5) &= 5 \\
\underline{round}(-4.5) &= -5 \\
\underline{round}(67.0) &= 67
\end{aligned}$$

<u>odd</u>(I), where I is an integer value, returns a Boolean value that is <u>true</u> if I is odd and <u>false</u> if I is even.

<u>ord</u>(C), where C is a character value, returns an integer value equal to the ordinal number of C within the character set.

<u>ord</u> applies to scalar and subrange types (including <u>Boolean</u>) as well as to <u>char</u>. See Section III.3.

<u>chr</u>(I), where I is an integer value, returns a character value equal to the character with ordinal number I within the character set.

These functions are inverses of each other:

$$\begin{aligned}
\underline{ord}(\underline{chr}(I)) &= I \\
\underline{chr}(\underline{ord}(C)) &= C
\end{aligned}$$

The following expressions are <u>true</u>:

$$\begin{aligned}
\underline{ord}('A') &= 65 \\
\underline{ord}(' ') &= 32
\end{aligned}$$

$$\begin{aligned}
\underline{chr}(32) &= '\ ' \\
\underline{chr}(93) &= ']' \\
\underline{chr}(3) &\ \{= \text{ETX (which is not printable)}\}
\end{aligned}$$

<u>str</u>(L,S) is a procedure that sets the string variable S to a representation of the value of the integer or long integer L.

III.3   Scalars and Subranges

III.3.1   Scalars

Scalar types are types that consist of an enumeration of values.
The name of the type is an identifier.   The user may define
new scalar types, whose values are represented by identifiers.
A user-defined scalar is usually declared as a **type** -- it may
also be declared as a **var,** but this is less useful.

Here is a program fragment defining a few scalar types:

```
type
     color = (red, yellow, blue, green, lavender, purple,
               mauve, amber);
     month = (Jan, Feb, Mar, Apr, May, Jun,
               Jul, Aug, Sep, Oct, Nov, Dec);
     sex = (male, female);
     door_state = (open, closed);
```

Within the scope of the type declaration (see Chapter IV,
Section 2.1), a scalar value must be unambiguous: the same
identifier cannot appear in the definition of two different scalar
types.

The following program fragment is illegal:

```
type
     door_state = (open, closed);
     lock_state = (open, locked);
```

The values of a scalar type are ordered.   The relational
operators (=, <>, >, >=, <, <=) are defined for scalar types,
and have their usual meanings, based on the order in which the
scalar values are declared.

Using the (legal) types defined above, the following expressions
would be <u>true</u>:

```
Jan <> Feb
blue <= lavender
female > male
```

III.3.2 Subranges

The programmer may define a type or a variable that is a subrange of a previously declared scalar type. The symbol '..' is used to denote intervening values: for 'red .. green', read "red through green."

Given our examples above, these are legal declarations:

type
      winter = Jan .. Mar;
      spring = Mar .. Jun;
      primary = red .. blue;
var
      summer: Jun .. Aug;
      palette: primary;

   {the following two declarations
    describe equivalent subranges:}

      tag: sex;
      gender: male .. female;

... note that subranges may overlap.

Subranges of predeclared scalar types are also frequently used:

type
      f_index = 1..77;   {subrange of <u>integer</u>}

var
      Kinsey: 1..7;   {subranges of <u>integer</u>}
      state: 0..5;
      grade: 'A' .. 'F';   {subrange of <u>char</u>}

Any legal operations on a predeclared type are always legal on a subrange of that type, but the overflow conditions may vary:

state:= 3;   {this is ok}
state:= state+1;   {result is 4; no problem}
state:= state-10;   {result < 0; a value range error
                           occurs at runtime}

Note that the types <u>real</u> and long <u>integer</u> are not considered scalar types, and cannot be used to construct subranges.

III.3.3 Simple Types Declared as Scalars or Subranges

Some of the simple types we have discussed may be thought of as scalar or subrange types, For example:

    integer = -maxint .. maxint
... or ...
    integer = -32767..32767
        {for UCSD Pascal, this is
            an equivalent declaration}

    Boolean = (false, true)

This is not the way that these types are represented internally (see Section III.6), but they do behave as though they were declared this way.

Note that the types real and long integer are not considered scalar types.

III.3.4 Scalar and Subrange Routines

Three intrinsic functions are provided for manipulating scalar and subrange values: ord, pred, and succ.

ord(V), where V is a value of a scalar type, returns an integer that is the ordinal value of V in the sequence of values declared for that type.   All scalar types are ordered (as the name implies), and their values are numbered starting from zero.

We have already seen (in Section III.2.7.2) ord used to convert character values to integer values.   This is a special case of the use of the ord function.

Given the declarations earlier in this section, the following expressions are true:

    ord('Z') = 90   {using ASCII characters}
    ord(blue) = 2
    ord(Jan) = 0
    ord(true) = 1

Note that <u>ord</u> has no inverse function, except for the special case of <u>chr</u>: see Section III.2.7.

<u>pred</u>(V), where V is a value of a scalar or subrange type, returns the value that PRECEDES that value. <u>pred</u> stands for "predecessor."

Given the declarations earlier in this section, the following expressions are <u>true</u>:

    <u>pred</u>('Z') = 'Y' {in ANY character set}
    <u>pred</u>(blue) = yellow
    <u>pred</u>(Dec) = Nov
    <u>pred</u>(true) = <u>false</u>

If the value V is the first value in the scalar type (that is, if <u>ord</u>(V) = 0), then <u>pred</u>(V) results in a value range error at runtime (unless range-checking has been turned off: see Chapter X).

<u>succ</u>(V), where V is a value of a scalar or subrange type, returns the value that SUCCEEDS that value. <u>succ</u> stands for "successor."

Given the declarations earlier in this section, the following expressions are <u>true</u>:

    <u>succ</u>('A') = 'B' {in ANY character set}
    <u>succ</u>(blue) = green
    <u>succ</u>(Jan) = Feb
    <u>succ</u>(false) = <u>true</u>

If the value V is the last value in the scalar type (that is, if <u>ord</u>(V) is the greatest possible value for that type), then <u>succ</u>(V) results in a value range error at runtime (unless range-checking has been turned off: see Chapter X).

III.4   Structured Types

A 'structured type' in Pascal is a single type built out of
simple types in certain ways, and given a single name.   This
section discusses arrays, strings, records, and sets.   Files are
discussed in Section III.5.

An 'array' is a table of values all of the same type.   It
corresponds to the notion of a matrix in mathematics, and may
have one or more dimensions.

A 'string' is a sequence of characters.   Unlike an array, the
length of a string may change during the execution of a
program.   UCSD Pascal provides several intrinsics for the
manipulation of strings.

A 'record' is a group of values of (possibly) mixed type.
Records are useful for maintaining information that is logically
grouped together, but best represented by a variety of types.

A 'set' is, in the mathematical sense, the powerset of its base
type.   In other words, a set value is an (unordered) collection
of values from the base type.   Sets are useful for truth tables
and tests of membership.

III.4.1   Arrays

An array is a table of values.   The values in an array must all
be of one type, which is called the 'base type' of the array.

An array may have one or more dimensions.   The number of
dimensions and the size of each dimension cannot change during
the execution of the program.

The individual elements in an array are also called
'components'.   Each individual element may be referenced in a
program by the name of the array, followed by an 'index' (also
called a 'subscript') surrounded by square brackets ([ ]).

These are expressions that reference array elements:

        directory[45]
        year[month]
        TokenList[i+4]
        CubePoints[0,0,0]
        Hexagram [Upper3] [Lower3]

III.4.1.1   Array Format

An array is declared in the following way (using Extended BNF):

        array-type = **"array"** "[" ordinal-type {"," ordinal-type } "]"
                        "of" base-type

... where the 'ordinal-type's define the bounds of the array, and 'base-type' is either a type declaration, or the name of a type that has already been declared.

Each 'ordinal-type' is a subrange expression, or the identifier of a scalar or subrange type.   This is called the 'index type' of the array.

The 'base-type' may be any type except a file type.   It may well be another array.

These would be legal array declarations:
    var
        Students: **array** [1..ClassSize] **of** Grade;
        logout: **array** [day] **of** time;
        LastQuarter: **array** [1..ClassSize] **of** Boolean;
        state: **array** [0..49] **of** 1..7
        schedule: **array** [day] **of**
                        array [9..18] **of** initials;
        Cube: **array** [0..2, 0..2, 0..2] **of** color;

Arrays with multiple dimensions may be indexed by, for example:

        schedule [monday] [13]

... or by the shorter form:

        schedule [monday, 13]

66

Cube[1,1,0]

... as in the expression:

Cube[1,1,0]:= red;

An array declaration may be preceded by the keyword **packed,**
as in:

surname: **packed array** [0..19] **of** <u>char</u>;

... the semantics of using **packed** are described in Section
III.6.1.

The size of an array is limited only by the maximum number of
words that may be local to a routine or compilation unit (unit
or main program). This is 16383 words in all current versions.

Standard Pascal requires that a **packed array of** <u>char</u> have at
least two elements. UCSD Pascal does not have this
restriction.

III.4.1.2   Array Comparisons

Two arrays may be compared using the operators = (equals) and
<> (not equals). This is not legal in standard Pascal. The
arrays must have the same dimensions and same base type, and
should NOT be packed.

Any other comparisons involving arrays must be done element
by element, for example:

```
same:= true;
i:= 0;
while (i <= maxelement) and same do
   if a[i] = b[i]
      then i:= i+1
      else same:= false;
```


III.4.1.3   Array Operations

A single assignment may be used to assign an entire array
value to another array, provided both arrays have the same
dimensions and the same base type. This is a UCSD extension.

67

A **packed array of** char may be assigned another **packed array of** char value of the same length.

There are no Pascal operations that apply to arrays. The individual elements of an array may be operated upon, following the rules that apply to the base type of the array.

For example:

    vector[5]:= vector[5] + table[5, 12];
        {the base type could be a numeric type or a set}

III.4.1.4   Array Routines

UCSD Pascal provides four intrinsic routines for the rapid manipulation of arrays. They are most frequently used to handle packed arrays of character, but they do no type checking on their operands, and so are generally applicable. This section describes the procedures fillchar, moveleft, and moveright, and the function scan.

These four intrinsics have certain parameters that may be of any type at all (much like parameters to read and write). These are described below (not quite accurately) as 'typeless' parameters. Because of Pascal syntax, these parameters must be declared as having a specific type, but the intrinsics merely operate on main memory at the location of the parameter, and do not check what type it is.

If a typeless parameter is an array, it may have a subscript. If it is a record, it may have a field specification. These specify a location in memory where the intrinsic will operate.

Because of the generality of these routines, and because they do no type checking or range checking whatsoever, they should used with extreme **caution**, lest valuable information be destroyed.

fillchar(DESTINATION, LENGTH, CHARACTER) fills an area of memory with a single character.

> DESTINATION is a typeless parameter. LENGTH is an integer.

CHARACTER is a single char, or an integer (fillchar ignores the 8 most-significant bits of the integer, so it should be in the range 0..255).

fillchar fills memory with LENGTH instances of CHARACTER (two characters per word), starting from DESTINATION.

For example, given the declaration:

var buf: **packed array** [0..19] **of** char;

... the statements:

for i:= 0 **to** 19 **do** buf[i]:= '*';
fillchar(buf, 10, 'e');

... set buf to this value:

'eeeeeeeeee**********'

moveleft(SOURCE, DESTINATION, LENGTH) moves LENGTH bytes from SOURCE to DESTINATION. The bytes are moved from left to right.

SOURCE and DESTINATION are typeless parameters. LENGTH is an integer.

For example, given the array initializations:

src:= '1234567890';
dst:= '**********';

... the call:

moveleft(src, dst, 5);

... sets dst to: '12345*****'

moveright(SOURCE, DESTINATION, LENGTH) moves LENGTH bytes from SOURCE to DESTINATION. The bytes are moved from right to left.

SOURCE and DESTINATION are typeless parameters.

LENGTH is an integer.

moveleft and moveright both accomplish the same thing, except when bytes are moved to an overlapping location within the same array.

For example, given the same value of the array src, the call:

moveright(src, src[3], 5);

... correctly sets src to: '1231234590'

On the other hand, the call:

moveleft(src, src[3], 5);

... sets src to: '1231231290'

... because bytes are modified before they have been moved.

scan(LENGTH, <partial expression>, SOURCE) is a function that returns the location of a character within an array.

LENGTH is an integer.

<partial expression> is an = or <> symbol followed by a single character expression.

SOURCE is a typeless parameter.

scan scans SOURCE until the partial expression is satisfied, or until LENGTH characters have been scanned: whichever comes first. It returns an integer value that is the offset from the beginning of SOURCE to the point at which it stopped scanning.

If LENGTH is negative, scan scans from right to left rather than left to right, and returns a negative offset.

For example:

    var test: string;
    ...
        test:= 'For he on honey dew hath fed,';

70

```
index:=  scan(10, = 'h', test[11]);
         {index is set to 0}

index:=  scan(10, = 'h', test[12]);
         {index is set to 9}

index:=  scan(-9, = 'h', test[9]);
         {index is set to -4}

index:=  scan(10, <>'h', test[11]);
         {index is set to 1}
```

III.4.2   Strings

A string is a sequence of characters that has an associated length. The length of a string may change during the execution of a program.

Several intrinsics are provided to simplify the manipulation of strings.

Strings and string intrinsics do not appear in standard Pascal.

III.4.2.1   String Format

string is a predeclared type. A string value is a sequence of characters with an associated length. A string constant is typed as a sequence of characters surrounded by single quotes (apostrophes).

These are string constants:

```
'hello there'
'And whether pigs have wings.'
{embedded quotes are typed twice:}
''''     {a single apostrophe}
'The sixth sick sheik''s sixth sheep''s sick'
''       {the empty string}
```

The empty string is allowed, and has a length of zero.

Each string variable has a maximum length. The default is 80 characters. This can be overridden when the string is declared,

71

by following the identifier string with a length attribute in brackets ([ ]). A string may not be declared longer than 255 characters.

These are declarations of string variables:

>   heading: string; {default maximum length is 80}
>   graphline: string[200];
>   {... has a maximum length of 200}
>   surname: string[20];
>   abbrev: string[3]

III.4.2.2   String Comparisons

Strings are ordered, and may be compared with any of the comparison operators. The ordering of strings is lexicographical (that is, dictionary order): shorter strings precede longer strings, and upper case precedes lower case.

III.4.2.3   String Operations

Strings may be assigned.   No other operations are defined on strings.

The characters in a string are indexed from 1 up to the dynamic length of the string. The dynamic length of the string may not be greater than the string's maximum length (its 'static length').

If a string is indexed outside its bounds, a value range error occurs when the program is executed (unless range-checking is disabled: see Chapter X).   The empty string cannot be indexed at all.

III.4.2.4   String Routines

The simplest way to manipulate strings is to use the string intrinsics.   This section describes the functions concat, copy, length, and pos, and the procedures insert and delete.

concat(SOURCE1, SOURCE2, ..., SOURCEn) is a function.   It returns a string that is the value of the concatenation of strings SOURCE1 .. SOURCEn.

The SOURCE strings are string expressions, and there may be any number of them, separated by commas.

The length of the new string is the sum of the lengths of the sources.

For example:

concat('All in ', 'a garden ', 'green ...')

... returns the string:

'All in a garden green ...'

concat('There is a long poisonous ',
          concat('snake-like ','object'))

... returns the string:

'There is a long poisonous snake-like object'

copy(SOURCE, INDEX, SIZE) is a function.   It returns a substring of SOURCE that is SIZE characters long and starts at SOURCE[INDEX].   If SIZE is too long (INDEX + SIZE - 1 > length(SOURCE)), then copy does nothing.

SOURCE is a string variable; INDEX and SIZE are integers.

For example, if:

Long:= 'Fortune my foe, why dost thou frown on me?';

... then ...

copy(Long, 17, 19)

... returns the string:

'why dost thou frown'

delete(DESTINATION, INDEX, SIZE) is a procedure.   It removes

SIZE characters from DESTINATION, starting from
DESTINATION[INDEX]. If SIZE is too long (INDEX + SIZE - 1
> length(SOURCE)) then delete does nothing.

DESTINATION is a string variable; SIZE and INDEX are
integers.

For example:

delete(Long, 17, 19);

... replaces Long with the string:

'Fortune my foe, on me?'

insert(SOURCE, DESTINATION, INDEX) is a procedure.   It
inserts the string SOURCE into the string DESTINATION,
starting from DESTINATION[INDEX]. The new length of
DESTINATION is its old length plus length(SOURCE).

SOURCE is a string expression, and DESTINATION is a
string variable; INDEX is an integer.

For example, if:

Long:= 'There were three ravens,';
Short:= 'old ';

... then ...

insert(Short, Long, 18);

... replaces Long with the string:

'There were three old ravens,'

length(SOURCE) is a function that returns the current (dynamic) length of the string SOURCE.

SOURCE is a string expression; length returns an integer.

For example, if:

Long:= 'At noon Dulcina rested';

... then ...

length(Long)

... returns the integer 22.

pos(PATTERN, SOURCE) is a function. It returns an integer that is the location of the string PATTERN in the string SOURCE.

The integer that pos returns is the index of the first character of the matching substring.

If PATTERN cannot be matched, pos returns 0.

For example, if:

Long:= 'He that would an alehouse keep';
Short:= 'use';

... then ...

pos(Short, Long)

... would return the integer 23.

III.4.3 Sets

A set value is a collection of members that are values from some scalar or subrange type. In mathematical terms, a set type is the powerset of its base type.

III.4.3.1 Set Format

A set is declared in the following way (using Extended BNF):

    set-type = **"set"** **"of"** ordinal-type

... where ordinal-type is a scalar type or a subrange.

These are some set variable declarations:

    ASCII: **set of** char;
    palette: **set of** color;
    attribute: **set of** 1..5;
    lower_case: **set of** 'a' .. 'z';

The value of a set may be represented in the following way (again using EBNF):

    set-value = "[" [member {"," member }] "]"

    member = expression [".." expression]

In other words, a set value is an enumeration of values or subranges of values, enclosed in square brackets. The empty set is denoted by [ ].

For example:

    palette:= [red, yellow, blue];
    attribute:= [1, 3];
    new_set:= []   {the empty set}

The following expression is <u>true</u>:

    [red, blue, green] = [green, red, blue]

... since set elements are not ordered.

A set may have up to 4080 elements (16 bits/word * 255 words). A set of a subrange of <u>integer</u> must have positive bounds, and the upper bound must be no greater than 4079, regardless of the value of the lower bound. These (generous) restrictions apply only to UCSD Pascal.

III.4.3.2   Set Comparisons

The following are legal comparisons on sets:

=	... means ... equal to
<>	not equal to
>=	includes (is a superset of)
<=	is included in (is a subset of)

The comparison **in** is also defined for sets.

        ⟨value⟩ **in** ⟨set⟩

... is a Boolean expression. ⟨value⟩ is a scalar or subrange expression from the base type of ⟨set⟩. If ⟨value⟩ is indeed a member of this ⟨set⟩, the value of the expression is <u>true.</u>

For example, if is_letter is <u>Boolean</u> and ch is a <u>char</u>, then:

    is_letter:= ch **in** ['A'..'Z', 'a'..'z'];

... determines whether ch is in the alphabet.

Comparisons of sets are only legal if the two sets have the same base type (or if the subranges on which they are based have the same base type).

III.4.3.3   Set Operations

The following operations are defined on sets:

+	... means ... set union
*	set intersection
-	set difference

77

The following expressions are <u>true</u>:

['C', 'A', 'R'] + ['H'] = ['C', 'A', 'R', 'H']
['C', 'A', 'R'] * ['H'] = [] {the empty set}
['N', 'W'] * ['E', 'W', 'D'] = ['W']
['C', 'A', 'R'] - ['H'] = ['C', 'A', 'R']
['N', 'W'] - ['E', 'W', 'D'] = ['N']
[blue, red, green] + [gold] = [blue, red, green, gold]

As with set comparisons, set operations are only legal if the sets or their base subranges have the same base type.

III.4.3.4 Set Routines

There are no intrinsic routines for the manipulation of sets. Nor is there any provision in Pascal for the standard output of set values. The user must create routines that are appropriate to the purposes of a particular program.

III.4.4   Records

A record value is a collection of values that are (possibly) of different types.

III.4.4.1   Record Format

The following expressions in EBNF describe the declaration of a record:

    record-type = "**record**" field-list "**end**"

    field-list = fixed-part [";"]
             | variant-part [";"]
             | fixed-part ";" variant part [";"]

    fixed-part = id-list ":" type { ";" id-list ":" type }

    variant-part = "**case**" ordinal-type "**of**" variant
              | "**case**" tag ":" ordinal-type "**of**" variant

    variant = id-list ":" "(" field-list ")"
            { ";" id-list ":" "(" field-list ")" }

    id-list = identifier { "," identifier }

As indicated, variant-parts in a record must always follow fixed-parts, and there is only one of each at any given "level" of the record.

The id-lists in a variant must be constants of the type designated in the **case** heading of the variant-part.

Tag is an identifier.

Note that the keyword **end** pairs with the keyword **record.**

The field-list may NOT be empty.   In standard Pascal, it may be.

These are some record type declarations:

```
type
    complex = record
                   real_part,
                   imaginary_part: real
              end;

    student = record
                   surname: string[30];
                   score1, score2: integer;
                   grade: 'A'..'F';
                   repeat: Boolean
              end;

    disk = record
                   artist, composer: string[50];
                   size: (eight_inch, ten_inch, other);
                   release: integer;
                   condition:
                       record
                          chipped,
                          humor,
                          jazz,
                          tradeable: Boolean
                       end
              end;
```

... it is evident that records may be as simple or as complex as desired.

The elements of a record may be accessed by <record name>.<field name>. Given the declarations:

```
var
    class: array [1..50] of student;
    platter: disk;
```

... fields could be accessed by the following names:

```
class[1].surname
class[j].grade
platter.release
platter.condition.tradeable
```

III.4.4.2   Record Comparisons and Operations

As with arrays, the comparisons = and <> may be used to compare records of the same type that are NOT packed.   No other comparisons are defined for records.

No operations are defined on records.   Fields of records may be operated on, according to the type of the field.

III.4.4.3   Variant Records

Here are some examples of records with variants:

```
entry = record
            case head: Boolean of
                true: (number: integer);
                false: (identifier: string[5]);
        end;

choice = (addr, bits);
trix = record
            case choice of
                addr: (locn: integer);
                bits: (bmap: packed array
                              [0..15] of Boolean);
        end;
```

A variant record allows the programmer to treat a single field (a single memory location) as a variable that has a different type in different situations.

If the variant does not have a tag variable, then the names of the fields within the variant list are used as any other record field name.   For example:

```
var two_way: trix

begin
    ...
    two_way.locn:= 17760;
    ...
    two_way.bmap[0]:= false;
```

If the variant DOES have a tag variable, then the tag variable is itself a field. For clarity, it may be set to a particular value before the field corresponding to that value is used. For example:

```
var node: entry;

begin
    ...
    node.head:= true;
    node.number:= 57;
    ...
    node.head:= false;
    node.identifier:= 'WOOF0';
```

Because variant records can treat the same area of memory in different ways, their use can become involved; variant records can be a means of doing "dirty tricks." See Section III.6, and the Programmer's Guide, Chapter 8.

III.4.4.4   The With Statement

Specifying an element of a record by enumerating all the appropriate fields can become tedious, and interfere with the legibility of a program. The **with** statement provides a "shorthand" means of dealing with field names.

A **with** statement has the form:

   with ⟨record name list⟩ **do** ⟨statement⟩

⟨statement⟩ is usually a compound statement; see Chapter VI. ⟨record name list⟩ consists of one or more identifiers of record variables (separated by commas).

If multiple record names are used, the names of their fields must be unambiguous (that is, a field name cannot be used within the **with** if it is common to more than one of the records). If a simple variable has the same name as the field of a record, then within the **with** statement, the FIELD name takes precedence (and the simple variable cannot be used).

Here is an example of the **with** statement:

```
with class[n] do
    begin
        surname:= buffer;
        score1:= 0;      {initial values!}
        score2:= 0;
        grade:= 'A';     {benefit of a doubt}
        again:= false;
    end;
```

... and a slightly more complicated one:

```
with platter.condition do
    begin    {initializations}
        chipped:= false;
        humor:= false;
        jazz:= false;
        tradeable:= false;
    end {with};
```

We could also have the (unlikely) example:

```
with class[n], platter do
    begin
        grade:= 'C';
        artist:= 'Ellington';
    end;
```

III.5 Dynamic Types

In Pascal, 'dynamic types' are data structures whose size and configuration may change during the execution of a program. This section describes files, which store data serially, and pointers, which are a means of indirectly referencing data. Pointers may be used to build flexible data structures such as search trees.

III.5.1 Files

A file is a serial stream of data. The data may be read or written from within a Pascal program.

Files were originally restricted to serial access for the sake of simplicity. In the UCSD p-System, programs, text, and data are usually stored in random-access files on floppy disks. An 'external' disk file may be dealt with as an 'internal' file in a Pascal program. Some UCSD extensions take advantage of the p-System environment by providing for random-access files, interactive terminals, and so forth.

This section deals with internal files. The use of external files is described in Chapter VII.

III.5.1.1 Internal File Format

A file may be declared in the following manner:

file of <base type>

The base type of a file may be any type but another file type (this restriction does not apply in standard Pascal).

These are some file declarations:

var
        Chapter1: **file of** char;
        enrollment: **file of** student;
        seismic: **file of** integer;

A file consists of a serial stream of elements.

A file with no elements at all is allowed, and is called an 'empty' file.

A file may be modified only at a single location, which is called the file 'window'. The window is associated with a 'window variable', which contains the value of the file element at the window's location. If file_name is the name of a file, file_name^ denotes the window variable.

The window variable can be modified just as an ordinary variable (with an assignment, a routine call, and so forth). It is initialized when the file is opened, or by a call to the intrinsic get. Its value can be written to the file by a call to the intrinsic put.

In standard Pascal, the window is always at the end of the sequence of file elements. In UCSD Pascal, files can be accessed randomly by repositioning the window with a call to the intrinsic seek, which is described in Chapter VII.

The predeclared type text is defined as:

    text: **file of** char;

... files of type text are usually saved as p-System textfiles (a p-System textfile must have the suffix .TEXT in its external name).

In UCSD Pascal, a file may be declared without a type, for example:

    no_structure: **file;**

Input and output to untyped files can only be done with the UCSD intrinsics blockread and blockwrite; see Chapter VII.

Standard Pascal defines the predeclared files <u>input</u> and <u>output</u>. In UCSD Pascal, these files normally refer to the device 'CONSOLE:', which is an integral part of the p-System environment. (This is a default which may be overridden by the user: see the description of redirection in the <u>UCSD p-System Users' Manual</u>(3).)

"Character-oriented" devices (such as CONSOLE:, SYSTERM:, PRINTER:, REMOUT:, and REMIN:) are usually opened as textfiles when they are used within a Pascal program (see the <u>rewrite</u> and <u>reset</u> intrinsics in Chapter VII).

In UCSD Pascal, <u>input</u>, <u>output</u>, and the predeclared file <u>keyboard</u> are files of the predeclared file type <u>interactive</u>. An <u>interactive</u> file has the same structure as a <u>text</u> file, but is treated somewhat differently by the intrinsic routines <u>read</u>, <u>readln</u>, and <u>reset</u>. See Chapter VII.

A programmer may define a new interactive file:

      extra_terminal: <u>interactive</u>;

There are no inherent limits to the size of a file, but the storage device on which a file resides will be limited in size.

In UCSD Pascal, the restriction against a **file of file** (or <u>text</u> or <u>interactive</u>) is a special case of a general restriction against files being declared within ANY structured type: a file cannot be an element of an array, or a field within a record. In standard Pascal, this would be allowed. The chief reason for this restriction is so that the Compiler can easily generate code to automatically close files when a program (or routine) terminates.

III.5.1.2 Standard File Handling

This section describes the file-handling routines that are part of standard Pascal: <u>eof</u>, <u>eoln</u>, <u>put</u>, <u>get</u>, <u>reset</u>, and <u>rewrite</u>. <u>reset</u> and <u>rewrite</u> may also be used to associate internal files with external files. This use is nonstandard, and is described in Chapter VII.

Files are frequently accessed by using the standard routines read, readln, write, and writeln. These are described in Chapter VII.

eof(file_name) returns a Boolean value that is true if the window variable has been moved BEYOND the end of the file (eof stands for end of file). When eof is true, the value of the window variable is undefined.

If the file_name parameter is absent, the file input is assumed.

If the file is interactive, eof becomes true when a special end-of-file character is read. This character may be defined by the user; it is often referred to as <etx>, and frequently set to control-C (see the UCSD p-System Installation Guide(4), or equivalent documentation for your hardware).

If the file is a p-System textfile, eof= true implies eoln= true.

Warning: If eof(file_name) becomes true during a call to get(file_name), read(file_name, ...), or readln(file_name, ...), the data obtained from the get or read is not valid and must not be used.

eoln(file_name) is defined only if the file is of type text or interactive. It returns a Boolean value that is true if a <return> character (ASCII CR, chr(13)) has just been read (eoln stands for end of line). The window variable contains a blank (´ ´).

If the file_name parameter is absent, the file input is assumed.

If eof is true, eoln is true.

put(file_name) writes the value of the window variable to the file file_name.

The file_name parameter MUST be included.

In standard Pascal, put is only defined if eof is true, in other words, one may only write to a file by appending values to its end.

In UCSD Pascal, a put may be performed anywhere in the file. If eof is indeed true, the value of the window variable is appended. If eof is false, the value of the current record in the file is replaced by the value of the window variable. In other words (other jargon?), UCSD Pascal allows random-access updates of file records; see the description of seek in Chapter VII.

If a put is used to append an element to the file, and there is no more room on disk, a runtime error occurs.

get(file_name) is defined only if eof = false. It advances the file window by one file record; the value of the window variable is replaced by the value of the next element in the file sequence. If there is no following record, eof is set to true, and the value of the window variable is undefined.

The file_name parameter MUST be included.

reset(file_name) resets the file window to the beginning of the file. If the file is not empty, eof is set to false, and the window variable is set to the value of the first record in the file.

The file_name parameter MUST be included.

If the file is empty, eof remains true, and the value of the window variable is undefined.

If the file is interactive, eof is set to false, but the value of the window variable remains undefined. The reason for this is that the interactive file might well be an input device or an input/output device, and not have any pending data: trying to define the value of the window variable before the user has typed in any data would be difficult!

reset in UCSD Pascal may be called with an optional second parameter that defines an external p-System file to be associated with the internal file_name. This use of reset is described in Chapter VII.

<u>rewrite</u>(file_name) clears the file file_name by creating a temporary file that is empty. <u>eof</u> is set to <u>true</u>.

The file_name parameter MUST be included.

The temporary file can either replace the original file, or be discarded. This disposition depends on the way the file is closed: see Chapter VII.

As with <u>reset</u>, in UCSD Pascal <u>rewrite</u> may be called with an optional second parameter that associates an external file with file_name. This use of <u>rewrite</u> is defined in Chapter VII.

III.5.2   Pointers

Dynamic variables are allocated memory at runtime, rather than compile-time. A (nameless) variable of a given type may be created by declaring a pointer to that type, and then allocating space to the variable by calling the intrinsic <u>new</u>. Once the variable has been created, it can be referenced by pointers.

Pointers are used to build data structures such as linked lists and trees. For this purpose, they are typically embedded in record structures that contain both information and pointers to other records of similar type.

III.5.2.1   Pointer Format

A pointer is declared in the following way:

    <pointer type name> = ^<type identifier>

... such as:

    pool_ptr = ^<u>string</u>;

The pointer is said to be 'bound to' the type named by <type identifier>.

If we had variables of type pool_ptr:

    var   poolp, newpoolp: pool_ptr;

... we could then reference a string indirectly:

    poolp^:= 'isn''t this a nice test string?';

In a Pascal program, the <pointer type name> by itself refers to the pointer itself; the <pointer type name> followed by an up-arrow (^) refers to the object that is pointed to.

For example, if we made the following assignment:

    newpoolp:=poolp;

... then the following expression would be <u>true</u>:

```
newpoolp^ = 'isn''t this a nice test string?';
         {= poolp^}
```

The predeclared identifier nil is a pointer to nothing. It is usually used to signal the end of a linked list. For example:

```
poolp:= nil;
```

At this point, poolp^ would be undefined; a program which tried to access poolp^ would abort with a runtime error.

In standard Pascal, nil is a reserved word, not a predeclared identifier.

A pointer may be assigned the value of another pointer provided BOTH are pointers to the same data type.

Pointers may be compared with = and <>. There are no operations on pointers.

III.5.2.2 Building Data Structures

As stated before, pointers are most frequently used in conjunction with record structures that carry other information as well. This section illustrates the use of pointers to construct some familiar data structures.

Given the following declarations:

```
type
        arrow = ^name_rec;
        name_rec = record
                            name: string[30];
                            next: arrow;
                    end;
var
        head: arrow;
```

... we could construct a linked list of names. The start of the list is pointed to by the variable head, and the pointer field (next) in the last record of the list is equal to nil.

91

Note that arrow was declared as a ^name_rec before name_rec itself was declared. This is legal as long as both the pointer and the type it references are declared in the same **type** declaration part.

Note also that we did not declare any variables of type name_rec. We are able to build the list by allocating space that is pointed at by head and by subsequent next fields. This is done with the intrinsic <u>new,</u> which is described in Section III.5.2.3.

If the next field of the last record is changed to equal head^ instead of <u>nil,</u> we can turn our linear list into a circular queue.

By changing the declaration of name_rec, we can make our list doubly-linked:

```
name_rec = record
                name: string[30];
                fwd, back: arrow;
           end;
```

... provided the pointers are initialized correctly. In the first record of this list (head^), forward points to a new record, and back = <u>nil.</u> In the last record of this list, back points to the previous record, and forward equals either <u>nil</u> or head^, depending on whether the list is linear or circular.

Here are the declarations for a weighted binary tree:

```
type
        edge = ^node;
        node = record
                   weight: integer;
                   llink, rlink: edge;
               end;
var
        root: edge;
```

... in this example, the pointer called root would be the base of the tree, and in each node, llink would point to the left-hand subtree, and rlink to the right-hand subtree.

These small examples should give the reader some insight into how similar (and more complex) data structures would be

92

declared. The following section explains how to allocate a new data object to a pointer by using the intrinsic new. For a program example that uses pointers, refer to the Programmer's Guide, Chapter 2.

III.5.2.3 Standard Memory Management

This section explains how to allocate and de-allocate memory by using the standard procedures new and dispose. UCSD Pascal provides some further memory-management intrinsics that are more powerful, but more error-prone. These are described in Chapter VIII.

new(POINTER) allocates space for a variable of the type to which POINTER is bound, and sets the value of POINTER equal to the location of that variable.

If the bound type is a record with variants, new allocates enough space for the largest possible record of that type. This can be avoided by the following form of a call to new:

new(POINTER, TAG1, TAG2, ... , TAGn);

... where TAG1 .. TAGn are the tag fields for particular variants. If there are more variants than tag fields specified, the remaining variants are allocated the maximum necessary space. **Warning:** if a record has been allocated with a particular variant, and the program accesses the record using a LARGER variant, the program will encounter incorrect data. In UCSD Pascal, there is no runtime check to protect against this.

Note that a call to new with tag fields does NOT initialize the record, it merely specifies the variants which will be used. The record must still be initialized by a read or an assignment to pointer^.

<u>dispose</u>(POINTER) de-allocates the variable POINTER^, and sets POINTER equal to <u>nil.</u>

If the program does not use much data space, then <u>dispose</u> is probably unnecessary, but if the program's data occupies a lot of main memory, the use of <u>dispose</u>, along with some other memory management scheme, may be required (see Chapter VIII and the Programmer's Guide, Chapter 7).

<u>dispose</u> may be called with case variant tags, just as <u>new</u>. In fact, if <u>new</u> is called with particular variant tags, then <u>dispose</u> must be called with the SAME variant tags; otherwise, the Heap may be damaged and a runtime disaster (as opposed to an error) may result (see Chapter VIII).

III.6 Space Allocation for Data Types

This section outlines the space allocated to Pascal data types, and their overall format. All information here applies to UCSD Pascal, and not necessarily to any other implementation of Pascal. Finer details and implementation-specific details are not dealt with; programmers who need more information on System internals should refer to the UCSD p-System Internal Architecture Guide(5).

III.6.1 Packed Data

The declaration of an array or record may be preceded by the reserved word **packed,** for example:

TITLE: **packed array** [0..89] **of** char;

Declaring an array or record as **packed** does not alter the semantics of a program, it merely alters the way in which the data is stored.

Packed data is stored as tightly as possible. A single data item is never split across a word boundary, and an array or record within a **packed** array or record always begins on a word boundary.

Here are some examples:

TITLE: **packed array** [0..89] **of** char;

... occupies 45 words, rather than 90. Characters are packed two per word.

SAMPLE: **packed array** [0..9] **of**
 packed array [0..9] **of** 0..3;

... occupies 20 words, rather than 100. Each element of 0..3 requires only two bits, so each row of the matrix is 2 words long: 8 elements in the first word and 2 in the next, followed by blank space.

95

One_Word: **packed record**
                choice1, choice2, choice3, choice4,
                choice5, choice6, choice7, choice8:
                    Boolean;
                initial: char;
      end;

... occupies one word, rather than 9. The 8 Boolean bits are packed into one byte, and the character occupies one byte.

If an element in a packed array or record is too large to be effectively packed, the word **packed** is ignored. For example:

packed array [1..5] **of** integer;

Since an integer must occupy 16 bits, the example contains 5 words, just as it would if the word **packed** were not present.

If a field in a packed record happens to be allocated a full word (for example, the next field had to be word-aligned), then the field is "unpacked" and occupies the whole word.

A packed variable may not be compared to an unpacked variable, even if the underlying type is identical.

An element of a packed array or record may never be passed as a **var** parameter, but may be passed as a value parameter.

If a packed record contains a case variant, enough space is allocated for the largest possible variant.

In an array declaration, the appearance of the reserved word **array** WITHOUT the word **packed** in effect "turns packing off." If the entire array must be packed, it is safest to use **packed** in front of every instance of the reserved word **array.**

Standard Pascal defines the intrinsic procedures pack and unpack. Since packing and unpacking are done automatically in the UCSD p-System, there is no need for these procedures, and they are not implemented.

III.6.2 Simple Types

III.6.2.1 Integer

Integers are stored in 16-bit words (two 8-bit bytes) in two's complement format. The constant -32768 is illegal, and cannot be compiled.

When an operation on integers results in an overflow, a runtime error occurs (on most but not all implementations). This can sometimes be avoided by restructuring the expression, for example:

    big1 * big2 **div** big3   {causes an overflow}

    big2 **div** big3 * big1   {doesn't overflow}

Integers are "packed" one per word.

III.6.2.2 Real

In Version IV.0 of the p-System, real numbers are stored in either 2-word (32-bit) or 4-word (64-bit) formats. If the 2-word format is used, constants generated by the Compiler are also 2 words long. If the 4-word format is used, constants generated by the Compiler are from 4 to 6 words long. When a code segment is loaded into memory, real constants are converted to the real format of the host processor, which varies.

For PDP-11/LSI-11 machines, the format of real values is the canonical real format defined for those processors.

In p-System versions BEFORE IV.0, both real operations and real representations are machine-specific.

When an integer is compared to a real, the integer is converted to a real without changing its value.

Since integer values may appear in an expression whose result is real, it is possible for an integer overflow to occur while evaluating a real expression. This can be avoided by re-ordering the expression.

As with integers, real values are "packed" at their actual size (2 or 4 words).

III.6.2.3 Long Integer

Long integer formats vary with the implementation, but a long integer is always allocated an integral number of words.

As with real expressions, it is possible for an integer overflow to occur while evaluating an expression whose result is a long integer.

Long integers are "packed" at their actual size.

III.6.2.4 Boolean

Boolean values are stored in a 16-bit word: a 0 is <u>false</u> and a 1 is <u>true</u>.

The intrinsic function <u>odd</u> does not generate code to convert an integer to a Boolean: it merely allows an integer value to be treated as a Boolean. The low-order bit of the integer indicates whether it is odd or not; the other 15 bits of the word are left unchanged. See the Programmer's Guide, Chapter 8.

A Boolean value is packed into 1 bit.

III.6.2.5 Character

A character is stored as an integer in the range 0..255. Virtually all implementations use the ASCII character set. An unpacked character occupies the low-order byte of a full word.

ASCII codes are only 7 bits long. When ASCII characters are used in I/O to or from a character-oriented device, it is possible that the System will strip the characters' high-order bit.

The intrinsic function <u>chr</u> does not emit code to change the contents of the integer value it is passed: it merely allows that value to be treated as a character.

A character value is packed into a single byte.

III.6.3   Scalars and Subranges

Scalar values are represented as integers: the first value equals 0, the next 1, and so forth.

Values in a subrange are represented as the values of their (scalar) base type; only the boundary conditions for range-checking are altered.

The intrinsic function ord does not emit code to change the contents of the scalar value it is passed: it merely allows that value to be treated as an integer.

When scalar and subrange values are packed, each value is allocated the minimum number of bits necessary to store the MAXIMUM value of the type.

III.6.4   Structured Types

III.6.4.1   Arrays

The space allocated to an array depends on the space needed to store its base type.   All array entries are aligned on word boundaries, unless the array is **packed** (see above).   Elements in an array are stored in row-major order: a single row is stored in sequence, followed by the next row, and so forth. This is opposed to storing the array by columns, which is standard for some other languages.

Arrays are packed according to their base type.   A **packed array of** char contains 2 1-byte characters per word, and so forth.

III.6.4.2   Strings

A string is allocated enough words to contain its static (maximum) length.   The first byte contains the string's dynamic length (0..255).   The rest of the string consists of 1-byte characters packed two per word.

99

Since strings are already packed, packing does nothing.

III.6.4.3   Sets

Each value that may be present in a set is represented by a single bit. The location of the bit corresponds to its ordinal value: bits are numbered from zero, starting at the left. Zeroed bits are "padded" on the right of the "used" bits, so that each set occupies an integral number of words. The length of a set is not normally allocated with the set, but it is sometimes loaded with the set at runtime.

A set may contain at most 4080 elements (255*16 = 4080), and 4079 is the highest possible ordinal value in a set. The set [4078 .. 4079] is a full-sized set, NOT a set of one word.

Sets are already packed, so packing does nothing.

III.6.4.4   Records

Unless a record is packed, each field begins on a word boundary. The space allocated to each field depends on the type of the field.

Fields of a record are packed according to their type, but never cross word boundaries, as described in Section III.6.1.

III.6.5   Dynamic Types

Packing does nothing to dynamic types.

III.6.5.1   Files

Files are created as p-System disk files. If the program does not associate a Pascal file with an existing (or newly created) disk file, and does not use close to save that file, a temporary disk file is created that is removed from the directory when the scope of the file's declaration is exited.

For a typed file, the System allocates a 1-block (512-byte) area of memory as a buffer. No buffer is allocated for untyped files.

More details about disk files and disk directories may be found in the UCSD p-System Users' Manual(3) and UCSD p-System Internal Architecture Guide(5), respectively.

III.6.5.2   Pointers

A pointer is an address of a physical location.   The actual value of a pointer varies from implementation to implementation.   Since data items always begin on word boundaries, a pointer is always a word pointer; on byte-addressed processors, the low-order bit of a pointer is always zero.

The standard value nil also varies from processor to processor.

III.6.6   The Sizeof Intrinsic

sizeof(name), where name is the identifier of ANY variable or data type, returns an integer that is the number of bytes that have been allocated to that variable or data type.

sizeof does not appear in standard Pascal.

Warning: sizeof(ptr^) does not give the size of the object pointed to, but the size of ptr (always 1 word).   To find the size of the object pointed to, call sizeof with the name of the object's type.

Chapter IV
Overall Program Syntax

This chapter describes several topics that apply to the overall syntax of a program. First it covers a program's outline and declarations, then the scope of identifiers, and various restrictions. It ends with a discussion of **unit**s and separate compilation.

IV.1   The Outline of a Program

A Pascal program may be outlined in this form (using EBNF):

    "program" program-name
                ["(" identifier { "," identifier } ")"] ";"

    [label-declarations]
    [constant-declarations]
    [type-declarations]
    [variable-declarations]
    [routine-declarations]

    "begin"
        [statement { ";" statement }]
    "end" "."

EVERY identifier that is used in a Pascal program must be declared before it is used (predeclared identifiers are declared global to the entire program). Declarations must appear in the order they are shown above. A particular kind of declaration does not need to appear if it is not used (for example, a program may use variables, but no constants: only the variable declarations need be present).

UCSD Pascal allows one exception to the order of declarations. One or more include files that contain only declarations (in their proper order) may appear AFTER any **var** or **forward** routine declarations, and BEFORE any bodies of code. For more details, see Chapter X, Section 1.3.

IV.1.1 Program Heading

The first line in a Pascal program consists of the reserved word **program,** followed by an identifier, followed by a semicolon. Here is an EBNF description:

> **"program"** program-name
>   ["(" identifier { "," identifier } ")"] ";"

For example:

> **program** sample;

A list of identifiers may follow the program name, for example:

> **program** sample(input, output);

This feature is provided for compatibility with standard Pascal. In UCSD Pascal, these identifiers may be present, but they are ignored.

IV.1.2 Label Declarations

In Pascal, a label is an integer in the range 0..9999. Any labels that a program uses must be declared in a label declaration with the following scheme (using EBNF):

> **"label"** [label { "," label }] ";"

... such as:

> **label** 1, 13;

A label is a way of tagging a statement so that the statement may be jumped to by a **goto** statement elsewhere in the program. The use of labels and **goto**s is described in Chapter VI, Section 4. Every label that is declared must be referenced by at least one **goto** statement.

IV.1.3 Constant Declarations

A constant declaration associates an identifier with a value; this value does not change throughout the program. Constants are declared according to the following scheme (using EBNF):

```
"const"  { identifier "=" value ";" }
```

For example:

```
const
   file_number = 77;
   ListKey = 0;
   inv_fnum = -file_number;
   KEYLETTER = 'Y';
```

The value of a constant must be a numeric constant, a Boolean, a character, or a string.

The length of a string constant is fixed; it can be assigned to any string variable, or to a **packed array of** char that has the same length.

As shown, a numeric constant may be declared as the opposite (-) of a numeric constant that has already been declared. Other than this, no expressions or previously defined constants are allowed as values in constant declarations.

IV.1.4 Type Declarations

Type declarations are similar to constant declarations. They associate an identifier with a description of a type. Here is a description in EBNF:

```
"type" { identifier "=" type-description ";" }
```

For example:

```
type
   directions = (north, south, east, west);
   link = ^tree;
   tree = record
             height, girth: integer;
             locn: directions;
             next: link
          end;
   bulk = file of integer;
```

IV.1.5   Variable Declarations

A variable declaration associates an identifier with a type.   In EBNF, this is the scheme of a variable declaration:

    "var" { identifier-list ":" type ";" }

The type can either be the name of a type, or a type description (which need not have appeared in the **type** declarations).

For example:

    var
        compass: directions;
        i, j, k, l: <u>integer</u>;
        judgement: (bad, so_so, good);
        in_file: bulk

IV.1.6   Routine Declarations

The details of routine declarations (that is, declarations of procedures, functions, or processes) appear in Chapter V.   The scope of identifiers is affected by routine declarations, and is described in Section IV.2 below.   Some restrictions on routine declarations are described in Section IV.3.1.

In general, the format of a routine declaration is similar to the format of a program.   It contains a heading, followed by declarations, followed by a set of statements enclosed by the reserved words **begin** and **end.**

A routine heading consists of **procedure, function,** or **process** followed by an identifier, followed by an optional list of parameters, followed by a semicolon.   The heading of a **function** also contains the type of the value that is returned by the function.

Here are some routine headings:

        procedure bean;
        function maximum(i,j: <u>integer</u>): <u>integer</u>;
        process cold;
        procedure greater (a,b: <u>real</u>; **var** c: <u>real</u>);

IV.1.7 The Main Body

The main body of a program consists of the reserved word **begin,** followed by a list of statements separated by semicolons, followed by the reserved word **end,** followed by a period (.).

Every Pascal program must have a main body.

IV.2 Structure and Scope

Every routine in a Pascal program, and the Pascal program itself, is said to be a "block." A "block" consists of a heading (such as a program heading or procedure declaration), a list of declarations, and a list of statements surrounded by the reserved words **begin** and **end.**

This structure allows blocks to be nested. A program may contain blocks in the form of routines, each routine may contain blocks in the form of nested routines, and so forth.

The nesting of blocks governs the scope of variables and routines.

IV.2.1 Scope

An item declared within a block is said to be "local" to that block. An item that has been declared in a block that contains a local block is said to be "global" to that local block.

If two procedures are declared in a Pascal program in the following way:

>   **procedure** initialize;
>   ...;
>
>   **procedure** terminate;
>   ...;

... then each of them is an independent block, and neither is local to the other (both of them are local to the program in which they are declared).

On the other hand, if two procedures are nested:

```
procedure scan;
    ...
    procedure get_char;
        ...
        begin {get_char} ...
        end;  {get_char}
    begin  {scan} ...
    end;   {scan}
```

...then the nested procedure belongs to its global procedure. In this example, get_char is local to scan, and scan is global to get_char.

Any item (variable, type, routine, and so forth) that is local to a block is invisible to all of a program except that block itself and any blocks it may contain.

Thus, a procedure (or function, or process) may call any procedures that are global to it, or any procedures that are declared within it, but it may not call procedures that are local to other blocks in the program.

These rules apply to all identifiers. Identifiers declared at the program level may be used anywhere in the program; identifiers declared local to a routine may be used only within that routine and its nested routines, and so forth. Predeclared identifiers are considered global to the entire program.

A global identifier may be re-defined within a subordinate block; the local meaning supplants the global one. For example:

```
program credits;
    ...
    var COUNT: integer;
    ...
    procedure DEBITS;
        ...
        var COUNT: real;
        ...;
    begin ... end.
```

The variable COUNT that is local to DEBITS is a different variable than the variable COUNT that is global to the program. Note that it does not need to be of the same type: in this example, it is not. Within the procedure DEBITS, COUNT would always refer to the local variable: the global COUNT could not be used.

Predeclared identifiers may be re-defined just as user-declared identifiers may be. The programmer should be cautious about doing this, since it impairs a program's readability.

A routine may not call a routine whose declaration FOLLOWS it in the source program. This restriction may be circumvented by using the reserved word **forward,** as described below.

IV.3   Restrictions

IV.3.1   Forward Declarations

It is sometimes necessary for two routines to call each other. It is also sometimes desirable, in order to make a program more readable, to list routine declarations in one place, and the body of the routine code elsewhere. These situations can be handled by use of **forward** declarations.

A routine may be declared with the reserved word **forward** in place of its "block" (its declarations and statements). The routine(s) that must call this routine (and be called by it) may then be declared, followed by a second declaration of the routine along with its full body.

If the routine has parameters, they must be specified in the **forward** declaration, and not in the second declaration.

Suppose the procedures grab1 and grab2 must call each other. The following declarations would allow this:

> **procedure** grab1 (x: <u>integer</u>); **forward;**
>
> **procedure** grab2 (x: <u>integer</u>);
>   {declarations and body of grab2};
>
> **procedure** grab1;
>   {declarations and body of grab1};

Note that the parameters to grabl are declared in the FIRST declaration of grabl. They must not be included in the second declaration of grabl.

IV.3.2 Size Limits

These limits apply only to UCSD Pascal (Version IV.0 or earlier):

A routine may contain no more than 16383 words of local variable space.

A given segment (see Chapter VIII) may contain up to 255 routines.

In versions that precede IV.0, a routine must compile to no more than 1200 bytes of object code (P-code).

IV.3.3 Segment Routines

A code segment is normally the object code (P-code) produced by a single compilation. A routine can be made to occupy a code segment of its own by preceding its heading with the reserved word **segment**. Code segments and segment routines are discussed in more detail in Chapter VIII.

Within a given code segment, the code bodies of all segment routines must precede the code bodies of all non-segment routines.

If a segment routine must call a non-segment routine, the non-segment routine must be declared by a **forward** declaration that precedes the segment routine's declaration.

IV.4 Units and Separate Compilation

Portions of a program in UCSD Pascal may be separately compiled, and "packaged" into a **unit** that may be used by programs or by other **units**.

The UCSD Pascal Compiler will compile:

a single Pascal program,

a single unit,

a number of units (separated by semicolons), or

a Pascal program with in-line units.

A **unit** is not a complete program.   Instead, it consists of an **interface** part, whose declarations may be used by code that **uses** the unit, and an **implementation** part, whose declarations and code are private to the unit.   It may also contain initialization and termination code.

A program or other unit may use the objects declared in a unit's **interface** part by naming the unit in a **uses** declaration.

When a unit is declared within a program, it must appear after the program heading and before any declarations.   A number of units may be declared in this way, each of them followed by a semicolon.   This is a simple way to compile units, but it defeats the advantages of separate compilation.

Units became available in Version I.5, and are present in all subsequent versions.   There are differences in the implementation of units between versions II.0, II.1, and IV.0. These are discussed in Section IV.4.3 below (units in Version III.0 are the same as units in II.0).

IV.4.1 The Uses Declaration

All units that a program uses must be declared in **uses** declarations.   All of these declarations must follow the program heading, and precede any other declarations (such as **label**, **const**, etc.).

For example:

program not_insane;
    uses small_plot, record_ops;
    ...

It is also possible for a unit to use other units. Within a unit, uses declarations immediately follow either the reserved word **interface** or the reserved word **implementation** (see below).

IV.4.2   The Format of a Unit

A **unit** has the following scheme (using EBNF):

"**unit**" identifier "**;**"

    "**interface**"
        [uses-declarations]
        [constant-declarations]
        [type-declarations]
        [variable-declarations]
        [procedure-and-function-headings]

    "**implementation**"
        [uses-declarations]
        [label-declarations]
        [constant-declarations]
        [type-declarations]
        [variable-declarations]
        [procedure-and-function-declarations]

    ["**begin**"
        [initialization-statements]
        ["*****;**"
            termination-statements]
    ] "**end**"

The data structures and routines declared in a unit's **interface** part are global to the program or unit that **uses** them; the data structures and routines declared in the **implementation** part are strictly private to the unit, and may not be used by any other code. This allows the programmer to separate the unit's interface (whose form is determined by the problem to which the unit is applied) from the implementation (which may vary from system to system or be improved over time).

When a unit is changed, it must be recompiled. If its interface section is NOT changed, the programs that use it do not need to be recompiled. If the interface section IS changed, then all programs that use the unit must be recompiled as well.

IV.4.2.1   Restrictions

When a procedure or function is to be part of a unit's interface, its heading must appear in the interface part. This heading must include all of the procedure's or function's parameters. The actual code for the procedure must appear in the unit's implementation part: the procedure or function heading must reappear WITHOUT any parameters. This scheme is analogous to the declaration of forward routines, although the word **forward** is not used.

Segment procedures and functions must be declared as such in the implementation part: the reserved word **segment** must not appear in the interface part. The same restriction applies to procedures and functions that are declared **external.**

An interface part may not contain an include file (see the string option $I, described in Chapter X, Section 1.3).

In Version IV.0, an include file may contain ALL of an interface part, followed by the reserved word **implementation,** and, possibly, the rest of the implementation part as well. An interface part is treated by the Compiler as if it were a single include file.

If **uses** declarations appear within the **interface** part of a unit, they must be ordered correctly: if unit first_level **uses** unit second_level, the interface part must specify:

uses second_level, first_level;

... to avoid a compilation error.

IV.4.2.2   Initialization and Termination Code

The "main body" of a unit may consist of a single **end,** or a compound statement (with a **begin end** pair).

The compound statement may contain the construct:

   ***;

This "pseudo-statement" is used to separate initialization code from termination code.   All statements which precede ´***;´ are initialization statements, and all statements which follow ´***;´ are termination statements.   If no ´***;´ is present, the entire compound statement is understood as initialization code; if the entire compound statement is intended to be termination code, ´***;´ must be the first statement to follow the **begin.**

Initialization code is executed BEFORE any code of the host that **uses** the unit (whether that host is a program or other unit).

Termination code is executed AFTER the host´s code has terminated.

The compound statement should not contain branches around ´***;´: branching past it from initialization to termination code has the effect of executing the termination code and skipping the host´s code entirely, while branching from termination to initialization code has the effect of re-executing the initialization code and locking the host´s execution in an "endless" loop!

If an exit(**program**) call appears in initialization code, the remainder of initialization code is skipped, and so is the host´s code: execution proceeds with the unit´s termination code.   If an exit(**program**) appears in termination code, the remainder of the termination code is skipped (this applies only to the unit in which the exit appears: if the termination code of other units is pending, it will still be executed).   The call exit(<unit name>) is not legal.

In versions that precede IV.0, the '***;' construct is not available: the main body of the unit, if present, is entirely initialization code.

The syntax '***;' was adapted from the Pascal dialect called Pascal Plus, by Welsh and Bustard (14).

IV.4.3   The Implementation of Units

When a program uses a unit in Version IV.0, the code for that unit must be either within the program itself, the file *SYSTEM.LIBRARY, a user library file, or the Operating System.   If the System can find the unit's code, it is automatically linked to the host's code.

If the unit is in a user library file, this file must be named with the $U compiler option (see Section X.1).   Library files are described in the UCSD p-System Users' Manual(3).

IV.4.3.1   Previous Versions

In versions prior to IV.0, the user must explicitly use the System's Linker to link unit code to its host's code.

Version II.0 allows the declaration of a **separate unit.**   With a separate unit, only the code for those procedures and functions that are actually called by the host is linked.   Separate units have never been fully functional.   Version IV.0 accepts declarations of **separate** units, but treats them like any other unit.

Version II.1 allows the declaration of an **intrinsic unit.** Intrinsic units, like current IV.0 units, do not need to be explicitly linked before they are used.   Version IV.0 does not accept declarations of **intrinsic** units.

115

Chapter V
Procedures and Functions

Routines are distinguished by the manner in which they are called. A **procedure** is called by a statement that simply consists of the procedure's name (and possibly a parameter list). A **function** is called from within an expression. A **process** is initiated by a call to the intrinsic procedure <u>start.</u>

This chapter describes procedures and functions. Processes are described in Chapter IX, which deals with concurrency.

V.1   Procedure and Function Declarations

In the previous chapter, we saw some examples of procedure and function headings. They may be described by the following EBNF expressions:

> **"procedure"** identifier [
>   "(" ["**var**"] id-list ":" type-id
>   { ";" ["**var**"] id-list ":" type-id }
>   ")"] ";"

> **"function"** identifier [
>   "(" ["**var**"] id-list ":" type-id
>   { ";" ["**var**"] id-list ":" type-id }
>   ")"] ":" type-id ";"

The list of parameters to a procedure or function is optional. Parameters are a means by which a procedure or function can communicate with other portions of a program.

The parameters declared in the routine heading are known as 'formal' parameters. When a routine is called, the program specifies the values and variables that the routine should actually use: these are known as 'actual' parameters.

Here is an example:

```
procedure max (a,b: integer; var result: integer);
   {determines the maximum of two integers}
   begin
      if  a >= b  then
         result:= a
      else
         result:= b;
   end {max};
```

... which could be called by the following statements:

```
max(bound1, bound2, compare);
...
max(7,346,maxval);
```

... and so forth.   Note that the declaration of the formal
parameter result is preceded by the reserved word **var**.   This
allows a value to be assigned to result, which changes the value
of the actual parameters used (in this example, compare and
maxval).   **var** parameters are discussed in more detail below.

We could use a function to do the same calculation:

```
function max (a,b: integer): integer;
   {finds the maximum of two integers and returns it}
   begin
      if  a >= b  then
         max:= a
      else
         max:= b;
   end {max};
```

Note in this example that the code is essentially the same, but
the result is assigned to the function name, rather than a
parameter.   This is how a function's result is returned.   The
type of the value assigned to the function name must be
assignment-compatible with the function's type, which is
declared in the function heading (for compatibility rules, see
Chapter III, Section 2.7.1).

The function could be called in the following ways:

```
higher:= max(threshold, 100);
...
result:= 134 + (max(term1,term2)*2)/reduce;
...
if  year <> max(date1, date2)  then ...
```

... and so forth.

In the routine heading, a parameter's type must be specified by a type identifier ('type-id' in the EBNF), and not a type description.

V.1.1 Value Parameters

A 'value parameter' is declared in a routine heading by including the name of the parameter and its type.

Value parameters are used as local values for the purpose of local calculations. If a value parameter is changed within a routine, only the local copy of the parameter changes.

An actual parameter that corresponds to a value parameter may be either a constant or a variable, provided it is of the correct type. If the actual parameter is a variable, its value is not affected by the called routine.

V.1.2 Variable Parameters

A 'variable parameter' or '**var** parameter' is declared in the same way as a value parameter, but the declaration is preceded by the reserved word **var.**

Variable parameters are used to pass the results of calculations from the routine (usually a procedure) to its caller. If, within the routine, a value is assigned to the formal name of a variable parameter, the value of the actual parameter also changes. (This form of parameter passing is also called "call-by-reference.")

An actual parameter that corresponds to a variable parameter MUST be a variable of the proper type. The programmer should assume that its value will by changed by the call to the routine.

The declarations of value and variable parameters may be lumped together, for example:

```
procedure many_parms (a, b, c, d: real;
                       var e, f, g, h, i: real;
                       j, k, l, m, n: real);
```

... where the first and last groups of parameters declare value parameters, and the middle group declares variable parameters. The **var** declaration applies to the declarations that immediately follow it: its "influence" extends to the next semicolon (;).

Constants, elements of a **packed array,** fields of a **packed record,** and **for** loop counters may not be passed as **var** parameters.

A file may ONLY be passed as a **var** parameter.

Range-checking is never performed on strings passed as **var** parameters.

Variable parameters, unlike value parameters, are not copied into a routine's local area. When very large variables (such as arrays) must be passed to a routine, memory space can be saved by passing them as **var** parameters, even when the routine is not meant to change their contents.

V.1.3 Procedures and Functions as Parameters

In UCSD Pascal, a procedure or function may NOT be passed as a parameter to another routine. This is allowed in standard Pascal.

V.2 Calling Procedures and Functions

As already illustrated, a procedure is called by a single statement, and a function is called by using it within an expression.

Procedures and functions may call themselves recursively. This is illustrated in the Programmer's Guide, Chapter 3. It is important that recursive routines be written so that they will eventually terminate; the calls must eventually reach a case where the procedure or function does NOT call itself. There is no way for the System to check this, so the programmer must use caution. A "runaway" recursive routine causes the program to halt with a Stack Overflow runtime error.

When the code of a procedure or function has finished executing, the procedure or function "returns" to the caller. Execution proceeds from the point at which the procedure or function was called.

The user can cause a routine to return immediately, from anywhere in its code body, by calling the UCSD intrinsic procedure exit, which is described in Chapter VI, Section 4.

A function must contain at least one statement that assigns a value to the name of the function, and at least one of these statements must be executed. There is no runtime checking to see whether this is done; it is the programmer's responsibility.

In a procedure or function call, the order of actual parameters, their number, and their type must correspond exactly to the order, number, and type of formal parameters.

Certain Pascal intrinsics have optional parameters that may be omitted when the intrinsic is called, but this is a peculiarity of intrinsic routines, and there is no way for a user-written routine to specify optional parameters.

Chapter VI
Control Statements

This chapter discusses the statements that can be used to direct a program's sequence of execution (its "flow of control").

VI.1   Compound Statements

A group of statements can be made to appear as a single statement by surrounding it with the reserved words **begin** and **end.** Such a group is called a 'compound statement'. Here is an EBNF description:

```
compound-statement =
    "begin" statement { ";" statement } "end"
```

As the expression shows, a semicolon serves to separate statements rather than terminate them.   Nonetheless, it is common practice to put a semicolon after the last statement in the statement list (it is considered to be followed by a null statement).   This simply makes it easier to add statements to the statement list while debugging or maintaining the program. Most of the code samples in this book show this optional semicolon.

These are compound statements:

```
begin
    initialize;
    calculate;
    print_report;
    terminate;
end {outer_proc}

begin
    sum:=  odd_int(sum,pile[i]);
    all:=  all+1;   choice[all]:= i;
    if   pile[i] = 1   then   ones:= ones+1
    else
        if   pile[i] > 1   then   p:= i;
end
```

A compound statement may appear anywhere a single statement can.

123

VI.2   Conditional Statements

Pascal provides two forms of decision-making statements: the **if** statement, and the **case** statement.

VI.2.1   The If Statement

An **if** statement has two forms.   Here is an EBNF description:

```
if-statement =
    "if" Boolean-expression "then" statement
 |
    "if" Boolean-expression "then"
        statement
    "else"
        statement
```

If the Boolean expression is <u>true</u>, then the statement that follows the reserved word **then** is executed.   If the **if** statement has an **else** part and the Boolean expression is <u>false</u>, then the statement that follows the reserved word **else** is executed.

In the **if then else** form of the **if** statement, a semicolon MUST NOT precede the reserved word **else**, since the semicolon indicates the end of the entire **if** statement.

if statements are often nested, and this can appear to be ambiguous:

```
if <Boolean exprl> then
    if <Boolean expr2> then <statementl>
    else <statement2>;
```

... does the **else** pair with the first **if** or the second **if**?   In Pascal, the rule is that an **else** pairs with the CLOSEST matching **if**.   Thus, this example is indented correctly.   An equivalent statement would be:

```
if <Boolean exprl> then
    begin
        if <Boolean expr2> then <statementl>
        else <statement2>
    end;
```

If the outer **if** statement has an **else** part but the nested **if** does not, then **begin** and **end** should be used:

```
if <Boolean expr1> then
    begin
        if <Boolean expr2> then <statement1>
    end
else <statement2>;
```

... or the nested **if** should use a null **else** part:

```
if <Boolean expr1> then
    if <Boolean expr2> then <statement1>
    else   {do nothing}
else <statement2>;
```

Here are two examples of **if** statements, one straightforward, one less so:

```
if found
    then   Classify:= sym_tab[m].kind
    else   Classify:= symbol;

if   sym_name = sym_tab[m].name
    then   found:= true
else if   sym_name < sym_tab[m].name
    then   r:= m-1
else if   sym_name > sym_tab[m].name
    then   l:= m+1;
```

It is common practice to indent long sequences of **else if**s so that they line up vertically: this makes them easier to read, and emphasizes the fact that they represent a series of cases of which only one will be executed.

VI.2.2   The Case Statement

A **case** statement has this form (using EBNF):

```
case-statement =
    "case" expression "of"
        constant-list ":" statement
        { ";" constant-list ":" statement } [";"]
    "end"
```

125

Note that the reserved word **end** pairs with the reserved word **case** (just as an **end** pairs with **record**); there is no **begin**.

The expression must evaluate to a scalar (or subrange) value. Each constant-list consists of one or more constants of the same type as the expression (if there is more than one constant, they are separated by commas). No constant may appear in more than one constant list.

If the value of the expression matches a constant in one of the constant lists, the statement that follows that constant list is executed.

Here is an example of a **case** statement:

```
read(letter);
case letter of
    'A': Assemble;
    'C': Compile;
    'D': Debug;
    'E': Edit;
    'F': File;
    'H': halt;
    'I': Re_Init;
    'L': Link;
    'M': monitor:= true;
    'R': begin
                codefile:= '*system.wrk.text';
                Execute;
           end;
    'U': Execute;
    'X': begin get_codefile; Execute end;
    end {case}
```

... we hasten to point out that this is merely an illustration, and NOT a portion of the actual Operating System! Similar code is used to handle single-character commands at the outer command level.

In UCSD Pascal, if the case expression does not evaluate to one of the given options (for instance, in the example, not all 26 letters are shown), then the **case** statement is bypassed, and the next statement in sequence is executed. The **case** is said to "fall through." This is contrary to standard Pascal, in which the result of a **case** is undefined if a selected option is not present.

There must be at least one statement preceded by a constant list. This is a restriction of UCSD Pascal, and is not required in standard Pascal.

Here are examples of **case** statements with more than one constant in a constant list:

```
case digit of
    0: resume;
    1: prompt;
    2: restart;
    3: quit;
    4, 5, 6,
        7, 8, 9: {do nothing};
    end;

case color of
    orange, brown: repaint;
    red: touch_up;
    blue, yellow, green: mix;
    end;
```

VI.3   Repetition

In Pascal, there are three forms of loop: **while, repeat,** and **for.** **while** and **repeat** statements execute indefinitely, until some terminating condition is met. In a **while** statement, the condition is tested before the loop is executed, while in a **repeat** statement, the condition is tested after the loop: these two statements complement each other. A **for** statement uses a variable as a counter, and loops for a given number of times.

VI.3.1   The **While** Statement

A **while** statement has the form (using EBNF):

```
while-statement =
    "while" Boolean-expression "do"
        statement
```

Before each iteration of the loop, the Boolean expression is tested: if it is <u>true</u>, the statement is executed, otherwise the loop ends.

Clearly, unless the statement itself contains some code which will eventually cause the Boolean expression to be <u>false</u>, the **while** loop will continue to execute indefinitely.

Since the **while** statement tests the Boolean expression BEFORE the statement is executed, it is often necessary to initialize variables that appear in the Boolean expression.

Occasionally, it IS desirable for a **while** to execute indefinitely (for example, some kinds of concurrent processes require this). In this case, the programmer may specify:

```
while true do <statement>;
```

Here are two examples of **while** statements:

```
go_on:= true;   {this initialization is necessary}
while go_on do
    begin
        GENERATE(half, whole);
        if half < 1 then go_on:= false;
    end;

num_piles:= 0;   {initialization}
while not eoln and (num_piles < pile_max) do
    begin
        num_piles:= num_piles+1;
        read(pile[num_piles]);
    end;
```

128

Note that the second example is guaranteed to terminate. Presumably, the first example will terminate as well, provided the procedure GENERATE does what it is supposed to do.

VI.3.2   The Repeat Statement

A **repeat** statement has the form (using EBNF):

```
repeat-statement =
    "repeat"
        statement { ";" statement }
    "until" Boolean-expression
```

The program executes the statement list, then tests the Boolean expression.   If the Boolean expression is <u>true</u>, the statement list is executed again, and so forth.   If the Boolean expression is <u>false</u>, the loop ends.

Since the Boolean expression is tested AFTER the statement list is executed, there is usually no need to initialize the variables used in the Boolean expression.

When a **repeat** must execute indefinitely, the programmer may use the form:

>   **repeat** <statement list> **until** <u>false</u>;

Here are two examples:

>   **repeat** <u>read</u>(remainder) **until** <u>eof</u>;

>   **repeat**
>   num_piles:= num_piles+1;
>   <u>read</u>(pile[num_piles]);
>   **until** <u>eoln</u> **or** (num_piles >= pile_max)

Note that the second **repeat** example accomplishes the same thing as the second **while** example in the preceding section, EXCEPT that the assignment and the <u>read</u> are always executed at least once.   Notice that the conditions for terminating the loop have been inverted.

129

VI.3.3   The For Statement

A **for** statement has two forms. Here is an EBNF description:

```
for-statement =
    "for" var-id ":=" start-value "to"
        stop-value "do"
            statement
  |
    "for" var-id ":=" start-value "downto"
        stop-value "do"
            statement
```

The 'var-id' is a variable of some scalar or subrange type. It is called the 'index' of the **for** loop. The 'start-value' and 'stop-value' are values of the same type as the index variable (typically integer).

When a **for to** statement is executed, the 'start-value' and 'stop-value' are evaluated ONCE. The index is assigned the value of the 'start-value'. The statement is executed, and then the index is replaced by its successor (if it is an integer, it is incremented by 1). This continues until the value of the index is greater than the 'stop-value'.

A **for downto** statement is executed in the same way as a **for to** statement, except that before each iteration of the loop, the index is replaced by its predecessor (if it is an integer, it is decremented by 1). The loop ends when the value of the index is less than the 'stop-value'.

If the 'start-value' is greater than the 'stop-value' (or less than, for the **downto** form), then the statement is not executed at all. If the 'start-value' equals the 'stop-value', the statement is executed once.

The index must be a local variable. It cannot be a **var** parameter. After the **for** statement has executed, the value of its index is undefined, and the programmer must re-initialize the index variable if it is to be used again.

Here are some examples:

```
for weekday:= Mon to Sun do
    print_schedule(weekday);
```

```
for j:= i-1 downto 2 do
    p[j]:= p[j] + p[j-1];

for j:= 1 to i do
    begin
        write(j,': ');
        writeln(p[j]);
    end;
```

VI.4   Branching

By "branching" we mean changing a program's flow of control
by some means other than the statements already described in
this chapter. This practice is discouraged in structured
programming, but there are times (usually error conditions)
when it is the least painful way to accomplish something. The
goto statement allows unconditional branching. UCSD Pascal
also provides the intrinsic procedures <u>exit</u> and <u>halt</u> to allow
emergency terminations.

VI.4.1   The Goto Statement

A **goto** statement has the form (using EBNF):

    goto-statement =
        "goto" label

The label must be declared, and must be local to the block (the
routine or main program body) in which the **goto** statement
appears (see Chapter III).   A label has the form of an integer
in the range 0..9999.

UCSD Pascal requires a **goto** statement to be in the same
block as the label it names.   Standard Pascal does not.

Execution proceeds from the labelled statement.   This may
cause some statements to be skipped, or some statements to be
repeated.

Using EBNF, the form of a labelled statement is:

    labelled-statement =
        label ":" statement

For example:

```
... {program code}
goto 1558;
... {more program code -- }
     {all of this is skipped}
1558: {execution continues here}
     report_disaster;
...
```

In UCSD Pascal versions that precede Version IV.0, **goto** statements may not appear in a program unless the programmer has enabled them by using the {$G+} compiler option (this is no longer implemented).

VI.4.2 Exit

A routine or a program may be terminated immediately by calling the UCSD intrinsic exit. exit may be called in three ways:

exit(<routine name>);

exit(<program name>);

exit(**program**);

When exit is used in a procedure or function, execution returns to the caller of that routine. Any local files still open are closed and purged (see Chapter VII). If exit is used within a function, and called before the value of that function has been defined, the function returns an undefined value. If exit is used in a procedure or function that has been called recursively, control returns to the previous call (the call stack is "popped").

When a process is exit´ed, its execution ends.

Within the initialization and termination code of a **unit**, exit behaves in particular ways. These are described in Chapter IV, Section 4.2.2.

When exit is called with the name of the program or the reserved word **program**, the program is terminated immediately and control returns to the Operating System. Any open files

132

are closed as if by a call to close(file_name, normal) (see Chapter VII, Section 2.1).

VI.4.3   Halt

A call to the UCSD intrinsic halt causes the program to abort with a runtime error: the effect is similar to that of hitting the <break> key while a program is running.

Control is transferred to the Operating System unless the Debugger is running, in which case control is transferred to the Debugger.   The Debugger is described in the UCSD p-System Users' Manual(3).

It should be evident that a call to halt is either an emergency measure or a means of deliberately invoking the p-System Debugger.

Chapter VII
Input and Output

This chapter first describes the standard Pascal I/O intrinsics. It then covers I/O for external files, and finally device I/O. Standard I/O for internal files is described in Chapter III, Section 5.1.

Standard input and output in Pascal is done with the intrinsics read, readln, write, writeln, eof, eoln, and page. See Section VII.1.

External files under the UCSD p-System may be opened with extended calls to the intrinsics reset and rewrite. They may be closed with the intrinsic close. Disk files may be accessed randomly with the intrinsic seek. Untyped files are handled with the intrinsics blockread and blockwrite. See Section VII.2.

In UCSD Pascal, device I/O may also be done with a group of lower-level intrinsics: unitbusy, unitclear, unitread, unitstatus, unitwait, and unitwrite. See Section VII.3.

VII.1 Standard Pascal I/O

For examples of the use of these intrinsics, the reader should refer to the Programmer's Guide, Chapter 4.

VII.1.1 Read and Readln

read(FILENAME, ITEM1, ITEM2, ..., ITEMn) reads characters from FILENAME, converts them into values, and sequentially assigns them to the variables ITEM1, ITEM2, through ITEMn.

> The FILENAME parameter need not be present. If it is absent, the standard file input is used. In the p-System, input defaults to the device CONSOLE:, but this default can be overridden by the user; see the description of redirection in the UCSD p-System Users' Manual(3).

> If FILENAME has been associated with an external file, it MUST be a textfile (that is, a file of type text, interactive, or **file of** char).

> There may be one or more ITEMs. Each is a variable. If the type of the data read from the file does not match the type of the corresponding variable, a runtime error results.

An ITEM must be of type integer (or subrange of integer), long integer, real, char (or subrange of char), string, or **packed array of** char. Boolean values and structured types other than string or **packed array of** char may not be read.

If the input file is interactive, read behaves a bit differently than it would with a standard textfile. A standard read(FILENAME,ch) is defined as the sequence:

ch:= FILENAME^; get(FILENAME);

... but since an interactive file normally contains no values until the user has started typing them in, this standard definition would result in a runtime error. UCSD Pascal therefore defines a read on an interactive file to be the opposite sequence from the standard:

get(FILENAME); ch:=FILENAME^;

... this altered order also affects the setting of eoln: see below.

When integer or real values are read, leading blanks and carriage returns (<return>, ASCII CR) are ignored until a non-blank character is read.

The entry of a value is terminated by a space (' '), a <return>, or a character that is not a digit (reals may be entered with an exponent such as 'e+24'). When entering a value from an interactive file, the user may correct it before it has been terminated by using the <backspace> key and re-typing; once a value has been read, there is no way to correct it.

When a string value is read, it must be terminated by a <return>. For this reason, strings should be read by readln rather than read: see below.

readln(FILENAME, ITEM1, ITEM2, ..., ITEMn) is identical to read, except that the ITEM parameters are optional, and readln expects to read a <return> after all the ITEMs have been read; readln will wait until this <return> is read.

Since string values must be terminated with a ⟨return⟩, readln is the proper way to read strings: only one string value per call to readln.

A call to readln without parameters may be used to ignore the rest of a line. This is especially useful for stepping to the next line of a file after a series of reads:

```
n:= 0;
while  not eoln  do
    begin
        read(a[n]);
        n:= n+1;
    end;
readln;
```

VII.1.2 Write and Writeln

write(FILENAME, VALUE1, VALUE2, ..., VALUEn) sequentially writes VALUE1, VALUE2, through VALUEn to the file FILENAME.

The FILENAME parameter need not be present. If it is absent, the standard file output is used. In the p-System, output defaults to the device CONSOLE:, but this default can be overridden by the user; see the discussion of redirection in the UCSD p-System Users' Manual(3).

If FILENAME is associated with an external file, it MUST be a textfile (that is, a file of type text, interactive, or file of char).

There may be one or more values.

In UCSD Pascal, a value to be written must be of type integer, long integer, real, char, string, or packed array of char. Boolean values and structured types other than string or packed array of char may not be written. In standard Pascal, Boolean values may be written.

writeln(FILENAME, VALUE1, VALUE2, ..., VALUEn) is identical to write, except that the VALUE parameters are optional, and it writes a carriage return (⟨return⟩) after all other VALUEs have been written.

137

It is common practice to write several VALUEs to a single line with repeated calls to <u>write</u>, and then finish the line by a call to <u>writeln</u> that has no parameters:

```
for i:= 1 to 10 do
    write(a[i]:5);
writeln;
```

VII.1.2.1   Field Specifications

When a value is written, it is written within an 'output field' that is some number of characters wide. The default width of an output field is automatically wide enough to contain the value being printed. The user may override the default field width by explicitly specifying a field width within the call to <u>write</u> or <u>writeln</u>.

Values may be formatted by entering them in this manner:

```
value1:m
realvalue:m:n
```

... where m is a positive integer that specifies the output field width. If the value is real, n may be included: it is a positive integer that specifies the number of decimal places to be written.

If the printed format of the value is shorter than the field width m, the value is right-justified, and blanks are written on the left. If the value is numeric and m does not specify enough spaces, the full value is written, and m is ignored.

Real values must have at least room for the number plus a sign on the left. If the real value is too large for the specified format, it is written in exponential form.

Values of type <u>string</u> are always written with a field length equal to their dynamic length, unless a field length m is specified. If m is greater than the string's dynamic length, the string is right-justified, and spaces are written on the left. If m is less than the string's dynamic length, the string is truncated on the right. The length of a **packed array of** <u>char</u> is not dynamic, but otherwise it is written exactly as a <u>string</u>.

VII.1.3   Eof and Eoln

The intrinsic functions eof and eoln have already been described
in Chapter III, Section 5.1.   They are both Boolean functions:
eof(FILENAME) returns true when the end of FILENAME has
been reached, and eoln(FILENAME) returns true when a <return>
character has just been read.

The FILENAME parameter may be omitted, in which case eof
and eoln refer to the predeclared file input.

When reading from an interactive file, eoln is initially false,
and is set to true only when a <return> character is read.   The
value received by the read is a space (' ') rather than a
<return> character.

VII.1.4   Page

page(FILENAME) writes a form feed character (ASCII FF,
chr(12)) to the textfile FILENAME.

VII.2   Handling External Files

Files in Pascal programs may be associated with external files in the p-System.   To the UCSD p-System, a file is any source of data or sink for data.   Thus, a file may be a file on a block-structured device such as a floppy disk, an interactive device such as a terminal, a write-only device such as a printer, and so forth.

More information on p-System files and devices may be found in the UCSD p-System Users' Manual(3).

VII.2.1   Opening and Closing Files

This section explains how to open an external file (whether a device or disk file) with the procedures reset and rewrite.   It also describes how to save or remove a file with the close intrinsic.   The standard use of reset and rewrite is described in Chapter III, Section 5.1.

reset(FILENAME, EXT_FILE) does a standard reset on FILENAME, and also associates the Pascal (internal) file FILENAME with the p-System (external) file EXT_FILE.

The parameter EXT_FILE is a string expression that specifies the name of a p-System file.

If EXT_FILE is nonexistent, or the device is offline, or the file is already open, a runtime error results (unless I/O-checking has been disabled: see Chapter X, Section 1).

If EXT_FILE is a write-only device (such as PRINTER: or REMOUT:), a runtime error results, because reset attempts to initialize FILENAME^ for all files that are not interactive.

Here are some examples:

```
{opening disk files:}
    reset(bookfile, 'CHAPTER2.TEXT');
    reset(seismic, '#5:MARCH.12.DATA');
{opening an interactive device:}
    reset(talk, 'CONSOLE:');
{opening a file with a variable name:}
```

```
        userfile: = '*PROJECT.TEXT';
        reset(bookfile, userfile);
```

rewrite(FILENAME, EXT_FILE) does a standard rewrite on
FILENAME, and also associates the Pascal (internal) file
FILENAME with the p-System (external) file EXT_FILE.

The parameter EXT_FILE is a string expression that
specifies the name of a p-System file.

If EXT_FILE is not the name of an existing file, a new file
is created with that name.

If EXT_FILE is a file that already exists, rewrite creates a
temporary file to operate on while the program executes.
This temporary file can supplant the original file (as with a
rewrite in standard Pascal), be discarded, or be saved under
a new name. This depends on how the close intrinsic is
used; see below.

If EXT_FILE is a device that is offline, or a file that is
already open, a runtime error results (unless I/O-checking
has been turned off: see Chapter X, Section 1).

If there is no EXT_FILE parameter, rewrite(FILENAME) is
equivalent to rewrite(FILENAME, 'FILENAME'), for the first
8 characters of the FILENAME identifier.

Here are some examples:

```
    {clearing a disk file:}
       rewrite(bookfile, 'CHAPTER2.TEXT');
    {creating a new disk file:}
       rewrite(seismic, '#5:MARCH.31.DATA');
    {resetting an I/O device:}
       rewrite(talk, 'REMOUT:');
    {clearing a file with a variable name:}
       userfile: = '*PROJECT.TEXT';
       rewrite(bookfile, userfile);
    {creating a temporary file:}
       rewrite(scratch)  { = rewrite(scratch, 'scratch')}
```

Files opened with reset or rewrite may be closed by the
intrinsic close.

close(FILENAME [, OPTION]) closes the file FILENAME. After the close, the value of FILENAME^ is no longer defined.

If present, OPTION must be one of these words:

> normal
> lock
> purge
> crunch

The OPTION parameter may be omitted. If it is not present, close(FILENAME) is equivalent to close(FILENAME, normal).

close(FILENAME, normal) closes FILENAME. If FILE_NAME was associated with a disk file by a previous call to rewrite, then the call to close deletes the temporary version from the directory, and the original file is unaffected.

close(FILENAME, lock) is equivalent to a normal close unless FILENAME was associated with a disk file by a previous call to rewrite. In that case, the temporary file is saved, and the original version deleted.

close(FILENAME, purge) is equivalent to a normal close unless FILENAME was associated with a disk file or a device. If FILENAME is associated with a disk file, that disk file is removed from the directory. If FILENAME is associated with a device, the device goes offline.

close(FILENAME, crunch) is equivalent to a lock close, except that the file is truncated where it was last accessed: the position of the last get, put, read, or write to the file becomes the last record in the file.

When a Pascal program finishes its execution normally (that is, no runtime error occured), a close(FILENAME, normal) is done on all files. This does not affect files that have already been closed by the programmer.

VII.2.2   Random Access to Files

Unlike standard Pascal, where files are strictly sequential, UCSD Pascal allows file records to be accessed in random order, by use of the intrinsic <u>seek</u>, which is described in this section.

<u>seek</u>(FILENAME, INDEX) sets the file window to the INDEX'th record in FILENAME; <u>eof</u> is set to <u>false</u>.

>FILENAME cannot be a textfile or an untyped file. An internal file is a textfile if it is of type <u>text</u>, <u>interactive</u>, or **file of** <u>char</u>. Trying to <u>seek</u> on a textfile or untyped file causes a runtime error.

>INDEX is an integer. File records are numbered starting from zero. If INDEX is less than zero or greater than the largest record index in the file, <u>seek</u> accepts this: the next <u>get</u> or <u>put</u> to FILENAME will cause <u>eof</u> to be set to <u>true</u>.

>A <u>get</u>(FILENAME) or <u>put</u>(FILENAME) call MUST be made between two consecutive calls to <u>seek</u>: if this is not done, the contents of the window will be undefined and unpredictable.

>Note that <u>seek</u> does not set the value of the window variable (FILENAME^). That must be done by a call to <u>get</u> or <u>put</u>.

VII.2.3   Untyped Files

In UCSD Pascal, a file may be declared in the following way:

>file_name: **file;**

This is called an 'untyped' file. An untyped file does NOT have a window location or a window value. It must be associated with an external file by <u>reset</u> or <u>rewrite</u>, and the only way to manipulate it is by the UCSD intrinsic functions <u>blockread</u> and <u>blockwrite</u>, which are described in this section.

<u>blockread</u> and <u>blockwrite</u> do no type checking or range checking at all, so their use can lead to errors. The programmer must take care that they do not destroy any valuable data.

<u>blockread</u>(FILENAME, BUFFER, COUNT, RELBLOCK) attempts to read COUNT blocks from FILENAME into BUFFER, starting

from RELBLOCK. It returns the number of blocks that were actually transferred.

FILENAME is an untyped file that has been associated with an external file by a call to reset or rewrite.

BUFFER is a typeless parameter (typeless parameters are described in Chapter III, Section 4.1.4).

COUNT is an integer.

RELBLOCK need not be present. If it is present, it is a (zero-based) block index into FILENAME, and indicates the location from which the read should begin.

If the value returned by blockread does not equal COUNT, then either the end of the file was encountered, or a read error occurred. The programmer should check these conditions. If the end of file IS encountered, blockread sets eof to true.

Successive blockreads on the same file will continue to read blocks in sequence, unless RELBLOCK is used to explicitly name a location, or the file is re-initialized with reset or rewrite.

blockwrite(FILENAME, BUFFER, COUNT, RELBLOCK) attempts to write COUNT blocks from BUFFER into FILENAME, starting at RELBLOCK. It returns the number of blocks that were actually transferred.

FILENAME is an untyped file that has been associated with an external file by a call to reset or rewrite.

BUFFER is a typeless parameter.

COUNT is an integer.

RELBLOCK need not be present. If it is present, it is a (zero-based) block index into FILENAME, and indicates where the writing should begin.

If the value returned by blockwrite does not equal COUNT, then either the end of the file was encountered, or a write error occurred. The programmer should check these

conditions.   If the end of file IS encountered, blockwrite
sets eof to true.

Successive blockwrites on the same file will continue to
write blocks in sequence, unless RELBLOCK is used to
explicitly name a location, or the file is re-initialized with
reset or rewrite.

VII.3   The UCSD p-System Environment

VII.3.1   Keyboard

Files of type <u>interactive</u> have already been described (in Section VII.1, and Chapter III, Section 5.1).   The standard predeclared files <u>input</u> and <u>output</u> are interactive in UCSD Pascal.   So is the predeclared file <u>keyboard</u>.

When a character is read from the file <u>input</u>, that character is also echoed on the CONSOLE:.   <u>keyboard</u>, on the other hand, does NOT echo the character that is typed.   The most common use of <u>keyboard</u> is in reading a user's response to a promptline, since there is no need to redisplay that character on the screen.

A read from <u>input</u> (for example, <u>read(input</u>, character);) is equivalent to:

    read(keyboard, character);
    write(output, character);

VII.3.2   Device I/O

This section describes the UCSD intrinsics that may be used to control peripheral devices directly.   The use of these intrinsics is somewhat error-prone, and the programmer should be cautious with them.   On the other hand, they can be much faster than the standard Pascal I/O intrinsics, and are therefore indispensable for some applications.

For a programming example that uses these intrinsics, the reader should refer to the Programmer's Guide, Chapter 4.

All of these intrinsics require a parameter, DEVICE_NUMBER, which specifies the peripheral device that the routine call affects.   DEVICE_NUMBER must be in the range 1..255 (on some Systems the user may define device numbers greater than 12: see the <u>UCSD p-System Installation Guide</u>(4)).

These are the current standard device numbers in the p-System (they are also shown in the <u>UCSD p-System Users' Manual</u>(3)):

146

1	CONSOLE:	screen and keyboard (echoes)
2	SYSTERM:	screen and keyboard (no echo)
4	\<disk name\>:	the System disk
5	\<disk name\>:	user's disk
6	PRINTER:	line printer
7	REMIN:	serial line input
8	REMOUT:	serial line output
9..12	\<disk name\>:	additional disk drives

Because the device I/O intrinsics reference devices directly, their I/O cannot be redirected (redirection is described in the UCSD p-System Users' Manual(3)).

unitbusy(DEVICE_NUMBER) returns a Boolean value that indicates whether the specified device is ready to perform I/O (true if it is, false if it is not).

unitbusy always returns false, except on machines that use PDP-11 or LSI-11 processors.

unitclear(DEVICE_NUMBER) resets the specified device to its power-up state.

unitread(DEVICE_NUMBER, BUFFER, LENGTH, BLOCKNUMBER, FLAG) reads LENGTH bytes from the specified device into BUFFER.

BUFFER is a typeless parameter. LENGTH is an integer.

BLOCKNUMBER and FLAG are optional parameters. If they are not present, they default to zero.

If BLOCKNUMBER is present, it indicates the block of the specified device from which the read will start (the offset is zero-based). If the device is not block-structured, this parameter is ignored.

147

If FLAG is present and equal to 1, the transfer is done asynchronously rather than synchronously. If the hardware does not support asynchronous I/O, FLAG is ignored. For other uses of FLAG, refer to the BIOS documentation in the UCSD p-System Internal Architecture Guide(5).

To specify FLAG but not BLOCKNUMBER, simply precede FLAG with two commas:

    unitread(5, name_array, count,, 1);

If FLAG equals 2 and the device is block-structured, unitread transfers one physical sector. BUFFER should be large enough to contain this sector. LENGTH must be set to 0. BLOCKNUMBER is the relative sector number (zero-based).

unitstatus(DEVICE_NUMBER, STATUS_RECORD, CONTROL) writes status information about the specified device to STATUS_RECORD.

STATUS_RECORD is a typeless parameter; it should be an area of at least 30 words.

CONTROL is an integer that is equal to either 0 or 1. If 0, the status information refers to output; if 1, the status information refers to input.

If the specified device is a character-oriented device (such as CONSOLE:, PRINTER:, REMOUT:, and so forth), unitstatus changes only the first word of STATUS_RECORD. This is set to the number of characters that are currently waiting to be read. If no characters are pending (or if unitstatus fails), this word is set to zero. No output status is defined for character-oriented devices.

If the specified device is block-structured, then the first four words of STATUS_RECORD are set in the following way:

word 1: the number of pending characters
        (as with a serial device)
word 2: the number of bytes per sector
word 3: the number of sectors per track
word 4: the number of tracks

The remaining 26 words of STATUS_RECORD are not currently used, but they are reserved for future use.

unitstatus is available only on Adaptable Systems, and PDP-11/LSI-11 systems. On PDP-11/LSI-11 systems, it only reports on console devices.

unitwait(DEVICE_NUMBER) waits until the specified device has completed any I/O in progress.

unitwait is equivalent to:

while unitbusy(DEVICE_NUMBER) **do** {nothing};

unitwait is currently a null operation except on machines that have a PDP-11 or LSI-11 processor.

unitwrite(DEVICE_NUMBER, BUFFER, LENGTH, BLOCKNUMBER, FLAG) writes LENGTH bytes from BUFFER to the specified device.

BUFFER is a typeless parameter. LENGTH is an integer.

BLOCKNUMBER and FLAG are optional parameters. If they are not present, they default to zero.

If BLOCKNUMBER is present, it indicates the block of the specified device where the write will start (the offset is zero-based). If the device is not block-structured, this parameter is ignored.

If FLAG is present and equal to 1, the transfer is done asynchronously rather than synchronously. If the hardware does not support asynchronous I/O, FLAG is ignored. For other uses of FLAG, refer to the BIOS documentation in the UCSD p-System Internal Architecture Guide(5).

To specify FLAG but not BLOCKNUMBER, simply precede FLAG with two commas:

   unitwrite(5, name_array, count,, 1);

If FLAG equals 2 and the device is block-structured, unitwrite transfers one physical sector. BUFFER should be large enough to contain this sector. LENGTH must be set to 0. BLOCKNUMBER is the relative sector number (zero-based).

VII.3.3   The Time Procedure

If the hardware has a clock that returns the time in 60'ths of a second, then the time intrinsic may be used.

time(HIWORD, LOWORD) sets HIWORD_LOWORD to a 32-bit unsigned integer that contains the current value of the system's clock in 60'ths of a second.

The programmer should be careful not to treat LOWORD as a negative two's complement integer.

The value returned is NOT correlated to the time of day. time is usually used for incremental time measurements, such as measuring a program's performance by calculating benchmarks.

VII.3.3   Ioresult

ioresult returns an integer that indicates the status of the last I/O operation performed.

The Compiler generates I/O checks for ALL I/O operations except device I/O intrinsics. An I/O error at runtime causes a program to abort. If the programmer would rather that the program itself checked ioresult and took steps to correct an I/O error, I/O checking must be turned off. This is done with the {$I-} compiler directive: see Chapter X.

These are the possible values of ioresult:

```
 0 = no error
 1 = parity error (CRC)
 2 = illegal device number
 3 = illegal I/O request
 4 = data-com timeout
 5 = volume went offline
 6 = file lost in directory
 7 = bad file name
 8 = no room on volume
 9 = volume not found
10 = file not found
11 = duplicate directory entry
12 = file already open
13 = file not open
14 = bad input information
15 = ring buffer overflow
16 = write protect
17 = illegal block
18 = illegal buffer
```

The interpretation of these values may change in the future; refer to the current UCSD p-System Users' Manual for current error messages.

At present, the value of ioresult is stored in a single System-wide variable. The user should be careful if there are concurrent processes using ioresult: an ioresult in one process can change the information expected by another.

I/O done by the p-System itself does not affect a user program's ioresult behind the user's back.

Note that the following:

writeln('ioresult is: ', ioresult);

... is wrong, since writing the string constant will alter ioresult. The safer way to write an ioresult is:

iocheck:= ioresult;
writeln('ioresult is: ', iocheck);

VII.3.5 Screen I/O

This section describes gotoxy, which allows the user to position the cursor anywhere on the CONSOLE: screen. More sophisticated screen control can be accomplished by using the Operating System's Screen Control Unit, which is described in the UCSD p-System Internal Architecture Guide(5).

gotoxy(x,y) positions the CONSOLE:'s cursor at (x,y), where x indicates a column and y indicates a row. x and y are integers. The upper left corner of the screen is assumed to be (0,0). If x or y is too large, the cursor is placed at the edge of the screen. Most (but not all) terminals are 80 * 24 characters.

It is possible for a user to write a customized gotoxy. The requirements for this are described in the UCSD p-System Installation Guide(4).

Chapter VIII
Memory Management

The information in this chapter applies only to UCSD Pascal. More specifically, it is oriented to the Version IV.0 implementation, which handles main memory differently from former versions. These differences are described where necessary.

For programming examples that illustrate the management of memory when this is critical to the success of a program, see the Programmer's Guide, Chapter 7.

These topics are also discussed in the UCSD p-System Users' Manual(3) and the UCSD p-System Internal Architecture Guide(5).

VIII.1 The p-System Runtime Environment

There are three dynamic data structures that are used to manage main memory while a program is running. These are the Stack, the Heap, and the Codepool.

The Stack is a last-in-first-out stack that is used for procedure and function calls, the storage of static variables, and (on most processors) temporary values during expression evaluation.

The Heap is essentially a last-in-first-out structure as well, but its management is more complex. It is used to store dynamic variables, the stacks of subordinate processes, and non-relocatable code segments.

The Codepool is a collection of active code segments, including the code segment that is currently running. A code segment is a portion of a codefile: code is swapped in and out of memory one segment at a time. Code segments are described in further detail in the following section.

In p-System versions that precede IV.0, there is no Codepool: program code is stored on the Stack.

Some implementations use a separate stack for expression evaluation.

In implementations that use extended memory, the Stack and Heap may occupy one area of memory, and the Codepool a totally different area.

VIII.2   Segmentation

VIII.2.1   Code Segments

A code segment is typically the product of a single compilation: a program or unit is compiled into a single code segment. The code segment that contains a program or a unit is called the ´principal segment´; the segments that contain segment routines are called ´subsidiary segments´.

A programmer may also create a subsidiary segment that contains a single routine (however complex) by use of the reserved word **segment**. This word must be the first word in a routine heading, for example:

> **segment procedure** initialize;
>
> **segment function** handle_store (priority: <u>integer</u>): <u>integer</u>;
>
> **segment process** switching(light: <u>semaphore</u>);

As mentioned before, program code is swapped in and out of memory one segment at a time. Thus, a programmer may improve the memory utilization of a program by designating certain routines as segment routines which need not be in memory at all times. In particular, routines which are only called once or twice during a program (such as initialization and termination code) are very good candidates for segment routines.

Within a program, the declaration of the code BODIES of all segment routines must precede the declaration of any non-segment routine code. If a segment routine must call a non-segment routine, the non-segment routine must be declared by a **forward** declaration that precedes the segment routine´s declaration.

In versions that precede IV.0, only segment routines are swapped, and only when they are called or exited. In IV.0, creating subsidiary segments is a valuable way of tuning a program's memory usage; in pre-IV.0 systems, it may be a NECESSARY means of keeping a program's memory utilization down to a manageable size.

The name of a code segment is the first 8 characters of either the program name, the unit name, or the segment routine name (depending on how the code segment was created).

VIII.2.2 Controlling Segment Residence

This section describes the UCSD intrinsic procedures memlock and memswap, which may be used to control a segment's residence in main memory. These routines are available only in Version IV.0.

memlock(SEGMENT_LIST) locks all the segments named in SEGMENT_LIST into main memory.

SEGMENT_LIST is a string that contains the names of segments, separated by commas. Names of nonexistent segments are ignored.

All segments named in SEGMENT_LIST must remain in the Codepool until they are released by a call to memswap: until that time, they cannot be swapped out of memory.

If a segment that is named is not in the Codepool, it is locked in memory the next time it is loaded.

memswap(SEGMENT_LIST) unlocks all the segments named in SEGMENT_LIST.

SEGMENT_LIST is a string that contains the names of segments, separated by commas.

All segments that are named in SEGMENT_LIST and have been locked in the Codepool are released, and may now be swapped out to disk (under the control of the Operating System).

If a segment that is named is not in the Codepool, or is in the Codepool and has not been locked, the name is ignored.

VIII.3 Free Space

This section describes the UCSD intrinsic functions memavail and varavail, which allow a program to discover how much free space remains in main memory. memavail is available in all current versions; varavail is available only in Version IV.0.

memavail returns an integer which is the number of unallocated words in main memory.

> This number is the sum of the number of words between the Codepool and the Stack, plus the number of words between the Codepool and the Heap.

> In versions that precede IV.0, memavail returns the number of words between the Stack and the Heap.

> Note that in Version IV.0, the number returned by memavail may be less than the number of total available words of memory space, since there may be segments in the Codepool that could be swapped out.

varavail(SEGMENT_LIST) returns the number of available words for a particular configuration of main memory. It is typically used in conjunction with varnew.

> SEGMENT_LIST is a string that contains the names of segments, separated by commas. These are segments for which the user wants space to be available.

> varavail returns the number of words that would be available IF all of the segments named in SEGMENT_LIST were loaded. It assumes that all memory-locked segments remain in main memory, along with all of the segments named in SEGMENT_LIST.

> If a name in SEGMENT_LIST is not known to the Operating System, it is ignored.

VIII.4   Free Space on the Heap

This section describes a number of intrinsics which allow a program to allocate and de-allocate free space on the Heap (remember that the Heap is used to store dynamic variables).

new and dispose are the standard means of allocating and de-allocating dynamic variables on the Heap. varnew and vardispose may be used to allocate/de-allocate variable-sized areas. These are System-level intrinsics which do no checking; they can cause problems if not used carefully. Finally, mark and release are a means of controlling still larger portions of Heap use: they are also System-level tools.

It is very important that the pairs varnew/vardispose and mark/release match up correctly while the program is running. If they do not, the integrity of the Heap may be lost: this usually causes the System to crash.

The intrinsics dispose, varnew, and vardispose are available only in Version IV.0.   new, mark, and release are available in all current versions.

new and dispose are described in Chapter III, Section 5.2.

varnew(POINTER, COUNT) does a new on COUNT words, and returns an integer that is the number of words actually allocated.

POINTER is a pointer to any type (it should point to the type of data for which space is being allocated). COUNT is an integer.

If it is possible to allocate COUNT words, then the number returned by varnew should equal COUNT. If COUNT words are not available, then no space is allocated, and varnew returns zero.

157

vardispose(POINTER, COUNT) does a dispose on COUNT words.

POINTER is a pointer to any type: it should be the same as the pointer in the varnew that corresponds to this vardispose. COUNT is an integer, and should be equal to the COUNT in the corresponding varnew.

If either POINTER or COUNT is incorrect, the Heap's integrity is destroyed.

mark(POINTER) marks a location on the Heap by creating and allocating a Heap Mark Record (HMR). POINTER is set to point to that record.

It is customary to declare POINTER as a ^integer.

Note that the only Heap space allocated by mark is the space occupied by the HMR itself. Space for dynamic variables beyond the HMR must be allocated by other means (such as new and varnew); such space can be freed by a subsequent call to release.

release(POINTER) cuts the Heap back to the HMR that POINTER points to.

Calls to mark and release should come in pairs. POINTER should equal the value of POINTER that was set by the previous call to mark.

POINTER is customarily declared as a ^integer.

All space on the Heap that was allocated (by new or varnew) since the previous mark is de-allocated.

If mark and release are not paired correctly, or release is called with an incorrect pointer, the integrity of the Heap is destroyed.

Chapter IX
Concurrency

This chapter describes the management of concurrent routines (processes).

Concurrency, like memory management, pertains more to the p-System than to the UCSD Pascal language, and more information about concurrency may be found in the UCSD p-System Users' Manual(3) and the UCSD p-System Internal Architecture Guide(5).

Concurrent processes are available as of Version III.0.

For programming examples which use concurrency, refer to the Programmer's Guide, Chapter 5.

IX.1   Concurrent Execution

Virtually all p-Systems are implemented on hardware that has only one central processor.   Processes do not truly run at the same time, but share the processor, which is switched between them.   Thus, using processes on conventional hardware can slow a program down somewhat: there is usually a compensating gain in logical consistency, or efficiency in handling certain problems such as interrupts.

The Interpreter controls concurrent processes, and initiates them depending on their priority.   Priority is discussed below.   Once a process is started, it continues to run until it is finished, until it is interrupted, or until it must wait for another process. At this point, the processor is given another process, and it runs in the same manner: the p-System does not (in most current versions) do any sort of "time-slicing" or "task-switching" among ready processes that have equal priority.

IX.2   Processes

A process is a form of routine, and is declared in the same general way.   Here is an EBNF description of a process heading:

"process" identifier [
                 "(" ["**var**"] id-list ":" type-id
                    { ";" ["**var**"] id-list ":" type-id }
                 ")"] ";"

For example:

     process example (**var** result: <u>integer</u>;
                        var pause: <u>semaphore</u>);

The remainder of a process declaration is identical to a procedure or function declaration.

Processes must be declared global to a program: they may not be declared within a procedure, function, or other process.

A process is not called as a procedure or function would be called. Instead, it is initiated by a call to the UCSD intrinsic procedure <u>start</u>.

The same process may be <u>start</u>'ed any number of times: each of these instances is a concurrent process that runs independently of any other (though it may by synchronized with other processes (including other instances of the same process) by the use of semaphores).

The p-System assigns each instance of a process its own <u>processid</u>. <u>processid</u> is a predeclared type whose values are represented by integers. A program may examine a process's <u>processid</u> (this may be useful for debugging purposes). There are no operations on <u>processids</u>.

Each instance of a process is also assigned a priority and a stacksize value.

A process's priority determines its position in the queue of processes that are waiting to be run. A priority is a value in the range 0..255; the priority of a user program is 128. 128 is the default priority for all user processes: this value can be changed by the user in the call to <u>start</u>. A priority of 255 should not be used, as this conflicts with the Operating System's FAULTHANDLER process.

Processes may have the same priority. If so, they are placed in the queue in the order in which they were entered.

The stack for a process is allocated on the Heap, rather than the Stack itself. The default size for this area is 200 words: this value can also be changed by the user in the call to start.

IX.3   Initiating a Process

As mentioned before, a single instance of a process is initiated by a call to the UCSD intrinsic procedure start; the same process may be initiated any number of times.   start is described in this section.

start(<process call>, PROC_ID, STACKSIZE, PRIORITY) initiates the process named in <process call>.

> <process call> is the name of a process followed by a parameter list, if necessary. It has the same appearance as a procedure call.

> The remaining three parameters are optional.

> PROC_ID is of type processid. If present, it is set to the processid value that is assigned to this instance of the process.

> STACKSIZE specifies the number of words that will be allocated (on the Heap) to the process's stack. If not present, a default of 200 is used.

> A process's stack must have enough room for:

>> 1.   5 words, plus
>> 2.   the number of words occupied by the process's local (static) variables, plus
>> 3.   room for the activation records of all procedures and functions that the process calls, plus
>> 4.   (on most machines) room to evaluate expressions.

> Activation records are described in the UCSD p-System Internal Architecture Guide(5).

> An overflow on a process's stack causes a runtime error.

161

The programmer should be cautious about using <u>release</u> when the Heap contains the stack of a <u>start'</u>ed process.

PRIORITY is in the range 0..255. If not present, this value defaults to the priority of its parent process (which is a user program whose priority is 128). A priority of 255 should not be used.

IX.4   Process Synchronization

A process must often wait for some event to occur, or some other process to complete an action. A process may also contain a sequence of statements that must not be interrupted: such a sequence is known as a "critical section." The programmer may handle these situations by the use of semaphores and the intrinsic routines which handle them.

IX.4.1   Semaphores

A semaphore is a variable of type <u>semaphore</u>. A semaphore consists of a queue of processes that are waiting on that semaphore, and a count in the subrange 0..<u>maxint</u>.

Such semaphores are called 'counting semaphores', as opposed to 'Boolean semaphores': a Boolean semaphore has only the values <u>true</u> and <u>false</u>, and can be simulated by restricting a counting semaphore to the values 0 and 1.

When a process must wait for an event to occur, it calls the UCSD intrinsic <u>wait</u>(SEM). This suspends the process until the semaphore SEM allows it to continue. For this to happen, another process must call the intrinsic <u>signal</u>(SEM).

When the value of a counting semaphore is equal to zero, it is unavailable, and a <u>wait</u> will continue to wait on that semaphore until it becomes greater than zero.

Every semaphore that is used in a program must be initialized by a call to the UCSD intrinsic <u>seminit</u>, which is described below in this section. If a program attempts to use a semaphore that has not been initialized, the results are unpredictable.

seminit(SEM, INITIAL) initializes the semaphore SEM, and sets its count equal to the value INITIAL. INITIAL must be an integer in the range 0..maxint.

IX.4.2   Signal and Wait

This section describes the UCSD intrinsic procedures signal and wait.

signal(SEM) signals the semaphore SEM.

> If no processes are waiting for SEM, the value of SEM is incremented.

> If one or more processes are waiting for SEM, then the process at the head of SEM's queue is activated by adding it to the queue of ready processes. (A task switch may take place if the process at the head of SEM's queue has a higher priority than the process that was running.)

wait(SEM) waits on the semaphore SEM.

> If the count of SEM is greater than zero, then it is decremented and the process that called wait continues.

> If the count of SEM equals zero, then the process calling wait is suspended until SEM is made available again by a call of signal(SEM) in another process.

IX.4.3   Interrupts

A program may associate a semaphore with a hardware interrupt by means of the UCSD intrinsic procedure attach.

attach(SEM, I_VEC) associates the semaphore SEM with the external interrupt vector I_VEC.

> Whenever the hardware raises the interrupt in question, the System automatically calls signal(SEM).

The possible values of I_VEC, and the hardware states they represent, vary widely from processor to processor. The user should refer to machine-specific documentation for further information.

To de-attach a semaphore from an interrupt, and free it for other uses, the programmer may call attach in the following way:

   attach(nil, vector);

... where the value of vector is the value that was previously attached to SEM.

A vector must be attached to only one semaphore at a time, and the semaphore must remain in memory for the entire time it is attached.

Chapter X
Compilation

When a UCSD Pascal program is compiled, it may contain directions to the Compiler that control the Compiler's output. Separate textfiles can be included in a single compilation, and portions of a program may be conditionally compiled. Under the p-System, it is also possible to call assembled routines (native code) from a Pascal program: this is done with the **external** construct.

X.1   Compiler Options

A compiler option appears in a 'pseudo-comment'. A pseudo-comment is a comment whose left delimiter ('{' or '(*') is immediately followed by a dollar sign ($). For example:

```
{$I+}
(*$Q-*)
```

A single pseudo-comment may contain several compiler options:

```
{$I+,Q-}
```

If a pseudo-comment contains more than one option, only the LAST option may be a string option (see below, Section X.1.2).

The default options for a compilation are:

```
{$R+, I-, L-, U+, P+}
```

Unless these are explicitly overridden, they remain in effect whenever a program is compiled. The meaning of each of these letters is described below.

X.1.1   Stack Options

The I (I/O-check), R (Range-check), and conditional compilation flags are known as 'stack options'. The on/off state of these options can be nested up to 15 levels deep.

Each of these options (and each individual flag) has its own stack. Whenever a + or - is specified in the pseudo-comment for one of these options, that value is pushed onto the stack.

The stack may be popped by using the character ^ in place of
+ or -.

If more than 15 values are pushed onto the stack, the bottom
of the stack is lost. If the stack is popped when it is empty,
the value is always - (off).

X.1.2   Switch Options

Switch options are compiler options that have either an on or
off state, as indicated by a + or - when the option appears in
the text.

I stands for I/O-check.

> This is a stack option. The default is I+.   When I- is
> specified, the Compiler stops generating the test code that
> normally follows every I/O statement (except for unitread
> and unitwrite).

> If the programmer wishes to test ioresult explicitly after an
> I/O operation, in order to correct any errors that may have
> occured, then I- must be specified before the operation is
> done.

L stands for Listing.

> The default is L-.   L+ causes the Compiler to write a
> source program listing to the file *SYSTEM.LST.TEXT.   L
> can also be used as a string option, in which case the user
> can specify a different name for the list file (see Section
> X.1.3).

P stands for Page.

> The default is P+.   This causes the listing to be paginated
> so that it can be legibly printed on paper that is 8-1/2"
> long.

> A pseudo-comment that contains only P (e.g., {$P}) forces
> the listing to start a new page.

Q stands for **Q**uiet compile.

Q defaults to - or +, depending on whether the HAS SLOW TERMINAL data item in the file *SYSTEM.MISCINFO is true or false, respectively. Typically, SLOWTERM is false and Q- is the default. (For more information on SYSTEM.MISCINFO, see the UCSD p-System Installation Guide(4).)

Q+ suppresses the Compiler's output to CONSOLE:, except for error messages.

Q- allows the Compiler to send information on its progress to CONSOLE:.

R stands for **R**ange-check.

This is a stack option. The default is R+. If R- is specified, the Compiler stops emitting code to check the range of array indices and subrange expressions, the type of assignments, and so forth.

Programs compiled with R- run slightly faster, but invalid assignments do NOT cause a runtime error, leading to unpredictable and sometimes disastrous results. Unless a program is extremely time-critical, and has been thoroughly debugged, R- should not be used.

The letter R is also used for the Realsize option.

R also stands for **R**ealsize.

This option is only present in Version IV.0.

Real numbers are either 32 bits (2 words) or 64 bits (4 words) long. The p-System defaults to a particular size for each particular processor. With the R option, a programmer may override this default.

R2 causes the Compiler to generate 2-word real numbers, regardless of the default.

R4 causes the Compiler to generate 4-word real numbers, regardless of the default.

The pseudo-comment that contains this option must appear BEFORE the reserved word **program** or **unit**.

U stands for **U**ser program.

The default is U+. U- specifies that the compilation may use unit names that belong to the Operating System. If U- is specified, the pseudo-comment it appears in must appear BEFORE the reserved word **program** or **unit**.

Most users will never need to use this option, except when compiling their own gotoxy (see the UCSD p-System Installation Guide(4)).

X.1.3 String Options

String options require the programmer to specify a string that is used by the Compiler. This is either the name of a file, or text to be included in a file. The string may be preceded by zero or more spaces: preceding it with a single space is customary.

If the pseudo-comment uses '(* *)' delimiters, the enclosed string may NOT contain a '*'.

If the filename begins with a + or - (which is unlikely), then there MUST be a space after the letter that indicates the option; otherwise, the Compiler will treat the option as a switch option and not a string option.

C stands for **C**opyright.

The string is placed in the copyright field of the codefile (this resides in the segment dictionary: see the UCSD p-System Internal Architecture Guide(5)).

For example:

{$C Copyright 1931 by Wholly Imaginary Systems}

I as a string option stands for Include File.

The string is the name of a textfile. The text of the specified file is compiled into object code at the position of the pseudo-comment.

If the compiler cannot open the file under the name that is given, it appends '.TEXT' to the name and tries again. If the second attempt fails or an I/O error occurs while reading the include file, the compiler generates a fatal syntax error and aborts.

In Version IV.0, include files may be nested up to three levels deep. In previous versions, they may not be nested.

Include files may contain **const, type, var,** and routine declarations (within the include file, they must be in their proper order). If this is the case, the pseudo-comment MUST precede any blocks of code that appear in the main program file. There may be more than one such include file; if so, only the LAST such include file may contain procedure code.

Here is an example of a program with an include file that contains declarations:

```
program FunnyDeclarations;

    const   a = 1;
    type    guess = integer;
    var     gosh: guess;

    procedure fancy (p, q: integer);
        forward;

    {$I MOREDECS}

    procedure fancy;
        begin ... end;

    begin {main program} ... end.
```

These are the contents of MOREDECS:

```
const  b = 2;
type   nonsense = (l, m, n);
var    stuff: nonsense;

procedure plain;
   begin
      writeln('plain was called');
   end;
```

L stands for **L**isting.

This corresponds to the switch option specified above.   The
string is the name of a textfile to which the listing is
written.   Note that this name may be any valid filename,
but if the user wishes to edit it later, it must be created
with a suffix of '.TEXT'.

T stands for **T**itle.

The string becomes the title of each new page in the
listing file.

U as a string option stands for **U**ses library.

The string is the name of a codefile.   The Compiler
searches that file for the code of any **units** used in
SUBSEQUENT **uses** declarations.   See the Programmer's
Guide, Chapter 6, for an example of the use of this option.
Note that U is also the name of a switch option (see
above).

X.1.4   Conditional Compilation

Conditional compilation is not available in versions prior to
IV.0.

Code to be conditionally compiled is bracketed by the options B
and E (which are described below).   Whether it is compiled or
not depends on the value of a flag, which is set by the D

option (also described below).   The state of each flag is saved on a stack, as described in Section X.1.1.

B stands for **B**egin.

> This is a string option.   The string is the name of a flag that has been defined by a previous D option.   If only the string appears, the following code is compiled if the flag is true.   If the string is followed by a -, the code is compiled if the flag is false.   If the string is followed by a + or ^, these characters are ignored.

> The section of code to be conditionally compiled must be delimited by a B option and an E option that names the same flag.   Sections to be conditionally compiled may not be nested.

D stands for **D**eclare.

> This is a string option.   The string is the name of a flag. Its initial value is true unless its name is followed by a -.

> All flags must be declared BEFORE the reserved word **program** or **unit**.   The D option may be used again in a subsequent portion of the program to redefine the value of a flag: + pushes a true value, - pushes a false value, and ^ pops the flag's stack.

> The names of flags follow the rules for Pascal identifiers.

E stands for **E**nd.

> This is a string option.   The string must be the name of a flag used in a previous B option.   Any characters that follow the flag are ignored.

Here is a code fragment that illustrates conditional compilation:

```
{$D DEBUG+}
program ToBeTested;

    ...

    {$B DEBUG}
    procedure test_routine;
        ...
        begin ... end;
    {$E DEBUG}

    ...

    begin
        ...
        {$B DEBUG}
        test_routine;
        {$E DEBUG}
        ...
    end.
```

X.2   External Routines

Under the p-System, a Pascal program may call an assembled routine. This routine must be declared as **external** in the Pascal source, for example:

procedure native_code (n: <u>integer</u>); **external;**

function speed (rush: <u>real</u>, direct: <u>Boolean</u>): status;
   external;

This construction is analogous to the declaration **forward.**

The assembly-language routine itself must correspond to standard P-code protocols: refer to the <u>UCSD p-System Users' Manual</u>(3) or other documentation on the p-System assembly language.

172

PART II

UCSD Pascal
A Guide
for Programmers

Chapter 0
Introduction

The purpose of this Guide is to introduce the reader to the techniques of using UCSD Pascal, and present a number of complete, or nearly complete, programming examples.

The programs in chapters 1 through 4 illustrate basic topics -- topics that are essentially common to all Pascal programmers, whether they use UCSD Pascal or some other dialect, although it is always UCSD Pascal that is described. The programs in chapters 5 through 9 are more advanced, and present programming problems that are essentially unique to UCSD Pascal, the UCSD p-System, and the microcomputer environment.

Chapter I of the Definition is a brief survey of the features of Pascal. You may wish to read it before you read Chapter 1 of the Programmer's Guide.

If you are not a programmer, you will probably find this Guide rough going, and we recommend that you start from some simpler text. The Bibliography contains some suggestions. We have assumed that you know the basic concepts of programming, and have written some programs of your own, probably in some other language.

If you have programmed before, but in a language which is not structured (BASIC or FORTRAN, for instance), you will find that Pascal requires you to pay more attention to the definition of data and the form (the structure) of algorithms. When reading this guide, pay special attention to the first three chapters. The payoff for this extra effort is programs that are more reliable and easier to maintain.

We have tried to cover as much ground as we could, but this Guide does not describe all of UCSD Pascal. The details of things we have left out may be found in the Definition.

Our approach is to present working programs, and a "working set" of programming concepts at each stage. Many samples introduce a variety of concepts that in the Definition would be listed under separate headings. The intention is to provide you with the tools to begin writing useful programs as soon as possible.

We don't guarantee that the sample programs are perfect, but they have been formatted and printed from source code that was actually tested. To the best of our knowledge, they run correctly. The sample outputs were also printed directly from program output.

Chapter 1
Bootstrapping the Programmer

This chapter introduces most of the topics involved in writing a UCSD Pascal program, but does not discuss any of them in detail. The intent is to illustrate the style of Pascal and the basic form of Pascal programs. By the end of the chapter, the reader should be able to write simple programs in UCSD Pascal, but will have to read further to learn about more powerful (and more subtle) aspects of the language.

Our first program is one that prints a table of factorials on the console:

```
program Fact;
   var
      i: integer;
      prod: real;
   begin
      writeln('n    factorial of n');
      prod:= 1.0;
      for i:= 1 to 20 do
        begin
           prod:= prod*i;
           writeln(i,'  ',prod);
        end;
   end.
```

Program 1

The factorial of a positive non-zero integer n is defined to be the product of all the integers between 1 and n. Fact prints the following table:

n	factorial of n
1	1.00000
2	2.00000
3	6.00000
4	2.40000E1
5	1.20000E2
6	7.20000E2
7	5.04000E3
8	4.03200E4

177

```
 9   3.62880E5
10   3.62880E6
11   3.99168E7
12   4.79002E8
13   6.22702E9
14   8.71783E10
15   1.30767E12
16   2.09228E13
17   3.55687E14
18   6.40237E15
19   1.21645E17
20   2.43290E18
```

(The output format of real numbers may be slightly different on your System.)

Program Fact is composed of three parts: a program heading, a variable declaration part, and a program body.

Fact begins with the heading:

program Fact;

... which notifies the Compiler that the following text will define a program, and that the program will have the name Fact.

The program heading ends with a semicolon. In Pascal, semicolons serve to end declarations and separate statements.

Following the program heading is the variable declaration part:

var
    i: <u>integer;</u>
    prod: <u>real;</u>

All variables in a Pascal program must be 'declared' before they may be used. When a variable is declared it is given a name and a type. In Program 1, two variables are declared: i is of type <u>integer,</u> and prod is of type <u>real.</u>

Various objects in a Pascal program (such as variables) are named by user-defined identifiers. Identifiers begin with a letter that is followed by any combination of letters, digits and the underscore character (_). They may be any length (up to the length of a source line), and may contain a mixture of upper- and lower-case. However, the case of a letter is ignored, and so is the underscore character. Also, identifiers are distinguished only by their first eight characters (not counting underscores); identifiers that are the same for eight characters and different after that are considered the same identifier.

Certain identifiers are reserved for the Pascal language and may not be defined by the programmer: these are called 'reserved words'; throughout this book they appear in **boldface.** Many more identifiers are 'predeclared': these have the same status as user-defined identifiers, but are standard to Pascal (or UCSD Pascal). They are available to the programmer, and there is no need to declare them explicitly. Throughout this book, predeclared variables are underlined.

Real, integer, and long integer (described in Chapter 2) are the numeric types available in UCSD Pascal. A variable of type integer can take on any integral value between -maxint and maxint. maxint is a predeclared constant in Pascal that may be different in each implementation. In UCSD Pascal, maxint equals 32767.

Real variables can take on a much wider range of values at a cost of precision. A real variable consists of a mantissa part and a scale factor (also called the exponent). The range of values of real variables in UCSD Pascal varies with each implementation. For 2-word reals, a typical implementation may have a maximum absolute magnitude of 1.0E+38, with 6 or 7 digits of precision. For 4-word reals, the maximum absolute magnitude may be 1.0E+308, with 15 or 16 digits of precision.

The body of Program 1 is the section of text between the first **begin** and the last **end.** The final **end** is followed by a period to indicate the end of the program.

The body of a program consists of a list of statements which are 'executed' essentially in order from top to bottom. Some statements cause this straightforward order to change, and are called 'flow of control' statements.

Program 1 contains examples of three statement types: the assignment statement, the writeln statement, and the **for** statement. Each statement is separated from the following statement by a semicolon (;).

179

The assignment statement is used to give a value to a variable. For example:

    prod:= 1.0

... assigns prod the value 1.0. Further down in the program there is another assignment statement:

    prod:= prod*i

This statement assigns prod a new value which is the product of i and the current value of prod. (The asterisk is used in Pascal to indicate multiplication.)

The assignment symbol in Pascal (:=) differs from the comparison operator (=). Assignment and comparison are two fundamentally different operations.

Another type of statement in Program 1 is the <u>writeln</u> statement. <u>writeln</u> is used to print data on the user's console. The statement:

    <u>writeln</u>('n   factorial of n')

... causes the text between the apostrophes to be printed. <u>writeln</u> may take a list of items to be printed. Each item must be separated from the next by a comma, as in:

    <u>writeln</u>(i,' ',prod)

This prints the value of i, followed by a space (for legibility), followed by the value of prod.

(The <u>writeln</u> statement is actually a call to a procedure: in this case, a predeclared one. Procedure calls are discussed in Chapter 3.)

Finally, Program 1 contains an example of a **for** statement. A **for** statement causes a statement that follows the **do** to be executed repeatedly for a given number of times. A **for** statement has the form:

    for <counter>:= <first> **to** <last> **do** <statement>

The index variable <counter> is assigned the value <first>. On each execution of <statement>, the index variable <counter> is replaced by its successor (if it is an integer, it is incremented by 1). When the value of <counter> is greater than the value of <last>, the loop ends.

For example:

```
for i:= 1 to 10 do
    writeln(i)
```

... prints ten lines on the console, numbered one through ten.

It is often the case that a whole group of statements must be executed repeatedly. Pascal allows a group of statements to take the place of <statement> through use of the 'compound statement'. A compound statement is a group of statements separated by semicolons and surrounded by a **begin end** pair.

The **for** statement in Program 1 contains a compound statement which is made up of two statements:

```
for i:= 1 to 20 do
    begin
        prod:= prod*i;
        writeln(i,' ',prod);
    end
```

The semicolon following the writeln statement is optional. However, programs are seldom static entities -- they are constantly changed to incorporate new features or to fix bugs, and a programmer frequently needs to insert statements between the last statement of a compound statement and its closing **end.** Typing a semicolon after the last statement eliminates the need to add one later (better yet, it forestalls the bug that would result from FORGETTING to put one there later!). Thus, typing a semicolon in the first place is a good habit to acquire. All our sample programs will contain this optional semicolon.

It should now be clear how program Fact works. First, a heading is printed, and prod is assigned the initial value of 1.0. Then i takes on the values 1 through 20, and for each value of i, two statements are executed: prod is updated to have the previous value of prod times the current value of i, and then i and prod are printed. As the output listing shows, a table of twenty items is printed. On the left are 1 to 20 (the values of i), and on the right are the factorials of these numbers (the values of prod).

We have a few more comments to make about Program 1. First, numeric expressions appeared in all three statement types we examined. Pascal expressions appear very much like standard algebraic expressions. For integers, the following operations are available.

+	addition
-	subtraction
*	multiplication
div	integer division (truncated)
mod	remainder after division

For reals also, +, -, and * are available. Real division is represented by:

/	division

Arbitrary expressions can be formed with these operators and numeric constants and variables. As in algebra, the multiplication operators (*, **div, mod,** and /) have precedence over the addition operators (+ and -). Parentheses may be used to set apart subexpressions, which are evaluated first.

In general, integers can be used anywhere in real expressions. Type conversion from integer to real is performed automatically. However, reals cannot be used with so much freedom. In order to use a real in an integer expression, it is necessary to convert the value to an integer by rounding or truncation. Two functions are available for this purpose:

trunc(x)	discards the fractional portion of x
round(x)	rounds x to the nearest integer

Here are a few assignment statements using the variables prod and i as declared in our program.

```
prod:= (i+6) * prod
i:= i + trunc(prod/4.5)
i:= round(prod)
```

As above, and as in Program 1, numeric constants (like 6) may appear in expressions. Integer constants are made up of one or more digits. Real constants must contain a decimal point, a scaling factor, or both. The following assignment contains a real constant with a scaling factor:

```
prod:= 10e-1
```

A scaling factor is similar to "scientific notation", and should be read as "times ten to the power of" the integer that follows the letter ʹeʹ or ʹEʹ.

The writeln statement may contain a list of items to print. For our present purposes, these items must be expressions that yield a value of type integer, real, char (character), or string.

The type string will be described in more detail later, but for right now, string constants are a very useful way to print text on the console. A string constant is formed by surrounding text by a pair of apostrophes (single quote marks). String constants must not cross line boundaries. A single quote character may appear in a string constant by entering two quote marks at the desired position. For example:

```
ʹyou canʹʹt mean thatʹ
```

... is a string constant that contains the word "canʹt".

The next example introduces several new constructs, including input (<u>readln</u>) and two new flow-of-control statements: the **if**, which is a means of making simple decisions, and the **while**, which is a loop like the **for** statement, but does not have a control variable, and so repeats for some indefinite number of times.

```
program Factors;
    { Computes prime factors of an integer
      read from keyboard }
    var
      n,factor: integer;
    begin
      write('enter number to factor: ');
      readln(n);
      factor:= 2;
      while n > 1 do
         if n mod factor = 0
            then
               begin
                  write(factor,' ');
                  n:= n div factor;
               end
            else factor:= factor+1;
      writeln;
    end.
```

Program 2

This program finds the prime factors of a number. It does this in a rather "brute force" way. A possible factor is chosen (starting with 2), and if that divides the number then the factor is printed. If the possible factor does not divide the number it is incremented (by 1), and the search continues. This ensures that factors are printed in increasing order. The loop repeats until the last factor has been divided out (n = 1).

The number to be factored is entered by the user (it is "read in" to the program). In this way, the program achieves some generality: it will factor any integer, not merely integers that were chosen when the program was compiled. Of course, the larger the number, the more time the program will take in figuring what its prime factors are.

Both input and output are done on the console. Some runs of the program might produce the following output:

```
enter number to factor: 36
2 2 3 3

enter number to factor: 1719
3 3 191

enter number to factor: 210
2 3 5 7

enter number to factor: 16384
2 2 2 2 2 2 2 2 2 2 2 2 2 2
```

Immediately following the program heading is a comment that describes (briefly) what the program does. Comments are just that: they are meant to be read by the programmer (either the original programmer or someone else), and they are skipped over by the Compiler. A comment is any text enclosed in the delimiters (* *) or { }. Comments may cross line boundaries (as the one in the example does), and may appear anywhere in the program, except in the middle of a token such as an identifier or constant.

A comment at the beginning of a program or routine that describes what that program or routine does is always a good idea. A Pascal program is usually more readable if there are not too many comments -- it should make use of intelligible identifiers and clear algorithms: comments can then be judiciously used to explain what a piece of code does, or better yet, why it does what it does.

It is also a good idea, especially in long programs, to accompany variable (and constant) declarations with a comment that indicates the intended use of each variable. This helps prevent "abuses" of variables when the program is maintained later.

If several variables are of the same type, they can be declared together, as illustrated in the example by:

    n, factor: <u>integer;</u>

185

The variable names must be separated by commas.

Within the example program's **while** loop, values are printed by a call to write rather than writeln. write prints a new value, but does not start a new output line. When a line of output is complete, a new line can be started by the simple call:

writeln;

The effect of this may be seen in the sample output for the program.

The call to readln allows a value to be read from the console. readln can read real and integer values (it can read some other values as well: we will discuss these later). Unlike some languages (such as BASIC), Pascal does not automatically print a prompt when a value is to be read: the programmer should create a prompt appropriate to the situation. Thus, in the example program, the call to readln is immediately preceded by:

write('enter number to factor: ');

The main loop of this program is a **while** statement. While a **for** statement continues to execute a statement for a specific number of times, a **while** statement continues indefinitely as long as some condition is met. The **while** statement is thus a simpler, more general construct than the **for** statement.

The general scheme of a **while** statement is:

while ⟨Boolean expression⟩ **do** ⟨statement⟩

(Remember that the ⟨statement⟩ can be a compound statement).

Each time through the loop, the ⟨Boolean expression⟩ is tested: if it is true, the ⟨statement⟩ is executed, and if it is false, the loop ends.

A ⟨Boolean expression⟩ is often (though not necessarily) a comparison of some sort:

```
n > 1      {as in the sample program}
(n>1) and not eoln
(date <= 0) or (date >= 4000)
```

A Boolean value is equal to either true or false. These are operators that can be used in Boolean expressions:

and   logical and
or   logical or
not   logical negation (a unary operator)

These are numeric comparisons as they appear in Pascal:

>   greater than
<   less than
>=   greater than or equal to
<=   less than or equal to
=   equals
<>   not equals

The operands for these comparisons may be any numeric values.

The **while** statement in Program 2 contains a single **if** statement. The **if** statement is a means of making a simple decision. The form of an **if** statement is:

   if <Boolean expression> **then** <statement>

... or:

   if <Boolean expression>
      then
         <statement 1>
      else
         <statement 2>

In the first form, <statement> is executed only if <Boolean expression> is true. In the second form, <statement 1> is executed if <Boolean expression> is true, and <statement 2> is executed if <Boolean condition> is false.

Once again, <statement> may be a compound statement.

The indentation of the sample program indicates our preferred indentation for both **while** and **if** statements. In general, indentation should be chosen so as to (1) make the program legible, and (2) reflect the lexical nesting of the program. For example, the **if** appears within the **while,** and therefore it is indented more deeply.

We have one further point to make about this program. If you should run it and make a mistake while typing the value of n (such as typing letters instead of numbers), you may be confronted with a message such as this:

    enter number to factor: v

    User I/O error
    Segment PASCAL   Proc# 1   Offset# 15
    Type <space> to continue

A number of things can cause a runtime error; reading an illegal value is one of them. When a runtime error occurs, you must type a <space> before using the System again, and the program must be restarted, or corrected and recompiled. The command U(ser restart can (usually) be used to restart a program that has just been run. Other situations that may result in runtime errors will be mentioned when we come across them.

The next sample program prints a Pascal's triangle (this seemed an appropriate example!). It introduces the notion of constants, and the form of structured variable called an array.

```
program Pascal;
    { Pascal prints a Pascal's Triangle of size n
      on the terminal. }
    const
      n = 10;                    {size of triangle}
    var
      i,j: integer;
      p: array[1..n] of integer;
    begin
      for i:= 1 to n do
        begin
          p[i]:= 1;
          for j:= i-1 downto 2 do
            p[j]:= p[j]+p[j-1];
          for j:= 1 to i do
            write(p[j]:4);
          writeln;
        end;
    end.
```

Program 3

A Pascal's triangle is a triangular array, where the elements along the outer edges are equal to 1, and all other elements are equal to the sum of the two elements above them. Readers familiar with probability will recognize these values as the binomial coefficients. The triangle was a discovery of Blaise Pascal. The program's output looks like this:

```
1
1   1
1   2   1
1   3   3   1
1   4   6   4   1
1   5  10  10   5   1
1   6  15  20  15   6   1
1   7  21  35  35  21   7   1
1   8  28  56  70  56  28   8   1
1   9  36  84 126 126  84  36   9   1
```

The program accomplishes this by an outer loop that is repeated once for each line of the triangle. First the "right edge" of the line is initialized to 1, then a "backward" loop generates the elements of the line by summing elements from the previous line. Finally, a "forward" loop writes the elements of the line (capped off by a single writeln).

The size (the "depth") of the triangle is declared as a constant:

const
    n = 10;   {size of triangle}

To create a Pascal's triangle of another size, the constant could be changed. The program would have to be recompiled. Constants can be constant values of type integer, real, Boolean, char, or string. Note the similarity to **var** declarations, except that an equals sign (=) is used instead of a colon. All **const** declarations MUST precede all **var** declarations.

Also note that the declaration of n is accompanied by a comment that explains its use.

The program does not store the ENTIRE Pascal's triangle: only one line at a time. This is done with an **array**, which is a concept you are probably familiar with from other languages. An **array** in Pascal, like a matrix in mathematics, is a table of values grouped together under a single name. Arrays may have one or more dimensions. The array in our program is quite simple:

p: **array** [1..n] **of** integer;

This declares p to be an array with a "base type" of integer. The "bounds" of the array are 1 and n. Since n is a constant equal to 10, p contains 10 elements: each of them is an integer.

Note that the upper bound of the array is specified as a constant (n) (n also appears in the outer **for** loop below). One advantage of using an identifier to name the constant is that when the value of n is changed, no other part of the program need be changed. In Pascal, array bounds must be constants, not variables.

We will encounter multidimensional arrays in Chapter 2.

Within the main body of the program, p refers to the entire array (the program does not use this construct), and p followed by a value in square brackets specifies an individual element of the array. The value in brackets is called a "subscript." Thus, we could write:

    p[1]:= 1;

... or, as in the program itself:

    p[i]:= 1;

... and so forth.

When a program specifies an array subscript that is out of range, such as:

    p[0]   {... or ...}
    p[23]

... a runtime error occurs, much like the one we illustrated for Program 2. (This does NOT happen if the programmer has turned off range-checking: see the Definition, Chapter X, Section 1).

Using variables as subscripts is a very important practice. Our program does this in three statements:

    p[i]:= 1;
    p[j]:= p[j]+p[j-1];
    write(p[j]:4);

The second **for** statement that appears in the program has the form:

    for j:= i-1 **downto** 2 **do**

Note the reserved word **downto** instead of **to**. This is why this loop was described as "backward." The loop counter j is DECREMENTED (by 1) rather than incremented. This is the other form of the **for** statement, and is also frequently used. We cannot use a "forward" loop here, because that would

191

destroy values in p before they were used.

The outer loop of the program contains two **for** loops nested within it. The outer loop uses the index 'i', and the inner loops each use the index 'j'. This is a very common way of handling arrays. The important thing to remember is that once a **for** loop has completed its execution, the value of the loop counter is UNDEFINED: before the loop counter variable can be used again, it must be re-initialized. In Program 3, this is accomplished by the second nested **for** statement itself.

In the call to write:

write(p[j]:4);

... the number which follows the array element expression (':4') is called a "field specification," and indicates that the value should be printed within 4 spaces. If this specification were not there, the number would be printed without any surrounding spaces, and the Pascal's triangle would be illegible. Numbers are always right-justified within the output field. If the number is too large for the output field (e.g., if it were longer than 4 digits, which would not occur in so small a Pascal's triangle) the field specification is ignored.

Before we go on to Program 4, we have a few more things to say about arrays. It is very important to remember that declarations do not initialize variables. A declaration of an array does NOT initialize the array: all elements of an array are undefined until they have been initialized by a statement within the program.

An attempt to use an undefined (uninitialized) variable is not necessarily detected by the System, but it frequently results in a runtime error, since the space that is allocated to that variable contains "garbage" values left over from previous programs: these variables do not always correspond to what the programmer intends to to find there!

The situation can even be a bit more subtle than this. If you look at Program 3, you may notice that the array p contains undefined values all the way up to the last iteration of the outer loop: for each pass through the loop, p[1] through p[i] are defined, while p[i+1] through p[n] are undefined. There is no problem with this, since we never attempt to USE the undefined values in an expression or a call to <u>write</u>.

The other important point about Program 3 concerns the very first iteration through the loop. In this case (as is evident from the output), the output line (and hence the defined portion of p) is only 1 element long. Such a simple case of our loop (and it is necessary for the initialization of the Pascal's triangle) is called a "degenerate case."

Here is what happens on the first time through the loop:

1. i is set to 1.

2. p[1] is set to 1.

3. The next **for** loop specifies:
    for j:= i-1 **downto** 2 **do** ...
    ... since i-1 = 0, which is already less than 2, the loop is NOT executed.

4. The next **for** loop specifies:
    for j:= 1 **to** i **do** ...
    ... since i = 1, this loop is executed only ONCE.

5. writeln is called, which ends the output line that contains only the single value p[1] = 1.

Something similar occurs in the second iteration, where only 2 values are printed: again, the first nested **for** loop is skipped. The reader may wish to work through the steps for this case.

It is always important to pay attention to degenerate cases while programming. In some algorithms, such as this one, they are a necessary part of the problem's solution. In some algorithms, they are not crucial, but can be elegantly handled with no extra code. In some algorithms, degenerate cases are a nuisance and require that the programmer insert additional code to detect them and correct for their effects: this latter sort of algorithm should be avoided if at all possible. In addition to being inefficient (because of the extra test and correction code), an algorithm that must explicitly account for degenerate cases is frequently an algorithm that is not a good solution to the problem at hand, and often contains additional inefficiencies or bugs.

When an algorithm seems to be too complicated, it may be the case that the data structures you are using are not quite appropriate: remember that data structure and program structure are two sides of the same coin.

The next sample tests a string to see whether it is a palindrome: that is, a string that is the same both forwards and backwards, such as the popular 'able was I ere I saw elba'. It introduces the UCSD type string, and some new uses of the type Boolean.

```
program Palin_1;
    { Palin_1 tests to see if string s is a
      palindrome (reads the same forwards and
      backwards). }
    var
        s: string;
        i: integer;
        is_palindrome: Boolean;
    begin
        write('enter string to test: ');
        readln(s);
        is_palindrome:= true;
        for i:= 1 to length(s) div 2 do
            if s[i] <> s[length(s)+1-i]
                then is_palindrome:= false;
        if is_palindrome
            then writeln('    a palindrome')
            else writeln('    not a palindrome');
    end.
```

Program 4

The program prompts a user to enter a string, and then tests the string to see whether it is a palindrome by comparing the characters in the string, starting at either end and working toward the center. A Boolean variable is used to represent whether the string is a palindrome or not: if any characters are not equal, the variable is set to false. Finally, a message is printed that reports what the program found.

Some runs of the program might look like this:

```
enter string to test: aba
    a palindrome

enter string to test: curious
    not a palindrome
```

```
enter string to test: able was I ere I saw elba
a palindrome
```

The program input is contained in a variable of type <u>string</u>. A <u>string</u> is a sequence of characters. Single characters are represented by the type <u>char</u>, so a <u>string</u> is similar to an **array of** <u>char</u>. The difference is that an array must have a fixed length, while a string has a dynamic length that may change during a program's execution.

The individual characters in a string may be indexed by a subscript, just as the elements of an array. The index may range from 1 up to the dynamic length of the string. This dynamic length may be determined in the program by a call to the intrinsic function <u>length</u>. In the program above, we have the expression:

<u>length</u>(s) **div** 2

... which results in half the length (truncated) of the string s. The program MUST use a construct like this, since the string itself is typed in by the program's user, and we cannot know beforehand how long the string might be.

All strings have a maximum length (also called the "static length"). Unless the program specifies otherwise (Program 4 does not), this is equal to 80 characters. If we wanted to limit the string s to, say, 20 characters, we could have declared it in the following way:

s: <u>string</u>[20];

In a string declaration, if the predeclared word <u>string</u> is followed by a number in brackets, that number is the string's maximum length. No string may have a maximum length greater than 255.

The use of the function <u>length</u> is our first use of an intrinsic function; we will see many more of them. A programmer may also write new functions, as illustrated in Program 5.

When a string is read, as in the statement:

<u>readln(s);</u>

... the characters that the user types are placed in s, up to the
<return> character. While typing the string, the user may use
<backspace> to make corrections. Since the input of a string
must be terminated by a <return>, strings should always be read
by a call to <u>readln</u>, never <u>read</u>.

We encountered Boolean expressions in Program 3. A Boolean
value is equal to either <u>true</u> or <u>false</u>. Program 4 introduces a
Boolean variable called is_palindrome.

In the program, is_palindrome is initialized to <u>true</u>, and only set
to <u>false</u> if a non-matching pair of characters is encountered.
We assume the string to be a palindrome unless proven
otherwise. The important comparison is:

$s[i] <> s[length(s)+1-i]$

... which appears in the first **if** statement.

Boolean values cannot be printed in UCSD Pascal (in standard
Pascal they can). Thus, the last statement in our program
tests the value of is_palindrome, and prints a message
accordingly.

Note that the **for** loop only loops for HALF of the length of
the string. The **div** operation is an integer divide, and
truncates its result. If the string has an odd number of
characters, the center character is ignored, which is as it
should be, since the center character will be the same either
forwards or backwards (we hope!), and has no effect on whether
the string is a palindrome or not.

Also note that we have decided that the null string " is a
palindrome: this keeps our algorithm simple. There is no
question that the null string is the same both forwards and
backwards.

Here is the palindrome problem again, but this time we have placed the palindrome test in a function. This is our first example of an important technique: breaking a program down into independent modules. This sample also introduces the **repeat** statement, and more about Boolean expressions.

```
program Palin_2;
   var
      sample: string;

   function Palindrome(s: string): Boolean;
      { Palindrome returns true if s is a palindrome,
        and false if not. }
      var
         is_pal: Boolean;
         i,j: integer;
      begin
         is_pal:= true;                {assume it is a palindrome}
         i:= 1; j:= length(s);
         while (i < j) and is_pal do
            if s[i] <> s[j]
               then is_pal:= false
               else
                  begin
                     i:= i+1; j:= j-1;
                  end;
         Palindrome:= is_pal;
      end; {Palindrome}

   begin
      repeat
         write('enter string to test: ');
         readln(sample);
         if Palindrome(sample)
            then writeln('    a palindrome')
            else writeln('    not a palindrome');
      until sample = '';
   end.
```

Program 5

It should be evident that this program is an elaboration on the last program. The code that tests whether a string is a palindrome has been placed in the function Palindrome, which returns the result as a value (the test itself has been improved -- we will discuss this later).

The main program now has a loop, so instead of testing just one string, we can test any number of strings. The loop ends when the user enters the empty string. This is accomplished by typing only <return> when the prompt 'enter string to test: ' appears.

Here is the output from a sample run of the program:

```
enter string to test: 12321
    a palindrome
enter string to test: drome
    not a palindrome
enter string to test: YREKA B AKERY
    a palindrome
enter string to test:
    a palindrome
```

The loop in the main program is our first example of a **repeat** statement. A **repeat** is similar to a **while,** but the test for the loop's termination appears at the end of the loop rather than the beginning. This is an important difference, because it means that the statements within the loop are executed at least once, no matter what. The scheme of a **repeat** statement is:

repeat
    [<statement> {; <statement>}]
until <Boolean condition>

Notice that there is no need to bracket the statements in a **repeat** loop with **begin** and **end,** since the reserved words **repeat** and **until** accomplish this.

The **repeat** statement is used when (as mentioned), we want the statements to be executed at least once, and when (as in Program 5), the test for termination depends on a value that is assigned within the loop.

It is customary to indent the statements within a **repeat** loop, as illustrated in Program 5.

The main thing to describe about this program is the function itself.

Creating a function (or a procedure) is basically a means of packaging some code so that it can be accessed from several locations in the program, or at several different times during execution (as in the example). Packaging code in this way is an example of "modularity." Modularity is an important way of structuring programs, by making code reusable in various contexts, and thus keeping code independent and easier to debug.

Two means of packaging code are procedures and functions. The distinctive feature of a function is that it returns a value; thus, a function call must appear within an expression.

In Program 5, the function Palindrome returns a Boolean value, and when it is called, it appears as a Boolean expression within an **if** statement.

Within a sequence of declarations, procedure and function declarations must appear after all variable declarations, and before the code body of the program or routine. The form of a procedure or function declaration is similar to the form of a program itself: there is a heading, a list of declarations, and then a body of statements enclosed by a **begin end** pair.

The declarations within a procedure or function appear just like declarations within the main program: they may even include nested functions and nested procedures. All objects declared within a procedure or function are considered "local" to the procedure or function. NO CODE in the program that is outside the procedure or function may use any identifiers that were declared within it.

On the other hand, variables and so forth that were declared in the main program are considered "global" to the procedure or function, and could be used within it. The scope of identifiers is described in more detail in the Definition, Chapter IV, Section 2.1.

In Program 5, the function Palindrome contains the variables is_pal, i, and j. These are local variables, and could not be used by the main program. The main program itself contains the variable sample. This is global to Palindrome, and could be used within the function (though it is not).

Local variables allow us to hide the workings of a function or procedure from the rest of the program. This too is an important aspect of modularity. Should we decide to change a function (for example, to replace it with a better algorithm), we can do so without affecting any of the program that calls it. It should be apparent that this is useful.

This is the function heading in our sample program:

function Palindrome (s: <u>string</u>): <u>Boolean</u>;

Palindrome is the name of the function. <u>Boolean</u> indicates the type of value returned by the function, and s, which is a <u>string</u>, is called a "formal parameter."

A formal parameter is an identifier that takes on the value of the actual parameter that is used when the function is called. In the main program we have:

if Palindrome(sample) ...

'sample' is the "actual parameter" that corresponds to 's'. When Palindrome is called, 's' takes on the value of 'sample'.

Within a function, formal parameters are treated as local variables. The difference is that each takes its initial value from the actual parameter that corresponds to it. These actual parameters MUST be present when the function is called, and their type MUST correspond to the type of the formal parameters as declared in the function heading.

For the function to return a value, it must contain an assignment statement that assigns a value to the function name itself. Palindrome contains the assignment:

Palindrome:= is_pal;

Note that both is_pal and the function itself are of type <u>Boolean.</u>

If this assignment to the function's name is absent (or the code skips it for some reason), then the value of the function is undefined, and the results (when the function is called) are unpredictable.

The algorithm used in the function itself is a bit different than the one in Program 4. Instead of one index i, there are two indices, i and j. i is initialized to 1, and j is initialized to <u>length</u>(s). Instead of the complicated expression:

s[i] <> s[<u>length</u>(s)+1-i]

... that appeared in the last program, we have:

s[i] <> s[j]

... which is much more readable. On each iteration through the loop, i is incremented and j is decremented.

We are able to do this in Program 5 by changing the condition of the **while** loop to:

while (i < j) **and** is_pal **do**

This is a more complicated Boolean expression than we have seen so far. The simple Boolean expressions i<j and is_pal are combined with the operator **and**. **and** is one of the Boolean operators that were introduced with Program 2. These operators have strict precedence when an expression is evaluated, namely:

not	highest precedence
and	high precedence
	{equivalent to *, /, **mod**, or **div**}
or	middle precedence
	{equivalent to + or -}
>, <, >=, <=, =, <>, and **in**	low precedence

(**in** is a relational operator that we will encounter when we discuss sets.)

202

Because of this precedence of operators, we must put parentheses in the expression:

   (i < j) **and** is_pal

... because if we were to write:

   i < j **and** is_pal

... this would be equivalent to:

   i < (j **and** is_pal)

... which is definitely NOT what we intended (it is also illegal, since j is an <u>integer</u> and is_pal is <u>Boolean</u>).

When in doubt, include parentheses in a Boolean expression to make sure it says what you mean it to say, and to make it more readable.

As the programs in this Guide (and in your own work) grow more complex, so will the Boolean expressions, but they should never be so long or so obscure as to be unintelligible to someone reading the program.

Another advantage of the algorithm in Program 5 is that the loop ends as soon as a mismatch has been found. In Program 4, the **for** loop tests the entire string, even if is_palindrome has already been set to <u>false</u>.

The last sample program in this chapter takes a year entered in decimal form (such as 1956), and converts it to Roman numerals (such as MCMLVI). This program introduces procedures, subranges, and the type <u>char</u>.

```
program Roman;
   type
      digit = 0..9; {decimal digit}
   var
 •    n: integer;

   procedure Write_Digit(d: digit; units, fives, tens: char);
      { Write digit d in Roman numerals, using the
         characters units, fives, and tens. }
      var
         i: integer;
      begin
         if d = 9
            then write(units,tens)
         else if d = 4
            then write(units,fives)
         else
            begin
               if d >= 5
                  then write(fives);
               for i:= 1 to d mod 5 do
                  write(units);
            end;
      end; {Write_Digit}

   procedure Write_Date(date: integer);
      { Write date in Roman numerals. Dates not in the
         range 1..3999 are printed as ***. }
      begin
         if (date <= 0) or (date >= 4000)
            then write('***')
         else
            begin
               Write_Digit(date div 1000,'M','*','*');
               Write_Digit((date div 100) mod 10,'C','D','M');
               Write_Digit((date div 10) mod 10,'X','L','C');
               Write_Digit(date mod 10,'I','V','X');
            end;
      end; {Write_Date}
```

```
begin
    write('enter date: ');
    readln(n);
    write('in Roman numerals: ');
    Write_Date(n);
    writeln;
end.
```

Program 6

The main body of our program is quite simple. It reads a
single date and prints it in Roman form. You should now be
able, if you wish, to convert it so that it works on a series of
dates, just as our last sample program worked on a series of
strings. In fact, some of our future programming samples will
show only the procedures and relevant declarations, and dispense
with the program heading and main body, since we are
concerned with the algorithms embodied in the procedures and
functions, not the program's superstructure, which should be
easy for the reader to supply.

The program accepts a year in the range 1 to 3999, and
converts it to Roman numerals. As the comment in the
procedure Write_Date points out, dates outside this range are
simply printed as '***'. Restricting the range of allowable
dates in this way is necessary, otherwise the algorithm we use
would become too complicated (longer dates require some nonstandard characters).

It is acceptable to restrict the range of allowable inputs to a
program, provided the program always tests the input to see
that it is valid. There is no way of knowing what the user of
a program will enter, so it is always a good idea to test input
before trying to operate on it. Bad input should not cause a
program to generate bad results.

Here is output from some sample runs of the program:

    enter date: 1492
    in Roman numerals: MCDXCII

    enter date: 1981
    in Roman numerals: MCMLXXXI

```
enter date: 1957
in Roman numerals: MCMLVII
```

The procedure Write_Date is the first that is called. It checks the input, and if this is within the accepted range, it then calls Write_Digit four times: one each for the thousands, hundreds, tens, and ones place of the date in decimal form.

Write_Digit is a bit complicated, because a single digit in a decimal numeral can be as long as 4 letters in a Roman numeral. Every "digit" in a Roman numeral is either:

a string of 1..3 'units'
a 'five' followed by 0..3 'units'
a 'five' preceded by a single 'unit', or
a 'ten' preceded by a single 'unit'

The actual characters for 'units', 'fives', and 'tens' are passed from Write_Date to Write_Digit when Write_Digit is called. For each decimal place, the characters vary.

It should now be evident how the program works. If you are still uncertain, try working through an example.

The two procedure headings in our program are:

procedure Write_Digit (d: digit; units, fives, tens: <u>char</u>);

procedure Write_Date (date: <u>integer</u>);

As mentioned before, a **procedure** is like a **function,** except that it does not return a value. No type may be specified in a procedure heading, and it is illegal to assign a value to the name of a procedure.

Since procedures do not return a value, they are not called from expressions, but instead from a single statement that consists only of the procedure's name, followed by the list of actual parameters, if there are any. For example, the call to Write_Date is:

Write_Date(n);

... and the calls to Write_Digit are:

```
Write_Digit(date div 1000, 'M', '*', '*');
Write_Digit((date div 100) mod 10, 'C', 'D', 'M');
Write_Digit((date div 10) mod 10, 'X', 'L', 'C');
Write_Digit(date mod 10, 'I', 'V', 'X');
```

We have already seen calls to intrinsic procedures: write, writeln, read, and readln are all examples of these. Intrinsic routines may often be called with different numbers or types of actual parameters. A user-written routine must always be called with actual parameters that exactly match the formal parameters.

One thing to notice about the calls to Write_Digit is that the actual parameters passed to a procedure may be expressions as well as variables or constants. Of course, the type of the actual parameter must always be the same as the type of the value parameter. (There is another type of parameter called a 'variable' parameter: an actual parameter that corresponds to a variable parameter must be a variable. Variable parameters are described in Chapter 3.)

Another thing to notice about Write_Digit is that in the first call, the fives and tens parameters are specified as '*'. The "thousands place" of the Roman numeral should not contain any fives or tens. The reason we pass these characters is that we must pass SOMETHING, since actual parameters must match formal parameters. We pass '*', because if by some error the procedure should print out fives or tens in this place, we want the output to look incorrect, so that we know there is a bug somewhere.

The formal parameters units, fives, and tens in Write_Digit are declared to be of type char. char, short for character, is another simple type like integer, real, or Boolean. The calls to Write_Digit have some examples of character constants: 'M', 'C', 'L', 'D', 'X', 'V', 'I', and '*'. Character constants may in fact be any printable character: letters (either upper or lower case), numerals, and special symbols. A character constant must be enclosed in apostrophes (') to distinguish it from a single-letter identifier or special symbol. A single apostrophe is represented by ''''. It is also possible to declare variables of type char, and assign values to them or read them. There are no operations on characters.

char is the base type of the type string, so that a single character in a string (such as s[i]) is of type char.

Virtually all implementations of UCSD Pascal use the ASCII character set: both printing and non-printing characters are shown in Appendix E. We will have more to say about characters in the next chapter.

In this program, we have declared a **type:**

type
    digit = 0..9; {decimal digit}

What this declaration indicates is that the program now has a new type called digit, which can only take the integer values 0 through 9.

The expression 0..9 is our first example of a type that is a "subrange," that is, a restricted range of some other type: in this case, integer. The type integer is itself an example of a "scalar" type. A scalar type is a simple type whose values are both finite and ordered. In Pascal, it is possible to declare subranges of any scalar type.

So far, the scalar types we have seen are integer, char, and Boolean (Boolean is a scalar type because by definition, true > false). The types real and long integer are NOT scalar. Strings and arrays are structured types, not simple types, so they are not considered scalar either.

For now, the important point is that in Pascal, new types can be declared. The advantage is that the programmer can tailor the structure of data to better match the problem at hand. The following chapter goes into this topic in much more detail.

New types can be associated with an identifier by defining them in a **type** declaration. Type declarations must come after constant declarations and before variable declarations.

In Program 6, the new type digit is used as the type of d, the first parameter to Write_Digit. This has two effects. First, declaring d as a digit makes the program more readable. Second, the Compiler normally generates code to check for range errors (as we have seen when using array indices), and

208

should Write_Digit be called with a parameter that is not in the range 0..9, a runtime error will be generated. Thus, declaring a new type buys us some extra protection against programming mistakes.

We have some final observations about Program 6. Since Write_Digit is only called from Write_Date, we could have declared it WITHIN Write_Date, making it a local procedure. But it is sometimes clearer not to nest things too deeply, and we feel that the program as written is more readable.

Write_Digit is a good example of a procedure that can be used in multiple ways, since it can write a Roman "digit" for a decimal thousands place, hundreds place, tens place, or ones place, all depending on the parameters it is passed.

This is the end of Chapter 1. If you have programmed before, you should now be capable of writing some programs in Pascal. We have touched on the basic tools, but have not gone into great detail about any of them, particularly not about the great variety and flexibility of data types, and the aspects of UCSD Pascal that make it a separate dialect that fits into the p-System. The first thing we will go on to discuss is data types.

Chapter 2
Data and Expressions

This chapter talks about various Pascal (and UCSD Pascal) data types and ways to use them. We have already seen some types and usages in Chapter 1, and since those are straightforward, we will tend to skim over them and move on to newer topics.

An understanding of the material in this chapter is essential to becoming a versatile Pascal programmer. Unfortunately, we cannot cover all topics with equal depth (without making this Guide a duplicate of the Definition!), and so we will refer you back to the Definition for full details.

Expressions and Assignment

We have already seen a large number of expressions in the previous chapter, and can reiterate some facts about them:

> An expression is code that returns a value of
> a particular type, including <u>integer</u>, long <u>integer</u>,
> <u>real</u>, <u>char</u>, <u>string</u>, <u>Boolean</u>, or a **set.**

> An expression may include constants, variables,
> and calls to functions.

> These elements may be combined with operators.
> Different operations are defined for different
> data types.

> Numeric expressions are similar to algebraic
> formulas, and have much the same meaning.
> In the same way, Boolean expressions are similar
> to logical formulas.

> The order in which an expression is evaluated
> depends on the precedence of the operators used:
> certain operators have higher precedence than others.

> Subexpressions can be grouped together with
> parentheses, in order to alter the order of
> evaluation.

We have also seen that a variable can be set to a value by an assignment statement, which consists of the name of the variable, followed by :=, followed by an expression of the appropriate type. This can be used to initialize a variable or to change its value. The new value can be based on the previous value, as in:

    count:= count + 1;

Declarations

We have also seen that all identifiers used in a program must be declared by the programmer (except for predeclared identifiers such as write). Declarations precede the main body of a program, and must follow a particular order.

The first kind of declaration we have seen is the **const** declaration. Constants are values that may not be changed. They may be numeric values, Boolean values, characters, or strings. The advantages of using constants are:

A constant name is easier to read than the value itself, and

If it is necessary to change a constant value, only the declaration need be changed, rather than every occurrence of the value within the program text.

Constant declarations may not contain expressions, but a numeric constant may be declared as the opposite of a numeric constant that has already been defined, for example:

    const
            hi_bound = 128;
            lo_bound = -hi_bound;

Next come **type** declarations. Type declarations are essential if more than one variable is to be of the new type, or the new type is to be used for routine parameters.

This chapter will go into more detail on the subject of declaring new types.

Next come **var** declarations. The name of each variable is associated with a particular type. Variable declarations cause

212

Furthermore, the order in which real expressions are evaluated can greatly effect the accuracy of the result. This is illustrated by our next sample program:

```pascal
program Quadratic;

    { This program finds the roots (real or complex) of
      the polynomial A*x*x + B*x + C = 0. If A = 0, then
      there are not two roots, and an error message is
      displayed. }

    var
      .A,B,C: real;     {coefficients}
      d: real;      {discriminant}
      large_root: real;     {real root with largest abs. value}
      small_root: real;     {root with smallest abs. value}
      real_part: real;     {real part of imaginary roots}
      imag_part: real;      {imaginary part of imaginary roots}

    begin
      write('enter coefficients a b c: ');
      readln(A,B,C);
      if A = 0
        then
          writeln('does not have two roots')
        else
          begin
            d:= sqr(B) - 4*A*C;
            if d >= 0
              then                {roots are real}
                begin
                  writeln('roots are real');
                  if B >= 0
                    then large_root:= -(B+sqrt(d))/(2*A)
                    else large_root:= (sqrt(d)-B)/(2*A);
                  small_root:= C/(large_root*A);
                  writeln(large_root,', ',small_root);
                end
              else                {roots are complex}
```

```
                begin
                    writeln('roots are imaginary');
                    real_part:=  -B/(2*A);
                    imag_part:=  sqrt(-d)/(2*A);
                    write(real_part,' + ',imag_part,'i, ',
                              real_part,' - ',imag_part,'i');
                end;
            end;
        end.
```

Program 8

Here is some output from sample runs of the program:

```
enter coefficients a b c: 1 -1 -12
roots are real
 4.00000, -3.00000

enter coefficients a b c: 5 2 1
roots are imaginary
-2.00000E-1 +  4.00000E-1i, -2.00000E-1 -  4.00000E-1i

enter coefficients a b c: 0 1 3
does not have two roots
```

The structure of this program is straightforward and by now should be familiar; we will not discuss it. The important thing to observe is that it does NOT use the conventional formulas for finding quadratic roots. The traditional formulas for finding the real roots of the equation $A*x*x + B*x + C = 0$ are:

```
x1:=  (-b+sqrt(d))/(2*a);
x2:=  (-b-sqrt(d))/(2*a);
```

The problem with this lies in the nature of real representations. Regardless of the number of digits of accuracy, these are always finite. When two values of similar magnitude are subtracted, there is always a danger that precision will be lost (the same happens when a number is added to a value of similar magnitude but opposite sign) because the significant digits cancel each other, and only the digits of low significance (which usually contain roundoff error) remain. This cancellation error may propagate through future calculations.

Thus, if b and sqrt(d) have similar values, the formula for x1 may give drastically poor results.

The program deals with this problem by finding only the LARGER of the two roots in this way:

large_root:= -(B+sqrt(d))/(2*A)

... or:

large_root:= (sqrt(d)-B)/(2*A)

The smaller root is found by:

small_root:= C/(large_root*A)

... which uses only multiplication and division. These operations cannot cause cancellation errors of the kind we are worried about.

The point of Program 8 is that one should use caution (rather than faith!) in dealing with real quantities. We will encounter another example of real calculation in Program 18.

The type char is used to represent single characters. In virtually all implementations of UCSD Pascal, the character set is represented by the ASCII code, which is shown in Appendix E. ASCII stands for American Standard Code for Information Interchange.

In the ASCII code, digits, uppercase letters, and lowercase letters are all in contiguous groups, and in their usual order. This is required by standard Pascal, although the standard does not actually stipulate a particular character code.

The next sample program is actually just a procedure that translates lowercase characters into uppercase:

```
procedure U_Case(var s: string);
    { converts all lower-case letters in s
      to upper-case }
    var
        i: integer;
    begin
        for i:= 1 to length(s) do
            if (s[i] >= 'a') and (s[i] <= 'z')
                then s[i]:= chr(ord(s[i])
                    - ord('a') + ord('A'));
    end; {U_Case}
```

Program 9

U_Case accepts a string and translates all of its lowercase characters into their uppercase equivalent.

The algorithm does NOT assume that we are using ASCII. If it were re-written to avoid using the type string, it would work on any standard Pascal implementation. This generality comes from the (baroque) assignment:

s[i]:= chr(ord(s[i]) - ord('a') + ord('A'));

... which we will explain piece by piece:

ord(s[i])
        is the numerical equivalent of a character in the string
        (we know it is lowercase because of the **if** statement).

ord(s[i]) - ord('a')
>   results in an "offset" into the lowercase alphabet:
>   if s[i]= 'a', then this offset = 0,
>   if s[i]= 'b', then this offset = 1,
>   ... and so forth up to 25.

ord('A')
>   is the numerical equivalent of uppercase A.
>   This is the base of the upper-case alphabet.

ord(s[i]) - ord('a') + ord('A')
>   converts to upper case by adding the offset
>   into the alphabet (which has nothing to do
>   with case) to the base of the uppercase alphabet.

chr(...)
>   converts the whole mess back into a character.

Note that throughout this whole rigmarole, we have never depended on the exact value returned by the calls to ord, we have simply assumed that the uppercase alphabet and the lowercase alphabet were each contiguous, and in normal alphabetical order.

Scalars and Subranges

This section is an introduction to user-defined scalar and subrange types. Scalars and Subranges are covered in the Definition, Chapter III, Section 3.

The predeclared scalar types (integer, char, and Boolean) have already been introduced. The programmer may also create new scalar types, with declarations similar to these examples:

```
phase = (new, quarter1, half, quarter2, full);
grade = (A, B, C, D, E, F);
knot  = (square, granny, hitch, half_hitch, cloverleaf);
```

A declaration of a scalar type is an enumeration of values, enclosed in parentheses. The order of the values is the order in which they are declared.

The advantage of declaring a scalar type is that both the variable and the name of its possible values describe the data on which the program is working.

Because scalar types are ordered, the comparisons =, <>, >, >=, <, and <= apply with their usual meanings.

User-defined scalar types cannot be read or written with the standard Pascal procedures.

The standard functions on scalar types are:

pred(v)   returns the "predecessor" of v,
          that is, the value that precedes it

succ(v)   returns the "successor" of v,
          that is, the value that follows it

If v is the first value in the scalar type, then pred(v) causes a runtime error, and if v is the last value, succ(v) causes a runtime error.

ord(v)   returns an integer that is the
ordinal value of v in the list of
scalar values

Scalar values are numbered starting at 0. For example, if we use the type phase as declared above, ord(new) = 0 and ord(half) = 2.

For user-defined scalars, there is no inverse of the ord function. For type char, the function chr is the inverse of ord, as we have seen.

For an example of a user-defined scalar type, refer to Program 15 and Program 16.

We can define a subrange of any scalar type. For example:

```
lcase  = 'a' .. 'z';    {subrange of char}
mark   = 10 .. 20;      {of integer}
not_new = quarter1 .. full;  {of phase}
passing = A .. C;       {of grade}
```

The scalar type from which a subrange is derived is called the 'base type'. Any input or output, operations, comparisons, procedures, or functions that are defined for the base type are also legal for the subrange, although the overflow conditions for calculations may vary.

Subranges are frequently used as the index type of an array.

Subranges are also useful for the automatic range checking they provide. A subrange was used for this purpose in Program 6.

More examples of subranges will appear in the programs to come.

Arrays

Arrays were introduced in Chapter 1. Our next sample program (actually a program fragment) introduces the notion of **packed,** and an array of multiple dimensions:

```
const
    max = 4;         {adjust for larger matrix size}

type
    matrix = packed array[1..max,1..max] of Boolean;

procedure Sqr_Matrix(var m: matrix);
    { squares Boolean matrix m }
    var
        n: matrix;
        i,j,k: integer;
        s: Boolean;
    begin
    n:= m;
    for i:= 1 to max do
        for j:= 1 to max do
            begin
                s:= false;
                for k:= 1 to max do
                    s:= s or (n[i,k] and n[k,j]);
                m[i,j]:= s;
            end;
    end; {Sqr_Matrix}
```

Program 10

Program 10 squares a Boolean matrix. This is the same as squaring a numerical matrix, that is, multiplying it times itself, except that + is replaced by the Boolean operator **or,** and * is replaced by **and.**

There are applications for this routine. Each entry of the array, if <u>true</u>, may represent a one-way route from, say, one city to another. Squaring the matrix produces a table of cities that can be reached by a road that passes through exactly one other city.

When a matrix M is squared, each element of the resulting matrix M´ is given by the formula:

   M[i,j] = SUM (M[i,k] * M[k,j])

... or using Boolean elements:

   M[i,j] = OR (M[i,k] **and** M[k,j])

... SUM and OR are defined over all k, where 1 <= k <= max.

For example, if the matrix to be squared was:

   1 0 0
   0 0 1
   1 1 0

... the result would be:

   1 0 0
   1 1 0
   1 0 1

Here is a matrix actually passed to Sqr_Matrix:

   1 0 0 0
   0 0 1 1
   1 1 0 1
   0 1 0 0

... and here is the result:

   1 0 0 0
   1 1 0 1
   1 1 1 1
   0 0 1 1

You should note that operations must be done element-by-element. The two indices into the 2-dimensional array are controlled by nested **for** loops. This is a very common way of handling multidimensional arrays.

The word **packed** only appears in the global declaration of the array type 'matrix': it does not appear in the body of the program, and has NO effect on the algorithm. Packing is a means of reducing the storage space of an array or record. In a Boolean array that is **packed,** each element consists of only 1 bit, so the array occupies very little space.

Strings

The type string is another type that we have already encountered. A string is a sequence of characters whose length may change dynamically. This is a UCSD Pascal extension. A number of intrinsic routines are provided to handle strings. See the Definition, Chapter III, Section 4.2.

All the comparisons may be used on string values: the result returned is based on lexicographic (dictionary) order.

Program 11 consists of two routines that demonstrate some common conversions using strings:

```
function Str_to_Int(s: string): integer;
   { converts s to an integer }
   var
     i, result: integer;
   begin
     result:= 0;
     for i:= 1 to length(s) do
        result:= result*10 + ord(s[i]) - ord('0');
     Str_to_Int:= result;
   end; {Str_to_int}

procedure Int_to_Str(n: integer; var s: string);
   { converts integer n to a string returned as s }
   begin
     s:= '';
     while n > 0 do
        begin
          s:= concat(' ',s);
          s[1]:= chr(n mod 10 + ord('0'));
          n:= n div 10;
        end;
   end; {Int_to_Str}
```

Program 11

227

The way that these two routines operate should be familiar from the uppercase conversion program (Program 9), and the Roman numeral problem (Program 6). Int_to_Str must be a procedure, because a string cannot be returned as a function result (only simple variables can be returned from user-written functions).

The intrinsic length(S) was introduced in Program 4. It returns an integer value that is the dynamic length of the string S.

The intrinsic concat is a function. It returns a string value that is the concatenation of all the string values passed to it.

Since the parameters to concat must be strings, it was not possible to append the next digit by a call such as:

s:= concat(chr(n **mod** 10 + ord('0')),s);

Instead, it was necessary to append a "dummy character:"

s:= concat(' ',s);

... and then replace it with the desired character. (In this context, ' ' is treated as a string constant of length 1.)

The intrinsic pos(SOURCE,PATTERN) attempts to match PATTERN to a substring of SOURCE. If it succeeds, it returns an integer that is the index in SOURCE of the first character of the matched PATTERN. If it fails, it returns zero. Program 12 illustrates a way in which pos might be implemented:

```
function Position(s,p: string): integer;
    { Finds first occurence of p in s and returns the
      start character position. Returns 0 if no
      occurence. }
    var,
        a: integer;      {position in s of current search}
        n: integer;      {offset in p of current search}
        same_so_far: Boolean;    {TRUE until mismatch}
    begin
        a:= 1; same_so_far:= false;
        while not same_so_far
            and (a <= length(s)-length(p)+1) do
            begin
                n:= 0; same_so_far:= true;
                while same_so_far and (n < length(p)) do
                    if s[a+n] = p[1+n]
                        then n:= n+1
                        else same_so_far:= false;
                a:= a+1;
            end;
        if same_so_far and (length(p) > 0)
            then Position:= a-1
            else Position:= 0;
    end; {Position}
```

Program 12

The techniques used here are ones we have seen before. Note how the two nested search loops are controlled by a single Boolean variable.

In the last **if,** Position is assigned a-1 rather than a. This is because the outer **while** loop increments a at the end of every pass through the loop. It is simpler to do this than to check the value of same_so_far every time the loop is repeated. If same_so_far ever becomes true, then the loop ends, and a-1 is the solution.

Sets and Records

This section contains three sample programs that briefly introduce sets and records, which are data-structuring constructs that we have not seen before.

A set value is similar to a mathematical set. It is a collection of membership assertions about values from a base type. The base type of a set is a scalar or subrange type. A value of the base type is either **in** the set or not in the set.

Set constants are a list of elements or subranges enclosed in brackets, such as:

[0..9]   {the set of digits}
['A'..'Z']   {the uppercase alphabet}
[new, half, full]
    {some values from the type phases}
[9, 3, 5..7] {some miscellaneous digits}

Set values of the same base type may be manipulated with these operators:

+   set union
-    set difference
*   set intersection

... and compared with these operators:

=   equals
<>   not equals
in   membership

in tests whether a value is in a set. It is illustrated in Program 13 below.

Sets are described in the Definition, Chapter III, Section 4.3.

The following re-write of Program 9 illustrates the use of sets for range-checking, and the comparison **in**:

```
procedure Ucase(var s: string);
   {converts s to upper-case}
   var
      i: integer;
   begin
      for i:= 1 to length(s) do
         if s[i] in ['a'..'z']
            then s[i]:= chr(ord(s[i])
                       - ord('a') + ord('A'));
      end; {Ucase}
```

Program 13

The only difference from the previous Ucase is the line:

if s[i] **in** ['a'..'z']

... which tests if the character s[i] is in the set of all lower-case letters. This has the advantage of being easier to read than the earlier construction.

Here is an example that also illustrates the use of sets, and contains a very general function that you may be able to use in more than one program (it appears again in Program 22):

```
program Prompt_Test;

    type
        charset = set of char;

    function Prompt(line: string;
            legal_commands: charset): char;

        { Prompt prints line, then waits for a
            character in legal_commands to be typed.
            Its uppercase equivalent is returned. }

        var
            ch: char;
        begin
            repeat
                write(line);
                read(ch);
                writeln;
                if ch in ['a'..'z']
                    then ch:= chr(ord(ch)
                        -ord('a')+ord('A'));
            until ch in legal_commands;
            Prompt:= ch;
        end; {Prompt}

    begin
        repeat
            case Prompt('G(urgle, W(hir, S(plat, Q(uit: ',
                    ['G','W','S','Q']) of
                'G': writeln('gurrggle');
                'W': writeln('wwhhhirrr');
                'S': writeln('sppplaaat');
                'Q': exit(program);
            end;
        until false;
    end.
```

Program 14

The parameters to Prompt specify two things: the promptline that is to be displayed, and the set of characters that correspond to valid commands. It reads characters indefinitely, until a valid command is typed, and then returns that character.

In the main program, the character that Prompt returns is used as the 'selector' in a **case** statement. We have not seen the **case** statement before. It has the form:

```
case <selector> of
    <constant list>: <statement>
    ...           : ...
    end
```

The constant lists contain values of a particular scalar or subrange type, and may not "overlap." The selector is a value of the same type as the constants in the constant lists. If the value of the selector matches one of the constants, the statement that follows the matching constant list is executed. If the value of the selector does not match any constant, the **case** statement "falls through."

Note that the reserved word **end** pairs with the reserved word **case.**

A **case** statement is a valuable way of handling a multi-way branch. If you are a FORTRAN programmer, you may recognize the similarity to an assigned GO TO.

In the set legal_commands that is passed to Prompt, only upper-case characters need be specified. Prompt translates lower-case to upper-case. If you wish to use both lower- and upper-case commands, you can remove the **if** statement from Prompt.

Here is some output from the test program:

```
G(urgle, W(hir, S(plat, Q(uit: g
gurrggle
G(urgle, W(hir, S(plat, Q(uit: w
wwhhhirrr
G(urgle, W(hir, S(plat, Q(uit: G
gurrggle
G(urgle, W(hir, S(plat, Q(uit: s
sppplaaat
G(urgle, W(hir, S(plat, Q(uit: Q
```

A record value is a collection of values. Each value occupies a 'field' of the record, and each field has a name. Different fields in a record may be of different types.

Here is an example of a record declaration:

```
type
    date_rec = record
                    day: day_range;
                    month: month_type;
                    year: year_range;
                end;   {date_rec}

var   date: date_rec;
```

Note that the reserved word **end** pairs with the reserved word **record**.

There are three fields in this record, each of a different type. Individual fields in a record are referred to by the name of the record variable, followed by a period (.), followed by the name of the field, for example:

```
date.day:= 15;
date.month:= march;
write(date.year);
```

This sort of notation can get tedious, especially when we have nested records, so Pascal provides the **with** statement. A **with** statement names a record; within the **with**, the field names can be used without their prefixes:

```
with date do
    begin
        day:= 15;
        month:= march;
        year:= 1905;
    end;
```

A record is usually declared as a **type** rather than a **var** (though either is possible). This way, more than one variable can be of the same type of record: the record can even be the base type of an array.

Users of FORTRAN or BASIC may be familiar with creating "parallel arrays," where data about a set of objects is stored in several arrays of different types. In Pascal, this construct can be simplified by declaring a record type that contains fields for the necessary types, then declaring a single array whose elements are of the record type.

A more complete description of records may be found in the Definition, Chapter III, Section 4.4.

The next sample program fragment illustrates the use of a record and the **with** statement. It is a procedure (with the necessary declarations) that accepts a record that contains a date, and changes it to the following date:

```
type
    day_range = 1 .. 31;
    year_range = 1980 ..2050;
    month_type = (jan, feb, mar, apr, may, jun,
        jul, aug, sep, oct, nov dec);
    date_rec = record
        day: day_range;
        month: month_type;
        year: year_range;
    end;   {date_rec}

var   date: date_rec;

procedure Up_Date(var date: date_rec);

    { Up_Date increments date to the next calendar day.
      The eventual overflow on the last day of the last
      year is ignored. }

    var
        last_day: day_range;
    begin
        with date do
            begin
                case month of
                    feb: if (year mod 4 = 0)
                        and (year mod 100 <> 0)
                            then last_day:= 29
                            else last_day:= 28;
```

```
                        apr,jun,sep,nov: last_day:=  30;
                        jan,mar,may,jul,
                            aug,oct,dec: last_day:=  31;
                    end;
                if  day < last_day
                    then  day:=  day+1
                else
                    begin
                        day:=  1;
                        if  month < dec
                            then  month:=  succ(month)
                            else
                                begin
                                    month:=  jan;
                                    year:=  year+1
                                end;
                    end;
            end;
    end;  {Up_Date}
```

Program 15

Note that the body of the procedure Up_Date is enclosed in a
with statement: the identifiers day, month, and year used
within that **with** are actually fields of the record date.

The algorithm first computes the last day of the current month:
if that is equal to the day passed it, it resets day (date.day) to
1, and increments the month and year accordingly; otherwise, it
merely increments day.

One further flexibility of field types in the record construct is
the ability to create 'variants' which allow a field to have
more than one format.   Here is an example:

```
    StockItem = record
                    Name: string;
                    PartNum: integer;
                    case InStock: Boolean of
                        true: (OnHand: integer);
                        false: (Ordered: Boolean;
                                        NumOrdered: integer)
                end;
```

236

In a value of type StockItem, the fields Name and PartNum are always present. InStock is another field. If it is <u>true</u>, then the field OnHand is present and indicates the number of items in stock. If it is <u>false</u>, then the fields Ordered and NumOrdered are both present: the first indicates whether replacements have been ordered, and the second indicates the number of replacements.

The variant field must be the last field in the record. Record variants (also called "case records") may be used for both "clean" and "dirty" programming purposes: in either case, they must be used with CAUTION. We will not go into detail here; record variants are fully described in the Definition, Chapter III, Section 4.4.3. A "clean" use of a variant appears in Program 22, and further examples of their use may be found in Chapter 8.

Dynamic Variables and Pointers

In Pascal, "dynamic variables" are variables that a program can explicitly allocate and de-allocate while it is running. They are usually used to implement linked lists (such as queues), search trees, and other (less or more complicated) data structures. This is accomplished by using "pointers" to the dynamic variables.

A pointer is usually used as one field of a record that contains other information; the pointer points to other records of the same type, creating a list, a tree, or some other data structure.

The declaration of a pointer "binds" it to another type:

    i_ptr, nu_ptr: ^integer;

These pointers can now be used to dynamically reference (nameless) integer variables. Within the program, i_ptr refers to the pointer itself, while i_ptr^ refers to the variable it points to.

Since the variable that a pointer refers to is NOT declared, the space it occupies must be allocated at runtime. This is done with the intrinsic procedure new:

    new(pointer)   allocates space for pointer^
                      (that is, for a variable of
                      the pointer's base type)

After a new, it is still up to the programmer to initialize the value of this new variable.

Thus, we could write:

    new(i_ptr); {creates an integer variable}
    i_ptr^:= 1812; {sets it equal to 1812}
    nu_ptr:= i_ptr; {nu_ptr^ now equals 1812}

In this example, both i_ptr and nu_ptr point to the same integer. But suppose we had written:

```
new(i_ptr);
new(nu_ptr);
i_ptr^:= 1812;
nu_ptr^:= i_ptr^;
```

In this case, i_ptr and nu_ptr each point to a separate variable.
i_ptr is initialized to 1812, as before. The last assignment sets
the variable that nu_ptr points to equal to the variable that
i_ptr points to. In the first example, there was only one
variable. In the second example, there are two.

Pointer values can be assigned, and compared using = and <>,
but cannot be operated on.

It is possible (and sometimes necessary) to remove a dynamic
variable that has been allocated:

> dispose(pointer) removes pointer^ from memory
> and sets pointer = nil

The predeclared word nil (in standard Pascal it is a reserved
word) represents a pointer to nothing, and is conventionally used
to mark the end of a list. A pointer value can be compared
to nil, but an attempt to use it as a reference to a variable
causes a runtime error or an operation on "garbage" data.

The next sample program fragment uses pointers in records, and
a user-defined scalar type:

```
type
    sym_kind = (not_found,reserved,
        predeclared,user_defined);
    sym_rec = record
        ID: string;
        Kind: sym_kind;
        LLink,RLink: ^sym_rec;
    end; {sym_rec}
var
    tab_head: ^sym_rec;
    i: integer;
    s: string;
```

239

```pascal
function Find_Sym(s_id: string): sym_kind;
   { Find symbol s_id in table, and return its kind. }
   var
      found: Boolean;
      p: ^sym_rec;
   begin
      p:= tab_head;
      found:= false;
      while (p <> nil) and not found do
        with p^ do
         if ID = s_id
            then found:= true
         else if s_id < ID
            then p:= LLink
         else p:= RLink;
      if found
         then Find_Sym:= p^.Kind
         else Find_Sym:= not_found;
   end; {Find_Sym}


procedure Enter_Sym(s_id: string; s_kind: sym_kind);
   { Enters symbol s_id in table and sets kind to s_kind. }
   var
      inserted: Boolean;
      p,q: ^sym_rec;
   begin
      new(q);                              {allocate record}
      with q^ do
        begin                             {initialize record}
           ID:= s_id; Kind:= s_kind;
           LLink:= nil; RLink:= nil;
        end;
      if tab_head = nil                   {enter record in table}
         then tab_head:= q
         else
            begin
               p:= tab_head;
               inserted:= false;
               while not inserted do
                  with p^ do
                     begin
                        if s_id < ID
                           then
                              if LLink = nil
                                 then
                                    begin
```

240

```
                                    LLink:= q;
                                    inserted:= true
                          end
                      else p:= LLink
              else
                  if RLink = nil
                      then
                          begin
                              RLink:= q;
                              inserted:= true
                          end
                      else p:= RLink
              end;
          end;
      end; {Enter_Sym}
```

Program 16

Enter_Sym enters identifiers into a symbol table, and Find_Sym finds identifiers in the table. The table itself is structured as a binary search tree. Each node of the tree is represented by the record:

```
    sym_rec = record
          ID: string;
          Kind: sym_kind;
          LLink,RLink: ^sym_rec;
      end; {sym_rec}
```

The ID field contains the identifier. The Kind field indicates what sort of an identifier it is. The fields LLink and RLink point to a left and right subtree, respectively. If no such subtree exists, the pointer is equal to nil.

One global pointer, tab_head, points to the top of the tree. The tree itself is allocated dynamically by Enter_Sym.

Enter_Sym firsts allocates a record for the tree. Then it initializes the record. The identifier and its kind are passed to Enter_Sym as parameters (s_id and s_kind), and the ID and Kind fields of the new record are initialized with these values. Both LLink and RLink are set to nil.

If tab_head = nil, then this is the first record in the tree, and tab_head is set to point to it. If tab_head is not nil,

241

Enter_Sym traverses the tree until it finds a record with a nil link, and places the new record there by updating the nil link to point to the new record. As it traverses the tree, it follows either an LLink or an RLink.

Whether Enter_Sym chooses an LLink or an RLink depends on the alphabetical order of the new identifier ('s_id < id'). The tree is a common form of binary search tree. For any node, all the identifiers in the left subtree (alphabetically) precede the identifier at the node, and all the identifiers in the right subtree follow the identifier at the node.

Thus, the structure of the tree is based on the order in which identifiers are entered, but when the tree is traversed, the identifiers always appear in alphabetical order. Find_Sym assumes that the tree may be traversed in this way.

Find_Sym is passed an identifier, and returns its kind. It does this by simply traversing the tree until it finds a record whose ID field matches the parameter (s_id). If no identifier matches s_id, Find_Sym eventually reaches a nil pointer, and halts its search, returning not_found as the symbol kind.

In both routines, note the use of a **with** statement to simplify the code.

The identifier's kind is the sort of information that could be used by a Compiler. We use it to illustrate the more general technique of associating information with an entry in a table by including that information as a field in the record type.

These routines, by the way, come from the program that we used to format the sample programs before printing them.

Chapter 3
Flow of Control

We have already encountered the major control constructs: **if,
case, while, repeat,** and **for.** This chapter will not go over
them, but will briefly deal with the **goto** statement, then move
on to the structure of procedures and functions.

Unconditional branching in a program is generally frowned upon,
because it is confusing to read and difficult to verify.
Occasionally it is useful, especially in dealing with emergency
situations. In Pascal, the **goto** statement causes an
unconditional branch.

A **goto** or similar statement may be a familiar construct in the
programming language that you have been using. In Pascal, the
variety of flow-of-control statements we have already discussed
usually makes the **goto** unnecessary.

Program 17 consists of two code fragments that accomplish the
same thing; the second of the fragments uses a **goto:**

```
        found:= false;
        i:= 0;
        while not found and (i < n) do
          if a[i] = '*'
            then found:= true
            else i:= i+1;
        if found
          then writeln('found at ',i)
          else writeln('not found');
```

... this code performs the same task as:

```
    label 1;
    ...
    for i:= 0 to n-1 do
      if a[i] = '*'
      then
          begin
          writeln('found at ', i);
          goto 1;
      end;
    writeln('not found');
    1: {next statement}
```

Program 17

The destination of a **goto** is a labelled statement. Labels are represented by integers in the range 1..9999. Every label that appears in a program must be declared. Label declarations PRECEDE constant declarations.

In UCSD Pascal, a label must be within the same "block" as the **goto** that names it (a block is the body of a main program or a routine). Standard Pascal does not have this restriction.

Virtually all Pascal programmers would describe the first example as "structured," and second as "unstructured." Even though using the **goto** saves us the use of a Boolean variable, the first fragment would be preferable: it is easier to read, both BECAUSE of the Boolean, and because the order of execution does not jump about. A program that is easier to read is easier to debug.

244

Functions and Procedures

To illustrate the use of routines in structuring a program, we have chosen a rather lengthy function. This function, Parse_Group, contains three nested procedures and one nested function.

What Parse_Group does is accept input that consists of integers or groups of integers, and build a set that contains them. The input format is relatively loose -- we attempt to compensate for the vagaries of human operators or programmers. Parse_Group is a simple illustration of the form of a "recursive descent" parser: such parsers are often important parts of compilers or interpreters for high-level programming languages, including the Pascal compiler itself.

Here is the program; we will say more about it below:

```
const
    item_max = 100;

type
    item_range = 1..item_max;
    item_set = set of item_range;

function Parse_Group
    (var members: item_set): Boolean;
    { Parse a group, which consists of fields separated by
        commas. The set of items selected is
        passed back in item_set. Parse_Group returns true
        only if a legal group was parsed. }
const
    EOS = '!';
var
    s,prompt: string;
    p: integer;

procedure Parse_Error(msg: string);
    { Points to the position in the line that the error
        was detected, and prints the error message. }
    begin
        writeln('^':p+length(prompt),' -- ',msg);
        exit(Parse_Group);
    end; {Parse_Error}
```

```pascal
procedure Skip_Spaces;
  begin
    while s[p] = ' ' do
      p:= p+1;
  end; {Skip_Spaces}

function Parse_Num: item_range;
  { Scan off an integer between 1 and item_max, and
    return its value. }
  var
    n: integer;
  begin
    Skip_Spaces;
    if not (s[p] in ['0'..'9'])
      then Parse_Error('expecting number');
    n:= 0;
    repeat
      n:= n*10 + ord(s[p]) - ord('0');
      p:= p+1;
      if n > item_max
        then Parse_Error('number out of range');
    until not (s[p] in ['0'..'9']);
    Parse_Num:= n;
  end; {Parse_Num}

procedure Parse_Field;
  { Parse a field, and add indicated items to the
    member set, provided there is no duplication. A
    field consists of a number, or number..number. }
  var
    item: integer;
    start_item, end_item: item_range;
  begin
    start_item:= Parse_Num;
    Skip_Spaces;
    if s[p] <> '.'
      then end_item:= start_item
      else
        begin
          p:= p+1;
          if s[p] <> '.'
            then Parse_Error('expecting "."');
          p:= p+1;
          end_item:= Parse_Num;
        end;
```

```
              if start_item > end_item
                  then Parse_Error('subrange must be in order');
              for item:= start_item to end_item do
                  if item in members
                      then Parse_Error('duplicate item in list')
                      else members:= members + [item];
          end; {Parse_Field}

    begin {Parse_Group}
      prompt:= 'enter group: ';
      write(prompt);
      readln(s);
    { tack on termination character }
      s:= concat(s,EOS);
      Parse_Group:= false;
      p:= 1;
      members:= [];

      Skip_Spaces;
      if s[p] <> EOS
          then
              begin
                  Parse_Field;
                  Skip_Spaces;
                  while s[p] <> EOS do
                      if s[p] <> ','
                          then Parse_Error('expecting ","')
                          else
                              begin
                                  p:= p+1;
                                  Parse_Field;
                                  Skip_Spaces;
                              end;
              end;
          Parse_Group:= true;
    end; {Parse_Group}
```

Program 18

The legal input to Parse_Group is any list of integers or
subranges of integer, provided it does not contain duplicate
numbers or bad syntax.

247

These lists would be accepted by Parse_Group:

    1,5,10
    13,6..9

These examples show bad input and the error message printed by Parse_Group:

    enter group: 7..4
                 ^ - subrange must be in order

    enter group: 1,3,5,,7
                      ^ - expecting number

    enter group: 2..6,5,8
                      ^ - duplicate item in list

Program 18 is the longest example we have seen so far, but it should not be intimidating. In brief outline, this is what the function does:

    accept a string from the user

    tack a termination character (EOS) onto the string

    execute a loop that calls:

        Parse_Field to read a single number
            or range of numbers

        Skip_Spaces to scan over any spaces that
            may intervene before the next entry

    ... the loop ends when the termination character
        is encountered

It is the function Parse_Num (called by Parse_Field) that actually converts a character string into an integer; Parse_Field is the procedure that places that number in the set.

The way in which errors are handled is of special interest. Parse_Group is a <u>Boolean</u> function: if it returns <u>false</u>, then parsing has failed in some way.

248

The procedure Parse_Error is called from within Parse_Group. It prints an error message, and then calls:

    exit(Parse_Group);

... which aborts the parsing function.

The intrinsic exit is a UCSD Pascal extension. When it is passed the name of a routine, the routine returns immediately. It can also be called with:

    exit(<program name>);

... or:

    exit(**program**);

... which causes the program to terminate.

Note that in the main body of Parse_Group, its return value is initialized to false, and is only set to true when parsing is completed and no error has occurred. If it were set before this time, the call to exit might cause Parse_Group to incorrectly return true.

Note that Parse_Num and Parse_Field use local variables, while the other nested routines do not. Parse_Error uses only a parameter, and Skip_Spaces uses the string 's' and the integer 'p', which are global to Skip_Spaces (but local to Parse_Group).

Program 18 uses sets in two ways. One is for range-checking, a use we have already seen. The other is to build the set 'members'. This is the main purpose of Parse_Group. The variable 'members' is actually used in only two statements: it is initialized to the empty set in the main body of Parse_Group:

    members:= [];

... and only modified in the last line of Parse_Field:

    else members:= members + [item];

By modifying 'members' in only two places, we reduce the chance of error.

249

Recursion

Recursion refers to the ability of a procedure or function to call itself. In Pascal this is possible, and can be a most powerful tool for keeping program code brief, elegant, and intelligible.

The limitation of recursion is that there is a certain overhead every time a procedure is called: parameters and addresses must be pushed onto the Stack.

The DANGER of recursion is that a procedure or function might go on calling itself until the Stack overflows: our objective instead is to write programs that terminate cleanly and correctly. As with a **while** or **repeat** statement, a recursive routine MUST contain code that ensures its termination. In other words, there must be a point at which it does NOT call itself recursively, but instead returns in a normal fashion.

The scheme of a recursive routine that will terminate might be sketched as:

```
procedure recurse;

begin
    if <terminating case> then
        {finish task} ...
    else
        begin
            ...
            recurse;
            ...
        end;
end {recurse};
```

Because of the overhead, recursive routines should be only written to solve problems that are "naturally recursive:" problems that lend themselves to a recursive solution, and that cannot be implemented otherwise without a good deal of overhead (such as an extra programmer-created stack).

Program 19 integrates a curve (finds the area under the curve) by a technique called "Adaptive Quadrature." Adaptive Quadrature is a naturally recursive algorithm that is relatively

fast. In the parlance of numerical analysis, it "conve
quickly."

In our program, the procedure Adap_Quad merely sets up the problem and then calls Find_Area. It is Find_Area that actually calculates area and calls itself recursively.

Find_Area first attempts to solve the integral using Simpson's rule (this is a common means of calculating an integral by approximating a curve with a parabola). If this result comes within the given tolerance, Find_Area returns it (this is Find_Area's terminating case). If the result is not good enough, Find_Area calls itself again TWICE: once for the left half of the interval, and once for the right half. This is often called "double recursion."

The effect of Find_Area's algorithm is to spend more time integrating a difficult interval of the curve, and less time on an interval that converges quickly. This is why the algorithm is called "adaptive." If Find_Area were not recursive, writing an adaptive algorithm would be very difficult (and very messy).

```
program Test;

   const
      min_interval = 0.01;
      { the smallest interval which will
      continue to recurse }


   var
      tol,a,b,area: real;

   function Func(x: real): real;
      { Replace this function with whatever function
        is to be integrated. }
      begin
         Func:= sqrt(x);
      end; {Func}

   function Simpson
      (a,fa: real; var m,fm: real;
       b,fb: real): real;
      { Compute the area of interval [a,b] by Simpson's rule.
        The value of the area is returned as the function
        result, and the mid-point (m) and
```

```
              associated function value (fm)
              are returned through var parameters. }
   begin
      m:= (a+b)/2;
      fm:= Func(m);
      Simpson:= (b-a)*(fa+4*fm+fb)/6;
   end; {Simpson}


function Find_Area
   (tol,aw,a,fa,m,fm,b,fb: real): real;
   { Compute the area of interval [a,b] by the method of
     Adaptive Quadrature. tol is the acceptable tolerance
     limit for this interval. aw is the area of the whole
     interval, as computed by Simpson's method. If the
     computation is within tolerance, then just return.
     Otherwise, recurse to compute the area more
     accurately, or print a warning that area cannot
     be computed within tolerance with
     the current minimum interval. }
   var
      l,fl,r,fr: real;
      { l is mid-point of [a,m],
        r is mid-point of [m,b] }
      al,ar: real;
      { areas of left and right intervals }
   begin
      al:= Simpson(a,fa,l,fl,m,fm);
      ar:= Simpson(m,fm,r,fr,b,fb);
      if abs((aw-al-ar)/aw) <= tol
         then Find_Area:= al+ar
      else if l-a < min_interval
         then
            begin
               Find_Area:= al+ar;
               writeln
                  ('warning: region [',a,
                   ',',b,'] not in tolerance');
            end
      else Find_Area:=
         Find_Area(tol/2,al,a,fa,l,fl,m,fm)
         + Find_Area(tol/2,ar,m,fm,r,fr,b,fb);
   end; {Find_Area}


procedure Adap_Quad
   (tol,a,b: real; var area: real);
   { Compute area bounded by interval [a,b] by setting
```

```
                 up and calling the recursive Find_Area routine. }
        var
            aw,fa,fb,m,fm: real;
        begin
            fa:= Func(a);
            fb:= Func(b);
            aw:= Simpson(a,fa,m,fm,b,fb);
            area:= Find_Area(tol,aw,a,fa,m,fm,b,fb);
        end; {Adap_Quad}

    begin
        write('left bound: ');
        readln(a);
        write('right bound: ');
        readln(b);
        write('tolerance: ');
        readln(tol);
        Adap_Quad(tol,a,b,area);
        writeln('area is: ',area);
    end.
```

Program 19

For the function to be integrated, we have arbitrarily picked Pascal's sqrt intrinsic (we could change Func to calculate some other function, but we would have to recompile the program).

Here is output from some sample runs of the program:

```
    left bound: 1
    right bound: 5
    tolerance: .001
    area is:  6.78679

    left bound: 0
    right bound: 3
    tolerance: .1
    area is:  3.41141

    left bound: 0
    right bound: 3
    tolerance: .01
    warning: region [ 0.00000, 2.34375E-2] not in tolerance
    area is:  3.46405
```

```
left bound: 0
right bound: 3
tolerance: .001
warning: region [ 0.00000, 2.34375E-2] not in tolerance
warning: region [ 2.34375E-2, 4.68750E-2] not in tolerance
warning: region [ 4.68750E-2, 7.03125E-2] not in tolerance
area is:   3.46405
```

One advantage of Adaptive Quadrature is that the function is evaluated only ONCE at any given point: the result is passed on as a value parameter in further calls to Find_Area. Our version of Func is very short, but if Func were a complicated calculation, we would still be able to integrate it relatively quickly.

Note that the tolerance is entered by the user, but is divided by 2 every time Find_Area calls itself. If we did not improve the tolerance in this way, we would run the risk of converging too quickly. Even with this precaution, we also set a minimum size for the interval we may integrate, and Find_Area terminates on this case as well, after printing a warning which says the value returned may not be accurate.

The min_interval precaution is necessary because we don't know beforehand what Func returns (it may not even be continuous!), and so we give ourselves a way out so that we don't continue calling Find_Area "forever".

The variable names in this program are short and not terribly readable, but we kept them short because a call to Find_Area has so many parameters; if the call were longer than one line of code, it would be less readable, not more so! This was a tradeoff. Note that the names of parameters and local variables in Adap_Quad are the same as the parameters to Find_Area and Simpson: this helps make them comprehensible, because they correspond to the same objects: nevertheless, each is local to its own procedure, and is NOT global.

Chapter 4
Input and Output

I/O (Input/Output) is concerned with transferring information to and from files. In the p-System, a file is either a file on a block-structured device (such as a disk file), or a peripheral device (such as the console or a printer). This chapter provides some practical illustrations of I/O operations.

UCSD Pascal provides four kinds of I/O: character I/O, record I/O, block I/O, and device I/O. The first two are part of standard Pascal, the second two are UCSD extensions that provide low-level operations. Here is a summary of the four kinds:

character I/O
> deals with character strings
>> (either numeric or literal)
>
> is sequential
> is automatically buffered

record I/O
> deals with information stored in
>> records on disk files
>
> is either sequential or random-access
> is automatically buffered

block I/O
> deals with blocks (512 bytes)
>> of 'untyped' files
>
> is either sequential or random-access
> is NOT buffered
> is used when speed is important

device I/O
> deals with sequences of bytes
> is either sequential or random-access
> is NOT buffered
>
> is used to directly control physical
>> devices (when speed or low-level
>> control is important)

(Random-access is only available on disk files. In the p-System, devices that are not block-structured are handled sequentially.)

The program examples illustrate the syntax for declaring files. The standard Pascal intrinsics <u>reset</u> and <u>rewrite</u> may be used to open scratch files. They are more frequently used in a way that is peculiar to UCSD Pascal: associating an internal (Pascal) filename to an external (p-System) filename. Files opened in this way may be either discarded or saved with the UCSD intrinsic <u>close</u>.

Remember that a physical file on the p-System may be either a disk file or an actual device (CONSOLE:, PRINTER:, REMIN:, REMOUT:, ...). This is described in the <u>UCSD p-System Users' Manual</u>(3), and summarized in the Definition, Chapter VII. We shall illustrate some of this usage in the examples below.

Character I/O

Character I/O consists of reading and writing information to and from files and character-oriented (serial) devices. We have already seen the intrinsics <u>read</u>, <u>readln</u>, <u>write</u>, and <u>writeln</u> used to perform I/O from the console. These intrinsics may be used in much the same way when performing I/O from other devices or disk files.

The two sample programs that follow deal with arbitrary files. The user enters the names of the files that are to be used.

```
program lc_filter;
   { This program converts a textfile to lower-case. }
   var
      i: integer;
      s: string;
      in_file,out_file: text;
   begin
      write('input file: ');
      readln(s);
      reset(in_file,s);
      write('output file: ');
      readln(s);
      rewrite(out_file,s);
      while not eof(in_file) do
         begin
            readln(in_file,s);
            for i:= 1 to length(s) do
               if s[i] in ['A'..'Z']
                  then s[i]:= chr(ord(s[i])
                       -ord('A')+ord('a'));
            writeln(out_file,s);
         end;
      close(out_file,lock);
   end.
```

Program 20

Program 20 converts a file of mixed upper and lower-case characters to all lower-case. The mechanism that does this:

s[i]:= chr(ord(s[i])-ord('A')+ord('a'))

257

... should be familiar from Program 14.

As shown, the names of both the input and output files are entered by the user. Both of them are declared as text, which is equivalent to **file of** char. In UCSD Pascal, a **file of** char may be either a serial device, or a .TEXT file on the p-System.

The input file may be either a device or a file that has already been saved on disk. We open it with the call:

   reset(in_file, s);

reset opens in_file, and associates it with the file named in the string s. (If the user typed an unusable filename, the System responds with a runtime error.) reset makes the file available to the program, and sets the implicit buffer at the beginning of the file, but it does not alter the file's contents.

The output file, on the other hand, is opened with:

   rewrite(out_file, s);

rewrite not only makes the file available and restores the buffer to the beginning, as reset does, it also opens a new (scratch) copy of the file that may supplant the old copy when the file is closed. We presume that the name the user gives for the output file will either be a new file, or an old file that is no longer needed. It could also be an output device.

In both the call to reset and the call to rewrite, the second parameter is optional (in standard Pascal, these intrinsics do not have a second parameter at all). When these routines are called without a second parameter, the p-System creates a scratchfile that is deleted when the file is closed or when the program has finished running. In actual practice, the second parameter is usually used: we are reading from an existing disk file, or creating a new one, or both, as in the sample program.

Note that once we have opened the files we need, readln and writeln are used just as they would be in console I/O, except that their first parameter is the name of a file.

The termination condition of the program's main loop is:

while not _eof_(in_file) **do**

The intrinsic function _eof_ stands for end of file. It returns _true_ after the last record in a file has been read or written. In other words, the program loops until all of in_file has been read.

When a routine or a program terminates, all files that were used during its execution are automatically closed by the p-System. If the files were new (such as scratchfiles), they are deleted. If they already existed on disk, then they are left unchanged.

In our program, the file out_file was new, but since it contains our program's output, we want to keep it. The System's automatic "housecleaning" can be overridden by a call to the UCSD intrinsic _close_. In Program 20, the call that is actually used is:

close(out_file, lock);

The parameter lock instructs _close_ to save the file on disk (under the name used to open it). _close_ can also be called with the parameter purge, which causes the file to be deleted from the directory. (There are other possible parameters to _close_: these are detailed in the Definition, Chapter VII, Section 2.)

For the file in_file, no call to _close_ appears, since it is not necessary.

Our next example of character I/O is a program that does a linear regression on a file of numeric data:

```
program Linear_Regression;
    { This program does a linear regression (closest line
      fit) on data in a file. The input file must be a text
      file with two items of data (x,y) on each line. }
    var
        s: string;
        data: text;
        n,x,y,y_intercept,slope,
        sumx,sumy,sumxy,sumxsq,temp: real;
    begin
        write('data file: ');
        readln(s);
        reset(data,s);
        n:= 0; sumx:= 0; sumy:= 0;
        sumxy:= 0; sumxsq:= 0;
        while not eof(data) do
            begin
                readln(data,x,y);
                n:= n+1; sumx:= sumx+x; sumy:= sumy+y;
                sumxy:= sumxy+x*y; sumxsq:= sumxsq+x*x;
            end;
        temp:= n*sumxsq - sumx*sumx;
        y_intercept:= (sumy*sumxsq - sumxy*sumx)/temp;
        slope:= (n*sumxy - sumx*sumy)/temp;
        writeln('closest fit: y = ',
            slope,'x + ',y_intercept);
    end.
```

Program 21

Instead of an output file, we write the results directly to the console. The input file is opened just as the input file in Program 20. Like that file, it is declared as text, but in this case each line of the textfile consists of two real constants, separated by one or more spaces.

If data1.text contains:

    1 1
    4 3
    7 8.2
    5 4

... the program produces:

    data file: data1.text
    closest fit: y =   1.14933x + -8.34666E-1

If data2.text contains:

    1 2
    5 10
    3 6
    40 80
    21 42

... the program produces:

    data file: data2.text
    closest fit: y =   2.00000x +   0.00000

The first column of numbers contains values of x, and the second column contains corresponding values of y. The closest fit to the data is:

$$y = slope * x + intercept$$

... where slope and intercept are calculated by the program. The formulas for these are:

$$slope = (n*SUM(x*y) - SUM(x)*SUM(y))$$
$$/ (n*SUM(sqr(x)) - sqr(SUM(x)))$$

$$intercept = (SUM(y)*SUM(sqr(x)) - SUM(x*y)*SUM(x))$$
$$/ (n*SUM(sqr(x)) - sqr(SUM(x)))$$

SUM is defined over all x and all y. Therefore the program keeps a running total for each sum, as it reads values from the disk file. When all the values have been read and summed, the slope and intercept are calculated using these formulas.

Record I/O

While character I/O is performed on textfiles and character devices, record I/O is performed on datafiles. The data is stored in its internal form (e.g., integers are 16-bit words, reals are multiple-word floating point representations, and so forth). Because of this, datafiles are not readable as text (the Editor cannot use them, for instance).

Print Queuing

Program 22 below illustrates the use of the record I/O intrinsics. It is a very long program, and you should not feel obliged to study all of it. We have included it because it illustrates so many practices that are typical of applications and systems programming in UCSD Pascal.

Print_Queuer maintains a file that is a "queue" (a first-in-first-out list) of names of files that are waiting to be printed. We presume that another program would do the actual printing. (This method of building a print queue, and then printing the files either later or concurrently, is known as "spooling.")

The Command Level

Like the p-System itself, Print_Queuer is menu-driven. When it is run, the first thing that appears on the screen is:

    L(ist, I(nsert, D(elete, C(lear, Q(uit

This prompt is controlled by the procedure Command:

```
procedure Command;
   var
      done: Boolean;
   begin
      done:= false;
      repeat
         case Prompt('L(ist, I(nsert, D(elete, C(lear, Q(uit ',
                   ['L', 'I', 'D', 'C', 'Q']) of
            'L': List_Command;
            'I': Insert_Command;
            'D': Delete_Command;
            'C': Clear_Command;
            'Q': done:= true;
         end;
      until done;
   end; {Command}
```

The function Prompt was introduced in Program 14. Command allows five different operations. The action of Q(uit should be obvious. The other four are described below. Before explaining them, we describe the structure of the print queue itself.

The Structure of the List

The print queue is contained in a single file:

   f: **file of** print_rec;

The file contains two lists: a list of allocated records, each of which contains a filename, and a list of free records that are available for allocation. Neither list needs to be contiguous: each record points to the record that follows it, much as a dynamic list is constructed with pointers. The "pointers" in f are simply integers that index records in the file, and are used by the intrinsic seek.

Each record in the file is of type print_rec, which is a type declared as:

```
print_rec = record
    case rec_kind of
        info: (alloc_tail,free_tail,
            last_block_alloc: integer);
        alloc,free: (name: string[30];
            link: integer);
    end;
```

This is our first full example of a variant record. Each
print_rec record can have one of two forms: a group of three
integers, or a string of 30 characters followed by an integer.

The form each record takes is determined by the "tag type"
rec_kind, which is declared as:

    rec_kind = (info,alloc,free);

In practice, only the FIRST record of the file is an info record.
All other records are either alloc(ated) or free. No tag
variable is needed for the field, since we can tell what type
the record is by its context.

The info record contains three integers:

    alloc_tail points to the tail of the list of allocated records.
    These allocated records are the names of files to be
    printed.

    free_tail points to the tail of the list of free records.

    (These values each point to the tail, rather than the head,
    in order to make inserting a record easier.)

    last_block_alloc points to the last allocated block in the
    file. This is so we can "shrink" the file if this record is
    deleted.

The remaining records in the file simply consist of a string of
30 characters, and an integer that points to the following
record in the list. If the record is allocated, then the string is
the name of a file to be printed. If the record is free, then
the string is never used (it contains "garbage").

```
```

Clearing the List

The simplest command is C(lear. It calls the following procedure:

```
procedure Clear_Command;
   { Empties the queue. }
   begin
      f^.alloc_tail:= 0;
      f^.free_tail:= 0;
      f^.last_block_alloc:= 0;
      seek(f,0); put(f);
      writeln;
      writeln('    queue cleared');
   end; {Clear_Command}
```

Clear_Command only alters the first (info) record of the file. It may be that the other records in the file contain information, but since the info record does not recognize that, they will be ignored.

Listing the List

The L(ist command prints all of the names in the allocated list. The procedure that does this is:

```
procedure List_Command;
   { Lists the names of files in the queue in
      reverse order (first file in the queue
      is at the bottom of the list). }
   var
      i: integer;
   begin
      seek(f,0); get(f);
      i:= f^.alloc_tail;
      writeln;
      writeln('files queued: ');
      while i <> 0 do
         begin
            seek(f,i); get(f);
            writeln('    ',f^.name);
            i:= f^.link;
         end;
   end; {List_Command}
```

We go to the info record to find out the index of the tail of the allocated list, and then traverse the list, printing each filename as we come upon it. The link field of the head of the list will be 0, and this terminates the loop. Note that the files are printed in reverse order.

Inserting Filenames

The I(nsert command has a much more complicated procedure:

```
procedure Insert_Command;
  { Inserts a file in the queue. If a free
    record is available, it is used. Otherwise
    a new block is allocated at the end of the
    queue file. }
var
  s: string[30];
  free_block, temp: integer;
begin
  writeln;
  write('    file to insert: ');
  readln(s);
  seek(f,0); get(f);
  if f^.free_tail <> 0
    then
      begin
        free_block:= f^.free_tail;
        seek(f,free_block); get(f);
        temp:= f^.link;
        seek(f,0); get(f);
        f^.free_tail:= temp;
        seek(f,0); put(f);
      end
    else
      begin
        last_block:= last_block+1;
        free_block:= last_block;
      end;
  seek(f,0); get(f);
  temp:= f^.alloc_tail;
  f^.alloc_tail:= free_block;
  seek(f,0); put(f);
  f^.name:= s;
  f^.link:= temp;
```

```
        seek(f,free_block); put(f);
    end; {Insert_Command}
```

First the procedure gets the name of the file to be added to the list. It does not check whether this is a valid filename, although that would not be a bad idea -- the reader may wish to contemplate how to write a filename-checking procedure.

Then the info record is examined to see if there is a free record. If there is, it is removed from the free list, and added to the tail of the alloc list. If there is not, the file is extended by a single record.

Finally, the index of the new record is put in the info block, and both the string and the link are put in the new record. The value of the link is the previous tail of the alloc list.

Note that if the free list is empty, the **if** statement only updates some bookkeeping information: the final put automatically extends the length of the file.

Deleting Filenames

The D(elete command is a little more involved than I(nsert, but involves the same basic operations:

```
    procedure Delete_Command;
        { Deletes a file from the queue. If the file
          deleted was in the last block of the queue,
          last_block is decremented, to shorten the
          resulting queue. }
    var
        temp,prev,i: integer;
        found: Boolean;
        s: string;
    begin
        writeln;
        write('    delete what file: ');
        readln(s);
        seek(f,0); get(f);
        prev:= 0; i:= f^.alloc_tail;
        found:= false;
        while (i <> 0) and not found do
            begin
                seek(f,i); get(f);
```

```
                    if f^.name = s
                       then found:= true
                       else begin prev:= i; i:= f^.link; end;
                 end;
             if found
                then
                   begin
                      temp:= f^.link;
                      seek(f,prev); get(f);
                      if prev = 0
                         then f^.alloc_tail:= temp
                         else f^.link:= temp;
                      seek(f,prev); put(f);
                      if i = last_block
                         then last_block:= last_block-1
                         else
                            begin
                               seek(f,0); get(f);
                               temp:= f^.free_tail;
                               f^.free_tail:= i;
                               seek(f,0); put(f);
                               seek(f,i); get(f);
                               f^.name:= '<free>';
                               f^.link:= temp;
                               seek(f,i); put(f);
                            end;
                      writeln('    file deleted')
                   end
                else
                   begin
                      writeln;
                      writeln('    not found');
                   end;
          end; {Delete_Command}
```

After accepting a filename, the procedure must search the alloc list for that record. If it is not there, it prints an error message, otherwise it places that record on the free list (setting the filename to '<free>' to avoid confusion), and updates the info record accordingly. Note that if the name to be deleted is the last in the file, the variable last_block is simply decremented.

The Main Program

We are now (finally, you might say!) ready to look at the main program:

```
begin
   {$I-}
   reset(f,'PRINT.FILES');
   if ioresult <> 0
      then
         begin
            rewrite(f,'PRINT.FILES');
            Clear_Command;
         end;
   seek(f,0); get(f);
   last_block:= f^.last_block_alloc;
   {$I+}
   Command;
   seek(f,0); get(f);
   f^.last_block_alloc:= last_block;
   seek(f,0); put(f);
   seek(f,last_block_alloc); get(f);
   close(f,crunch);
end.
```

The first line of the main program is:

{$I-}

This is our first example of a 'compiler option'. Normally, the Compiler generates code that automatically checks all I/O operations. In this case, we want I/O checking turned off so we can use the UCSD intrinsic function ioresult. When we have finished initializing the print queue file, we turn I/O checking back on with:

{$I+}

(The full set of compiler options is described in the Definition, Chapter X, Section 1.)

We want to turn off I/O checking because we want to be able to maintain the print queue file over several different runs of the program. If the file already exists, we must open it with a reset (rewrite would open a new copy). But if the file does

NOT exist, we are required to open it with a __rewrite__. The simplest way for the program to tell if the file is already on disk is to try opening it with a __reset__: if that fails, __ioresult__ returns an error number, and we know that we must use __rewrite__.

If we did not turn off I/O checking, any error values returned by __ioresult__ would be intercepted by the program at runtime, and cause the program to halt.

After calling __rewrite__, the program calls Clear_Command to initialize the info record.

Once the file has been successfully opened, the last_block variable is initialized, and then Command is called. Command monitors most of the program's work.

We use last_block to optimize the length of the file when it is closed. This is why its value is maintained by the I(nsert and D(elete commands. When the user Q(uit's and Command terminates, last_block is used to update the info record, and then we do a __get__ on the last_block record. The only purpose of this __get__ is to set things up for the call to __close__:

    __close__(f,crunch);

crunch is a close option we have not seen before. When a file is closed with the crunch option, all records from the last record accessed to the end of the file are deleted. If there are any unused records between last_block and the end of the file, they are deleted when the file is closed. This is a way of saving disk space.

Notice that even though the program is more than 170 lines long, we have only two global variables: f and last_block.

Here is output from a sample run:

    L(ist, I(nsert, D(elete, C(lear, Q(uit i

        file to insert: QUEUER.LST

    L(ist, I(nsert, D(elete, C(lear, Q(uit i

        file to insert: LINREG.OUT

L(ist, I(nsert, D(elete, C(lear, Q(uit l

files queued:
    LINREG.OUT
    QUEUER.LST

L(ist, I(nsert, D(elete, C(lear, Q(uit i

    file to insert: OWL.TEXT

L(ist, I(nsert, D(elete, C(lear, Q(uit d

    delete what file: LINREG.OUT
    file deleted

L(ist, I(nsert, D(elete, C(lear, Q(uit l

files queued:
    OWL.TEXT
    QUEUER.LST

L(ist, I(nsert, D(elete, C(lear, Q(uit q

The Whole Thing

Here is a listing of the entire program:

```pascal
program Print_Queuer;

   type
      charset = set of char;
      rec_kind = (info,alloc,free);
      print_rec = record
         case rec_kind of
            info: (alloc_tail,free_tail,
               last_block_alloc: integer);
            alloc,free: (name: string[30]; link: integer);
         end;
   var
      f: file of print_rec;
      last_block: integer;

   function Prompt
      (line: string; legal_commands: charset): char;
      { Prompt prints a promptline and returns a
         response character in legal_commands. }
      var
         ch: char;
      begin
         repeat
            writeln;
            write(line);
            read(ch);
            writeln;
            if ch in ['a'..'z']
               then ch:= chr(ord(ch)-ord('a')+ord('A'));
         until ch in legal_commands;
         prompt:= ch;
      end; {prompt}

   procedure List_Command;
      { Lists the names of files in the queue in
         reverse order (first file in the queue
         is at the bottom of the list). }
      var
         i: integer;
      begin
         seek(f,0); get(f);
         i:= f^.alloc_tail;
```

```pascal
       writeln;
       writeln('files queued: ');
       while i <> 0 do
          begin
             seek(f,i); get(f);
             writeln('      ',f^.name);
             i:=  f^.link;
          end;
   end; {List_Command}


procedure Insert_Command;
   { Inserts a file in the queue. If a free
     record is available, it is used. Otherwise
     a new block is allocated at the end of the
     queue file. }
   var
      s: string[30];
      free_block, temp: integer;
   begin
      writeln;
      write('    file to insert: ');
      readln(s);
      seek(f,0); get(f);
      if f^.free_tail <> 0
         then
            begin
               free_block:=  f^.free_tail;
               seek(f,free_block); get(f);
               temp:=  f^.link;
               seek(f,0); get(f);
               f^.free_tail:=  temp;
               seek(f,0); put(f);
            end
         else
            begin
               last_block:=  last_block+1;
               free_block:=  last_block;
            end;
      seek(f,0); get(f);
      temp:= f^.alloc_tail;
      f^.alloc_tail:=  free_block;
      seek(f,0); put(f);
      f^.name:=  s;
      f^.link:=  temp;
      seek(f,free_block); put(f);
   end; {Insert_Command}
```

```
procedure Delete_Command;
    { Deletes a file from the queue. If the file
      deleted was in the last block of the queue,
      last_block is decremented, to shorten the
      resulting queue. }
var
    temp,prev,i: integer;
    found: Boolean;
    s: string;
begin
    writeln;
    write('    delete what file: ');
    readln(s);
    seek(f,0); get(f);
    prev:= 0; i:= f^.alloc_tail;
    found:= false;
    while (i <> 0) and not found do
        begin
            seek(f,i); get(f);
            if f^.name = s
                then found:= true
                else begin prev:= i; i:= f^.link; end;
        end;
    if found
        then
            begin
                temp:= f^.link;
                seek(f,prev); get(f);
                if prev = 0
                    then f^.alloc_tail:= temp
                    else f^.link:= temp;
                seek(f,prev); put(f);
                if i = last_block
                    then last_block:= last_block-1
                    else
                        begin
                            seek(f,0); get(f);
                            temp:= f^.free_tail;
                            f^.free_tail:= i;
                            seek(f,0); put(f);
                            seek(f,i); get(f);
                            f^.name:= '<free>';
                            f^.link:= temp;
                            seek(f,i); put(f);
                        end;
```

```pascal
                    writeln('    file deleted')
            end
        else
            begin
                writeln;
                writeln('    not found');
            end;
    end; {Delete_Command}


procedure Clear_Command;
    { Empties the queue. }
    begin
        f^.alloc_tail:= 0;
        f^.free_tail:= 0;
        f^.last_block_alloc:= 0;
        seek(f,0); put(f);
        writeln;
        writeln('    queue cleared');
    end; {Clear_Command}


procedure Command;
    var
        done: Boolean;
    begin
        done:= false;
        repeat
            case Prompt('L(ist, I(nsert, D(elete, C(lear, Q(uit'
                        ,['L', 'I', 'D', 'C', 'Q']) of
                'L': List_Command;
                'I': Insert_Command;
                'D': Delete_Command;
                'C': Clear_Command;
                'Q': done:= true;
            end;
        until done;
    end; {Command}


begin
    {$I-}
    reset(f,'PRINT.FILES');
    if ioresult <> 0
        then
            begin
                rewrite(f,'PRINT.FILES');
                Clear_Command;
            end;
```

275

```
      seek(f,0); get(f);
      last_block:=  f^.last_block_alloc;
      {$I+}
      Command;
      seek(f,0); get(f);
      f^.last_block_alloc:=  last_block;
      seek(f,0); put(f);
      seek(f,last_block_alloc); get(f);
      close(f,crunch);
   end.
```

Program 22

Block I/O

Block I/O is used to transfer large portions of files. The block I/O intrinsics deal with multiples of 'blocks'. To the p-System, a block is 512 bytes. It is the unit of storage on 'block-structured' devices such as floppy disks.

Block I/O is intentionally fast, simple, and does little error checking. In other words, it is used when efficiency is important and structure is irrelevant. It follows that block I/O should be used with CAUTION.

Program 23 simply compares two files one block at a time, and prints a message that tells whether they are the same or different:

```pascal
program File_Compare;
    { File_Compare compares two files
    (of any type) for equality. }
    type
        block = packed array[0..511] of char;
    var
        a_file,b_file: file;
        a_buf,b_buf: block;
        s: string;
        same: Boolean;
    begin
    repeat
        write('file a: ');
        readln(s);
{$I-} reset(a_file,s); {$I+}
    until ioresult = 0;
    repeat
        write('file b: ');
        readln(s);
{$I-} reset(b_file,s); {$I+}
    until ioresult = 0;
    same:= true;
    while same and not eof(a_file)
                and not eof(b_file) do
        begin
            same:= (1 = blockread(a_file,a_buf,1))
                and (1 = blockread(b_file,b_buf,1));
            if same
                then same:= (a_buf = b_buf);
        end;
    if not same or not eof(a_file)
                or not eof(b_file)
        then writeln('files different')
        else writeln('files same');
    end.
```

Program 23

Note that the files are declared without a type. The block I/O intrinsics can only handle untyped files. As the comment at the beginning of the program indicates, the external files can be of any kind.

278

The third parameter to <u>blockread</u> is the number of blocks to transfer. <u>blockread</u> is a function, and it returns the number of blocks that actually were transferred. If this number is not equal to the parameter, then something went wrong. We infer from this that the files are not the same.

For more information about block I/O, refer to the Definition, Chapter VII, Section 2.3.

Device I/O

Device I/O is used for efficiency, or when direct control of a peripheral device is required. The UCSD intrinsics that perform device I/O are all described in the Definition, Chapter VII, Section 3.2.

Program 24 copies all of track 0 from one disk to another. On many implementations of the p-System, this track contains the System bootstrap program (and nothing else):

```
program Boot_Copy;

    const
        sectors_per_track = 26;
        bytes_per_sector = 128;
    var
        i: integer;
        buf: packed array[1..bytes_per_sector] of char;

    begin
        writeln;
        writeln('Bootstrap Copy Program');
        writeln;
        writeln('    place source disk in drive 4');
        writeln('    and destination disk in drive 5');
        writeln;
        write  ('    press <return> to continue --');
        readln;
        for i:= 1 to sectors_per_track do
            begin
                unitread(4,buf,0,i-1,2);
                unitwrite(5,buf,0,i-1,2);
            end;
        writeln;
        writeln('    copy complete');
    end.
```

Program 24

The parameters to <u>unitread</u> and <u>unitwrite</u> indicate:

the device number,

the memory buffer,

the number of bytes to transfer
(has no meaning when the transfer
is in physical sector mode),

the block number
(or sector number, in physical
sector mode), and

the "mode"
(2 indicates physical sector mode).

This program will only work if both disks have the same format. The format is "hard-coded" in the form of constants. For the program to run with disks of a different format, the values of sectors_per_track and bytes_per_sector would have to be changed.

Chapter 5
Concurrency

Code is said to execute "concurrently" when it runs at the same time as another piece of code. In UCSD Pascal, a routine called a **process** may be run concurrently with the main program and other **process**es. For concurrent execution to truly happen, each process must have its own processor. Since almost all current p-System applications run on only one processor, concurrent execution must be simulated: the System runs only one process at a time, but co-ordinates process execution to achieve the appearance of concurrency.

On hardware with multiple processors, concurrency can be a means of speeding up execution. This is not the case with the p-System. Because of the overhead involved in switching processes, using concurrency can even slow a program down somewhat. But concurrent algorithms can greatly improve the conceptual organization of a program, and should not be overlooked. Concurrency can be especially useful for systems programming, I/O handling, and interrupt handling.

The **process** construct and the intrinsics that handle concurrency are UCSD Pascal extensions available in versions III.0 and later. They are not found in standard Pascal. Concurrency is described in the Definition, Chapter IX.

A process is not called. An instance of a process is started by a call to the intrinsic start. The same process may be started a number of times: each time, a new instance of the process is begun.

When a process is started, it is given a unique value of the type processid. The program may examine this value, but may not change it. A started process is also given a stack of its own on the Heap, and a priority. The priority is an integer in the range 0..255.

A call to start may specify the size of the process's stack, and the process's priority. The default stack size is 200 words, and the default priority is 128.

Once a process has been started, it either runs to completion, runs until it must wait for another process to do something, or runs until it is interrupted. When one of these events happens, the processor is given to the waiting process with the highest priority.

It is important that a process be able to communicate with other processes in order to synchronize activity and ensure that one process does not interfere with another's operations. Process communication is accomplished with semaphores and the intrinsics signal and wait.

A semaphore consists of a count, which is a positive integer value, and a queue of processes that are waiting for that semaphore. If the count equals zero, a process waiting for the semaphore cannot run.

Before a semaphore may be used, it must be initialized by a call to the intrinsic seminit. For example:

seminit(my_turn,1);

The first parameter is the name of the semaphore, the second is its count.

Once a semaphore has been initialized, two or more processes may use it to co-ordinate their execution. The intrinsic procedures that allow this are:

wait(sem)
        if sem is available (count > 0)
        then decrement count and keep executing,
        otherwise wait until the count > 0.

signal(sem)
        if count = 0 and a process is waiting,
        then start another process,
        otherwise increment count.

The initial value of a semaphore's count can be thought of as the number of resources the semaphore controls. A process waiting for a semaphore only stops executing if count = 0.

It is common to initialize a semaphore's count to 0 or 1. This implies that only one process at a time may use the semaphore's "resource." A semaphore with an initial count of 1 or 0 is often called a "Boolean semaphore."

One important use of Boolean semaphores is to ensure the mutual exclusion of processes handling one resource. Suppose we have a number of processes which all use the printer. Only one process may do so at a time. We declare a semaphore printer_avail, and initialize it with:

    seminit(printer_avail, 1);

In each process, we bracket the printer-driving code with wait and signal:

    wait(printer_avail);
    {code that uses the printer}
    signal(printer_avail);

This ensures that no two processes will use the printer at the same time. A portion of code that is protected against interference in this way is called a "critical section."

Boolean semaphores may also be used to synchronize the activity of two co-operating processes ("coroutines," as opposed to "subroutines"). In the following sample program, there is a process called Player. Player is started twice, and each instance of Player plays one side of a simple two-person game.

```
program Nim;
  const
      stack_size = 2000;
      pile_max = 10;
  type
      pos_int = 0..maxint;
      pile_range = 0..pile_max;
  var
      turn_a,turn_b: semaphore;
      pid_a,pid_b: processid;
      pile: array[pile_range] of pos_int;
      num_piles: pile_range;

  function Random(lob,hib: integer): integer;
      { Random returns a random number between
        lob (low bound) and hib (high bound). }
      begin
        Random:= (lob+hib) div 2;
      end; {Random}

  function Odd_Int(a,b: pos_int): pos_int;
      { Odd_Int returns the exclusive-or of a and b. }
      begin
        Odd_Int:= ord((odd(a) and not odd(b))
                   or (odd(b) and not odd(a)));
      end; {Odd_Int}

  {= = = = = = = = = = = = Player = = = = = = = = = = = = =}

  process Player
      (name: string; var my_turn,
      your_turn: semaphore);
      { Player mimics a player of the game of Nim.
        Player is an expert at the game of Nim, and
        will force a win whenever it is possible
        to do so. }
      var
        i,p,ones,all,x: pile_range;
        sum,c: pos_int;
        choice: array[pile_range] of pile_range;
      begin
        repeat

          wait(my_turn);
```

```pascal
      ones:= 0; all:= 0; sum:= 0;
      for i:= 1 to num_piles do
         if pile[i] > 0
            then
               begin
                  sum:= Odd_Int(sum,pile[i]);
                  all:= all+1; choice[all]:= i;
                  if pile[i] = 1 then ones:= ones+1;
                  if pile[i] > 1 then p:= i;
               end;

{only one pile non-one}
   if all-ones = 1
      then
         if odd(ones)
            then c:= pile[p]
            else c:= pile[p]-1
      else if sum <> 0
         then
{can pick winning move}
         begin
            x:= 0;
            for i:= 1 to num_piles do
               if pile[i] > Odd_Int(sum,pile[i])
                  then
                     begin
                        x:= x+1;
                        choice[x]:= i;
                     end;
            p:= choice[Random(1,x)];
            c:= pile[p] - Odd_Int(sum,pile[p]);
         end
      else if all > 0
         then
{must make random move}
         begin
            p:= choice[Random(1,all)];
            c:= Random(1,pile[p]);
         end;

   if all <> 0
      then
         begin
            if (all = 1) and (ones = 1)
               then writeln
```

```
                        (name,´: I lost´)
                 else writeln
                        (name,´: pile = ´,p,´, count = ´,c);
               pile[p]:= pile[p] - c;
            end;

         signal(your_turn);

      until all = 0;
   end; {Player}

begin
   write(´enter piles: ´);
   num_piles:= 0;
   while not eoln and (num_piles < pile_max) do
      begin
         num_piles:= num_piles+1;
         read(pile[num_piles]);
      end;
   seminit(turn_a,1);
   seminit(turn_b,0);
   start(Player(´player a´,turn_a,turn_b),
      pid_a,stack_size);
   start(Player(´player b´,turn_b,turn_a),
      pid_b,stack_size);
end.
```

Program 25

The game this program plays is called Nim. The rules of Nim
are simple: there are a number of "piles" (up to 10) of
"matchsticks" (the quantity is represented by a positive integer).
At each turn, a player may remove as many matchsticks as
desired from a SINGLE pile. The player who is forced to
remove the last matchstick loses the game.

The process Player is an expert at Nim. The main program
starts two instances of this process, and they play against each
other. Each instance does its best to win. The turns are co-
ordinated by the semaphores my_turn and your_turn.

The semaphores are needed to ensure that each instance plays
in its proper turn. The turns are needed (as in a game played
by humans!) to ensure that the processes´ resource, the array of
matchstick piles, is not tampered with out of sequence.

The user determines the number of piles and the quantity of matchsticks in each: the first thing the main program does is read this data as a single input line of integers. Then it initializes the appropriate semaphores and starts the two instances of Player. Here is output from a sample run of Nim:

```
enter piles: 7 12 9
player a: pile = 1, count = 2
player b: pile = 2, count = 6
player a: pile = 3, count = 6
player b: pile = 2, count = 3
player a: pile = 1, count = 5
player b: pile = 2, count = 2
player a: pile = 3, count = 3
player b: I lost
```

Each player waits on my_turn and signals your_turn. Note that these are local to Player, and for the scheme to work, they must be called with the GLOBAL semaphores turn_a and turn_b. The main program must initialize turn_a and turn_b correctly.

A single semaphore would not work: only one process at a time would modify the piles, but there would be no guarantee that the turns alternated. The outcome of the game would be at the whim of the System's process queuing.

The purpose of Odd_Int is to do a Boolean XOR of its two parameters. All the piles are "summed" in this way: the result is an integer value where a 1 bit represents an odd number of 1's in that column. A winning move is one that makes all the column sums even.

Player's strategy (which is optimal) is this:

    if only one pile contains more than 1 matchstick,
    then make an odd number of piles by taking
        either the whole pile, or all but 1;

    else
        use odd_int to "sum" the piles:
        if its result is not 0,
        then choose a move that makes it 0;

    else

make a random move.

Odd_Int performs some dirty tricks. We will discuss these in Chapter 8. The function Random works, but does not pick a very random number: it could stand to be replaced with a better algorithm.

Handling interrupts is another use for semaphores. A semaphore can be bound to a hardware interrupt (or other implementation-defined event) by a call to the intrinsic <u>attach</u>:

   <u>attach</u>(sem, event_number);

The definition of event_number depends on the hardware you use. Refer to hardware-specific documentation for possible values. At present, up to 64 different event numbers may be used.

Once a semaphore has been attached to an interrupt, the semaphore must remain in main memory as long as it remains attached.

Program 26 is a simple example where a semaphore is attached
to the interrupt from a hardware clock. We assume that the
appropriate event number is 5:

```
program Clock;

   const
      clock_vector = 5;

   var
      s: semaphore;
      pid: processid;

   process tick_tock;
      begin
         repeat
            wait(s);
            writeln('tick');
            wait(s);
            writeln('tock');
         until false;
      end; {tick_tock}

   begin
      seminit(s,0);
      attach(s, clock_vector);
      start(tick_tock,pid,500,200);
      repeat
      until false;
   end.
```

Program 26

The process does a simple task: it notes the passage of two
clock "ticks," and prints an appropriate message for each.
Since its statements are enclosed in a:

repeat

   ...

until false;

... loop, and since the program does not terminate (it uses the
same construct), tick_tock executes indefinitely.

The endless loop construct is actually quite common when writing processes that handle I/O interrupts: we want them to continue doing their job until the program terminates or the System halts.

The only other thing to notice about this program is that we have given tick_tock a larger stack and a higher priority than the defaults. Having a high priority is common for an interrupt-signalled process. When the interrupt occurs, we want the process to do its job as soon as possible, and then go back to sleep.

Chapter 6
Units and Separate Compilation

Units in UCSD Pascal are a means of separate compilation. They can be used to:

create library packages
(which may contain both declarations and routines)

reduce the amount of code that needs to be
compiled at one time,

limit the amount of code that may need to
be recompiled during maintenance,

improve communication when more than one programmer
is working on the same project.

One example of all these advantages is the IV.0 Operating System, which is an extremely large program that consists of more than 20 units.

For a full description of units, refer to the Definition, Chapter IV, Section 4. Another example of a unit apears in Chapter 8 as Program 30.

The sample program for this chapter is a small package of routines that handle an integer stack:

```
unit Stack_Ops;

   interface

      procedure Push(n: integer);
      function Pop: integer;

   implementation

      const
         max = 100; {size of stack}
      var
         tos: integer;
         stack: array[1..max] of integer;

      procedure Error(message: string);
         { Prints message on stack overflow
           or underflow. }
         begin
            writeln(message);
            exit(program);
         end; {Error}

      procedure Push{n: integer};
         { Pushes n on stack. }
         begin
            if tos >= max
               then Error('stack overflow');
            tos:= tos+1;
            stack[tos]:= n;
         end; {Push}

      function Pop{: integer};
         { Pops top of stack and returns value. }
         begin
            if tos < 1
               then Error('stack underflow');
            Pop:= stack[tos];
            tos:= tos-1;
         end; {Pop}
```

```
   begin
       tos:= 0; {initialize stack}
   end.
```

Program 27

A program that uses Stack_Ops may use Push and Pop as though they were declared within the program. The program may NOT use objects declared within the **implementation** part: the constant ´max´, variables ´tos´ and ´stack´, and the procedure Error.

In the **implementation** part, the headings for Push and Pop show the parameter list and function type surrounded by comment delimiters. This is just a memory aid for the programmer and program reader.

The initialization code sets up the stack by setting tos (the top of stack) to zero.

Here is a brief program that uses this unit:

```
   program Uses_Unit;

       uses {$U Stack_Ops.CODE} Stack_Ops;

       begin
           Push(4);
           Push(5);
           Push(6);
           writeln(Pop,´ ´,Pop,´ ´,Pop);
       end.
```

The **uses** declaration must appear immediately after the **program** heading. In a unit that used this unit, the **uses** declaration could appear immediately after either the reserved word **interface** or the reserved word **implementation**.

If we were to change the **implementation** part of Stack_Ops (for example, we recompile it with max = 500), we would NOT need to recompile Uses_Unit. If we changed the **interface** part, on the other hand, Uses_Unit WOULD need to be recompiled.

When a unit is in a particular codefile (a "library") other than
*SYSTEM.LIBRARY, the program may specify this with the $U
compiler option, for example:

program Uses_Unit;

{$U STACK.CODE}
uses Stack_Ops;

More about referencing libraries may be found in the Definition,
Chapter IV, and in the UCSD p-System Users' Manual(3).

In earlier versions of the System, units often had to be
explicitly linked to other code by using the System's Linker.
As of Version IV.0, this is no longer necessary. Earlier versions
also implemented **separate** and **intrinsic** units. These no
longer exist. For information on these other types of units,
refer to the appropriate Users' Manual.

Chapter 7
Memory Management

This chapter is VERY IV.0-specific. Some of the features described here do apply to previous versions, but the appropriate Users' Manual, or an applications manual, should be consulted for the details on the version you are using.

Under the p-System, main memory is divided into three resources that all compete for space. These are:

The Stack
>Used for storage of static variables, expression
>evaluation, and bookkeeping information
>for procedure and function calls;
>Grows from high memory toward low memory;

The Heap
>Used for storage of dynamic variables, and stacks
>of subordinate processes;
>Grows from low memory toward high memory;

The Codepool
>Contains code segments;
>"Floats" between the Stack and the Heap.

When no more main memory space is available, a "Stack overflow" error occurs (even if it is the Heap that needs more space). This is a fatal error: the System halts and then re-initializes itself. Program results may be lost.

Little can be done to manage Stack and Heap space; internal System structures already attempt to be space-efficient. One thing a program can do is allocate a data buffer whose size is variable: we show how to do this below. It can also be helpful to pack records and arrays. For example, the declaration:

>example: **array** [1..1000] **of** Boolean;

... requires 1000 words, while the declaration:

>example: **packed array** [1..1000] **of** Boolean;

... requires only 63 words.

Often, the algorithm that the programmer chooses determines how efficient the program will be, in terms of both time and space.

In the Codepool, the "unit" of code is the segment. Only the segment that is currently executing need be in memory, and the programmer can take care that other segments are swapped out and do not occupy space that may be needed for data.

In general, a single program compilation creates a single code segment. Likewise, a unit occupies a single segment. The programmer may place a routine in a code segment of its own by preceding the routine heading with the reserved word **segment,** for example,

segment procedure memory_hog;

segment function save_space (size: <u>integer</u>): <u>integer</u>;

segment process seldom;

Since a segment routine must be read into memory whenever it is needed, routines that are declared as **segment**s should be routines that are rarely called (perhaps just once per execution, or not during every execution). Initialization and termination routines are good candidates for this.

The programmer can further control the residence of segments by using these UCSD intrinsic procedures:

<u>memlock</u>(seg_names)
    'seg_names' is a string of segment names,
    separated by commas; segments that are named
    cannot be swapped out;

<u>memswap</u>(seg_names)
    allows the segments named in 'seg_names'
    to again be swapped out to disk.

<u>memlock</u> may speed up a program, by forcing a segment that is frequently used to remain in main memory. Unless <u>memlock</u> is used, any segment is swappable. The programmer should be careful to call <u>memswap</u> once a locked segment is no longer

needed (otherwise, it will remain in memory and may cause a Stack overflow).

The name of a segment is the name of the program, unit, or routine (only the first 8 characters are used).

When a program must allocate a large data buffer, but is intended to run on many different machines whose memory requirements will differ, it is possible to make the buffer variable in size by using the intrinsics varavail and varnew. This is illustrated by the next program:

```pascal
program Myprog;

    const
        res_segs = 'myprog,fileops,pascalio';
        slop = 2000;
    type
        byte = 0..255;
        large_buf = array[0..32000] of integer;
    var
        buf: ^large_buf;
        buf_size: integer;

    begin
        buf_size:= varavail(res_segs) - slop;
        if varnew(buf,buf_size) = 0
            then Error('problem in allocating buffer');

        { A buffer of buf_size words has been allocated.
          buf^[0] through buf^[buf_size - 1] may now
          be accessed. }

        ...

    end.
```

Program 28

The intrinsic function varavail is passed a list of segment names. It returns the number of words of memory that would be available IF main memory were to contain both the segments named in the list, and any other segments that have already been memlocked.

In Program 28, varavail is passed the string 'myprog,fileops,pascalio'. MYPROG is the program itself. FILEOPS and PASCALIO are Operating System segments that are frequently called. If the buffer we wish to allocate were to prevent any of these segments from being loaded into memory, the program would have to halt with a stack overflow.

The buffer is allocated the number of words returned by varavail, plus a 'slop' of 2000 words. The slop allows for other uses of memory such as data space for the rest of the program, Operating System overhead that we cannot predict, processes that might compete with Myprog, and so forth.

The intrinsic function varnew(POINTER, COUNT) simply does a new(POINTER) on COUNT words. It returns the number of words allocated. If it cannot allocate the full COUNT words, it returns zero.

We provide for a VERY large data buffer by the declaration:

    large_buf = **array**[0..32000] **of** integer;

Note that this must be a type declaration. If it were a variable declaration, the entire area would be allocated. Instead, we declare:

    buf: ^large_buf;

This allows us to allocate as much or as little as we want.

Note that we must reference the array as a dynamic variable, for example:

    buf^[0]:= 1;

Chapter 8
Advanced Techniques

This chapter describes some techniques that are more powerful than the (relatively) straightforward programming practices we have already seen. These techniques are crucial to systems programmers and often to programmers of large applications. In general, they provide more efficient ways of solving certain problems. Some of them might be considered "dirty tricks."

The chief danger of these techniques is that they allow the programmer to write code that is almost unintelligible. This defeats most of the reasons for using Pascal in the first place! Another danger is that there is little error-checking, so the programmer must be quite cautious. Finally, because these techniques usually depend on some detail of implementation, they are not likely to be portable to other implementations of Pascal.

Character Intrinsics

The UCSD intrinsics moveleft, moveright, fillchar, and scan are provided for manipulating arrays of characters -- often large ones. In fact, they do no type checking on their arguments, so they can be used with any type of data. They are often used in conjunction with the sizeof intrinsic.

For example, fillchar can be used to quickly initialize an entire array:

```
fillchar(A,sizeof(A),0);
```

This would fill the array A with zeroes.

As a "sneakier" example, moveleft (or moveright) can be used to assign a value of one type to a value of any other type:

```
type
    I: integer;
    TWOBYTES: packed array [0..1] of 0..255;
...
moveleft(I,TWOBYTES,2);
```

This would assign the integer I to TWOBYTES, which is a pair of bytes. This would allow the program to examine the high byte and the low byte of the integer individually.

This technique requires both caution and a knowledge of how the data types are represented internally. See the Definition, Chapter III, Section 6.

Further examples of these intrinsics appear in Program 30, below.

Record Variants

Variant fields of a record may be used to convert data from one type to another. This can be useful when Pascal does not support a particular type conversion. A byte or a word can be constructed out of individual sub-fields: this is especially useful when the full word is to be used on the machine (or P-machine) level (e.g., the word is used as a single instruction or a memory address).

Program 29 is a procedure that shows a variant field used to construct a hexadecimal value from an integer:

```
procedure Write_Hex(n: integer);
  { Writes n as 4 hex digits. }
  var
    i: integer;
    hex: packed array[0..15] of char;
    both: record case Boolean of
          true: (w: integer);
          false: (h: packed array[1..4] of 0..15);
          end; {both}
  begin
    hex:= '0123456789ABCDEF';
    with both do
      begin
        w:= n;
        for i:= 4 downto 1 do
          write(hex[h[i]]);
      end;
  end; {Write_Hex}
```

Program 29

The variant field describes a memory location as both:

an integer (16 bits), and

a packed array of four 4-bit fields.

Each 4-bit field is directly converted to a hex digit by using its value to index the array 'hex'.

Memory Addresses

Pointers are implemented as 16-bit memory addresses. By using them in a record variant as described above, they may be made to point at anything in memory. This is an important technique in systems programming. Its pitfalls should be apparent.

Program 30 is a screen-handling unit for a computer that has a memory-mapped screen. The screen buffer is located at 1000H. Each byte in the buffer represents a character on the screen: all we need to do is update the buffer, and the hardware refreshes the screen. The screen displays 24 * 80 characters (as usual), so in our program we represent the buffer as an array of the same size.

```pascal
unit Screen_Routines;

    interface

        procedure Clear_Screen;
        procedure Set_Cursor(r,c: integer);
        procedure Write_Ch(ch: char);
        procedure New_Line;
        procedure Back_Space;

    implementation

        const
            row_max = 23;
            col_max = 79;
        type
            screen_map = packed array
                [0..row_max,0..col_max] of char;
        var
            screen: ^screen_map;
            row, col: integer;                {cursor position}

        procedure Clear_Screen;
            { Fills screen with spaces and homes cursor. }
            begin
                fillchar(screen^,sizeof(screen_map),' ');
                row:= 0; col:= 0;
            end; {Clear_Screen}

        procedure Scroll_Screen;
            { Scrolls screen up one line. }
            begin
                moveleft(screen^[1,0],
                    screen^[0,0],row_max*(col_max+1));
                fillchar(screen^[row_max,0],col_max+1,' ');
                row:= row_max;
            end;
```

```pascal
procedure Set_Cursor{r,c: integer};
  { Sets random cursor position. }
  begin
    row:= r;
    col:= c;
  end; {Set_Cursor}

procedure Write_Ch{ch: char};
  { Writes character on screen. }
  begin
    screen^[row,col]:= ch;
    col:= (col+1) mod (col_max+1);
    if col = 0
      then
        begin
          row:= (row+1) mod (row_max+1);
          if row = 0
              then Scroll_Screen;
        end;
  end; {Write_Ch}

procedure New_Line;
  { Performs carriage-return and
    line-feed on screen. }
  begin
    col:= 0;
    row:= (row+1) mod (row_max+1);
    if row = 0
      then Scroll_Screen;
  end; {New_Line}

procedure Back_Space;
  { Moves cursor back one space on line }
  begin
    if col > 0
      then col:= col-1;
  end; {Back_Space}

procedure Init_Screen;
  { Sets screen to point to buffer, and clears screen. }
  var
    mem_ptr: record case Boolean of
                true: (i: integer);
                false: (p: ^screen_map);
              end;
```

```
          begin
              mem_ptr.i:= 4096;   {address of buffer = 1000H}
              screen:= mem_ptr.p;
              Clear_Screen;
          end;

      begin
          Init_Screen;
      end.
```

Program 30

The only place in this unit where we do tricks with pointers is in the procedure Init_Screen. The record variant is used to make an absolute address (the field 'i') equivalent to a pointer ('p'). The pointer to the screen buffer ('screen') is then initialized to the value of 'p'.

In the procedure Clear_Screen, we use <u>fillchar</u> to quickly fill the entire screen with blanks. In the procedure Scroll_Screen, we call <u>moveleft</u> to move the screen up one line, and then call <u>fillchar</u> to set the last line to blanks. If we wanted a procedure that scrolled the screen DOWN one line, we could use <u>moveright</u> in a manner similar to <u>moveleft</u>.

The character intrinsics manipulate the array much faster than the usual assignments within **for** loops would. They are ideal for situations, like screen display, where speed is truly important.

Ord(odd)

Since Booleans are represented as 16-bit quantities, and since comparison operators only test the low-order bit of a Boolean value, the odd intrinsic actually does nothing more than allow an integer to be treated as a Boolean. In a similar fashion, the ord intrinsic merely allows its parameter to be treated as an integer, since this is the internal representation of all scalar types.

These facts can be useful, because the operators **and, or,** and **not** actually do logical operations on full words: each bit is set appropriately.

The combination of the odd function and the Boolean operators allow bit-wise operations on integer values.

For example, this expression:

    I:= ord(odd(I) **and** odd(15));

... has the effect of masking I down to its 4 low-order bits. The ord intrinsic allows the result to again be treated as an integer.

In Program 25, we already used this technique (and promised to explain it later) because our strategy for Nim required us to perform a bit-wise XOR on integers:

        function Odd_Int(a,b: pos_int): pos_int;
          { Odd_Int returns the exclusive-or of a and b. }
          begin
            Odd_Int:= ord((odd(a) **and not** odd(b))
                    or (odd(b) **and not** odd(a)));
          end; {Odd_Int}

The expression is complicated because there is no single operator that performs a bit-wise exclusive-or.

307

This is the end of the Programmer's Guide. While we hope that it has helped you, we hope that it is not the end of your study.

Among the many books available, one we would recommend most highly is Niklaus Wirth's <u>Algorithms + Data Structures = Programs</u> (19).

It seems that the most successful and innovative software (including languages and operating systems) has been invented, not with the grandiose aim of solving all programming problems for all time, but with the modest aim of solving a particular problem in the most elegant way possible. Pascal itself was invented for the purpose of teaching programmers.

In light of this, we encourage you to apply your skills toward problems that interest you, whatever those may be, and to approach them in a spirit of craftsmanship.

We wish you the best of luck, and thank you for the time you have spent with our scribblings.

Appendix A
Lexical Standards

1. The Character Set

The letters A..Z, a..z, the digits 0..9, the special characters:

( ) [ ] { } + - * / < = > : ; . , ´ ^ _

... as well as blanks (' ') and <return>.

The other printable characters are:

! @ # $ % & ? | ` ~ \ "

2. Special Symbols

. , ; : ´ ( ) [ ] { } + - * / = < > ^

:= .. <= <> >= (* *)

***

3. Reserved Words

An asterisk indicates reserved words not in standard Pascal.

and	goto	record
array		repeat
	if	
begin	*implementation	*segment
	in	*separate
case	*interface	set
const		
	label	then
div		to
do	mod	type
downto		
	not	*unit
else		until
end	of	*uses
*external	or	
		var
file	packed	
for	procedure	while
forward	*process	with
function	program	

4. Identifiers

May contain letters, digits, or the underscore (_)

The first character must be a letter

The underscore is ignored

Uppercase and lowercase are equivalent

Only the first 8 characters determine uniqueness

May not cross a line boundary

5. Comments

Are delimited by { } or (* *)

Delimiters may not be mixed

Comments with the same kind of delimiter may not be nested

Comments with different kinds of delimiter MAY be nested

A comment may be longer than one line

A comment with $ immediately after the left delimiter indicates a compiler option

6. Predeclared Identifiers

An asterisk indicates predeclared identifiers not in standard Pascal.

abs	*halt	page
arctan		*pmachine
*atan	*idsearch	*pos
*attach	input	pred
	*insert	*processid
*blockread	integer	put
*blockwrite	*interactive	*pwroften
Boolean	*ioresult	
		read
char	*keyboard	readln
chr		real
*close	*length	*release
*concat	ln	reset
*copy	*log	rewrite
cos		round
	*mark	
*delete	maxint	*scan
dispose	*memavail	*seek
	*memlock	*semaphore
eof	*memswap	*seminit
eoln	*moveleft	*signal
*exit	*moveright	sin
exp		*sizeof
	new	sqr
false	nil	sqrt
*fillchar		*start
	odd	*str
get	ord	*string
*gotoxy	output	succ

text
* time
* treesearch
  true
  trunc

* unitbusy
* unitclear
* unitread
* unitstatus
* unitwait
* unitwrite

* varavail
* vardispose
* varnew

* wait
  write
  writeln

Appendix B
UCSD Pascal Syntax

1. Comparisons

Comparisons are operators that return the type <u>Boolean.</u>

Comparisons on ordered types:

=	equal to
<>	not equal to
>	greater than
>=	greater than or equal to
<	less than
<=	less than or equal to

Ordered types include all numeric types, all scalar and subrange types, the type <u>string</u>, and **packed array of** <u>char.</u>

For <u>Boolean</u> values, these comparisons may be interpreted as:

=	equal to
<>	not equal to or XOR (exclusive or)
<=	implies
>	does not imply
>=	is implied by
<	is not implied by

Comparisons on unpacked **record**s or **array**s of the same type and dimensions:

=	equal to
<>	not equal to

Comparisons on **set**s:

=	equal to
<>	not equal to
>=	is a superset of
<=	is a subset of
in	membership

2. Operations

Integer operations:

+	addition
-	subtraction
*	multiplication
div	integer division
mod	remainder after division

The second operand of a **div** or **mod** cannot be zero.

*, div, and **mod** have precedence over + and -.

Real operations:

+	addition
-	subtraction
*	multiplication
/	real division

The second operand of a / cannot be zero.

* and / have precedence over + and -.

Long integer operations are the same as for integer, except that **mod** is not allowed.

Boolean operations:

not	negation (a unary operator)
and	conjunction
or	union (inclusive or)

not has precedence over **and**, which has precedence over **or**.

Set operations:

+	union
-	intersection
*	difference

* has precedence over + and -.

3. Statements

A statement may be a null statement. Among other things, this accounts for the extra semicolon at the end of a compound statement or the statement list in **repeat.**

assignment-statement = variable-name ":=" expression

case-statement =
    "case" expression **"of"**
        constant-list ":" statement
        { ";" constant-list ":" statement } [";"]
    "end"

compound-statement =
    "begin" statement { ";" statement } **"end"**

for-statement =
    "for" var-id ":=" start-value **"to"** stop-value
        "do" statement
    |
    "for" var-id ":=" start-value **"downto"** stop-value
        "do" statement

goto-statement = **"goto"** label

if-statement =
    "if" Boolean-expression **"then"** statement
    [**"else"** statement]

procedure-call = procedure-name ["(" parameter-list ")"]

repeat-statement =
    "repeat"
        statement { ";" statement }
    "until" Boolean-expression

while-statement =
    "while" Boolean-expression **"do"** statement

with-statement =
    "with" record-id-list **"do"** statement

4. Railroad Diagrams

These figures are a concise representation of UCSD Pascal syntax. They do NOT attempt to represent the inner workings of the Compiler.

Diagrams courtesy of SofTech Microsystems, Inc.

< compilation >

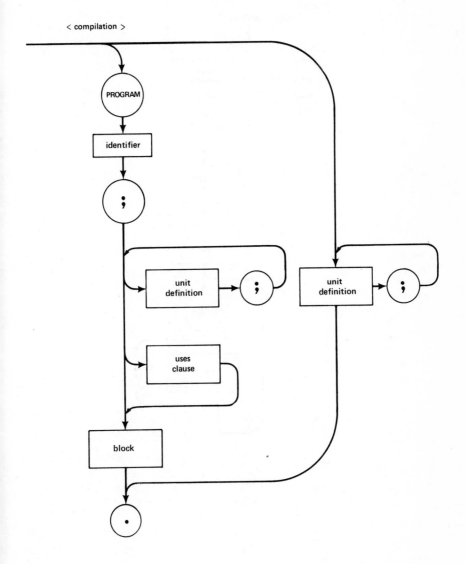

< unit definition >

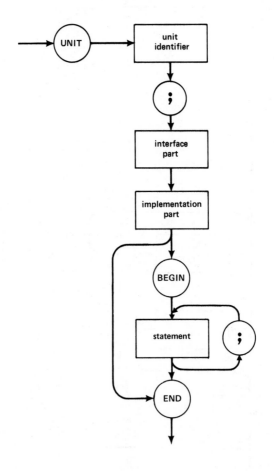

< block >

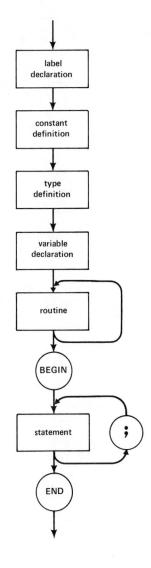

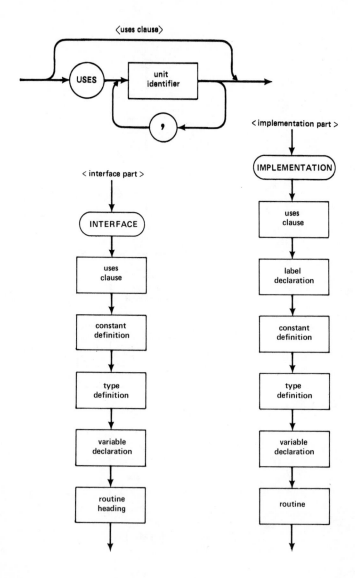

⟨routine heading⟩

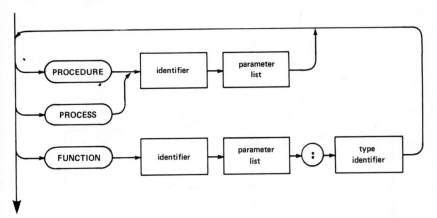

⟨label declaration⟩

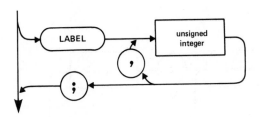

⟨constant definition⟩

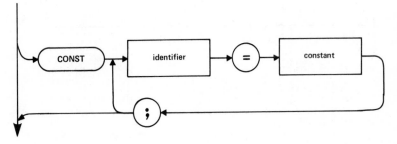

323

⟨type definition⟩

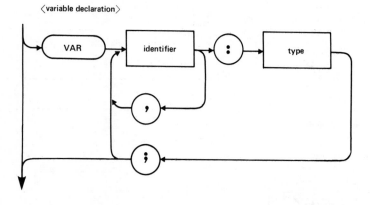

⟨variable declaration⟩

⟨type⟩

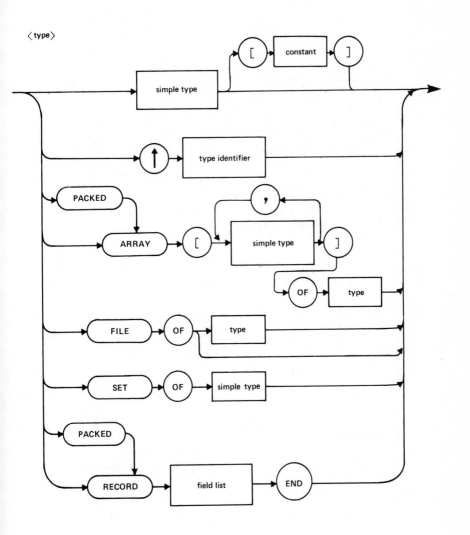

< field list >

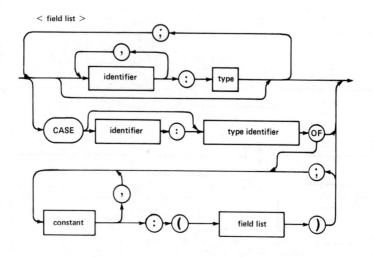

< simple type >

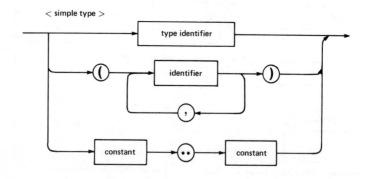

326

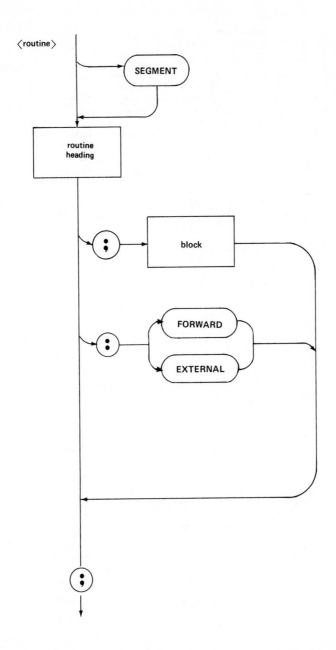

327

⟨statement⟩

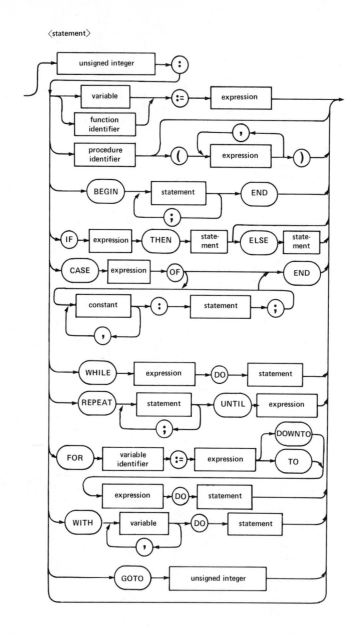

⟨expression⟩

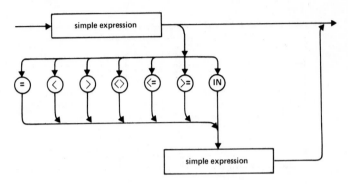

⟨simple expression⟩

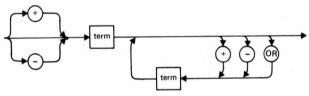

⟨parameter list⟩

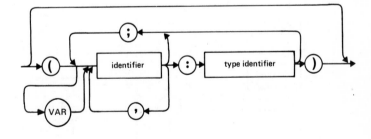

⟨ factor ⟩

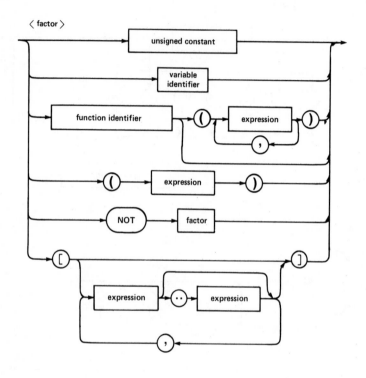

⟨ term ⟩

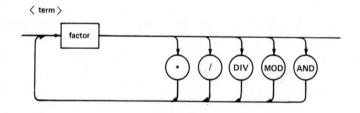

⟨constant⟩

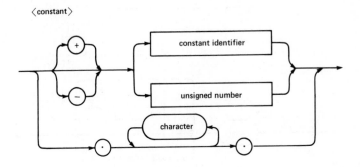

⟨unsigned number⟩

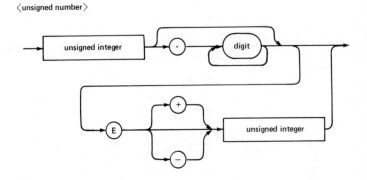

331

⟨unsigned integer⟩

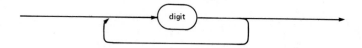

⟨identifier⟩

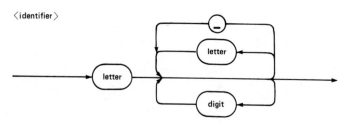

NOTE: The underscore character '—' is accepted but not significant

⟨unsigned constant⟩

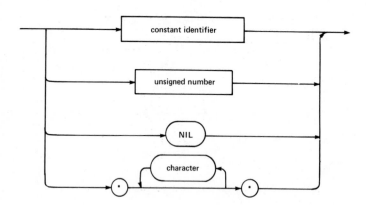

332

Appendix C
Intrinsics

Each intrinsic is followed by the number of the section or sections in the Definition that contain its description.

abs(X)	III.2.1.4, III.2.2.4
arctan(X)	III.2.2.4
atan(X)	see arctan
attach(SEM, I_VEC)	IX.4.3
blockread(FILENAME, BUFFER, COUNT [, RELBLOCK])	VII.2.3
blockwrite(FILENAME, BUFFER, COUNT [, RELBLOCK])	VII.2.3
chr(I)	III.2.7.2
close(FILENAME [, OPTION])	VII.2.1
concat(SOURCE1, SOURCE2, ... , SOURCEn)	III.4.2.4
copy(SOURCE, INDEX, SIZE)	III.4.2.4
cos(X)	III.2.2.4
delete(DESTINATION, INDEX, SIZE)	III.4.2.4
dispose(POINTER {, FIELD_TAG })	III.5.2.3
eof [(FILENAME)]	III.5.1.2, VII.1.3
eoln [(FILENAME)]	III.5.1.2, VII.1.3
exit(**program**)	VI.4.2
exit(PROGRAM_NAME)	VI.4.2
exit(ROUTINE_NAME)	VI.4.2
exp(X)	III.2.2.4
fillchar(DESTINATION, LENGTH, CHARACTER)	III.4.1.4
get(FILENAME)	III.5.1.2
gotoxy(X, Y)	VII.3.5
halt	VI.4.3
insert(SOURCE, DESTINATION, INDEX)	III.4.2.4
ioresult	VII.3.4
length(SOURCE)	III.4.2.4
ln(X)	III.2.2.4
log(X)	III.2.2.4

mark(POINTER)   VIII.4
memavail   VIII.3
memlock(SEG_LIST)   VIII.2.2
memswap(SEG_LIST)   VIII.2.2
moveleft(SOURCE, DESTINATION, LENGTH)   III.4.1.4
moveright(SOURCE, DESTINATION, LENGTH)   III.4.1.4

new(POINTER {, FIELD_TAG })   III.5.2.3

odd(I)   III.2.7
ord(SCALAR_VALUE)   III.2.7.2, III.3.4

page(FILENAME)   VII.1.4
pos(PATTERN, SOURCE)   III.4.2.4
pred(SCALAR_VALUE)   III.3.4
put(FILENAME)   III.5.1.2
pwroften(I)   III.2.2.4

read([FILENAME ,] VAR1, VAR2, ..., VARn)   VII.1.1
readln([FILENAME ,] VAR1, VAR2, ..., VARn)   VII.1.1
reset(FILENAME [, EXT_FILE])   III.5.1.2, VII.2.1
rewrite(FILENAME [, EXT_FILE])   III.5.1.2, VII.2.1
release(POINTER)   VIII.4
round(X)   III.2.7.2

scan(LENGTH, <partial expression>, SOURCE)   III.4.1.4
seek(FILENAME, INDEX)   VII.2.2
seminit(SEM, COUNT)   IX.4.1
signal(SEM)   IX.4.2
sin(X)   III.2.2.4
sizeof(VAR_OR_TYPE_ID)   III.6.6
sqr(X)   III.2.2.4
sqrt(X)   III.2.2.4
start(<process call>
      [, PROC_ID [, STACKSIZE [, PRIORITY]]])   IX.3
str(I, STR)   III.2.7.2
succ(SCALAR_VALUE)   III.3.4

time(HIWORD, LOWORD)   VII.3.3
trunc(X)   III.2.7.2

unitbusy(DEVICE_NUMBER)   VII.3.2
unitclear(DEVICE_NUMBER)   VII.3.2
unitread(DEVICE_NUMBER, BUFFER, LENGTH
        [, [BLOCKNUMBER] , FLAG])   VII.3.2
unitstatus(DEVICE_NUMBER,
        STATUS_RECORD, CONTROL)   VII.3.2
unitwait(DEVICE_NUMBER)   VII.3.2
unitwrite(DEVICE_NUMBER, BUFFER, LENGTH
        [, [BLOCKNUMBER] , FLAG])   VII.3.2

varavail(SEG_LIST)   VIII.3
vardispose(POINTER, COUNT)   VIII.4
varnew(POINTER, COUNT)   VIII.4

wait(SEM)   IX.4.2
write([FILENAME ,] VAL1, VAL2, ..., VALn)   VII.1.2
writeln([FILENAME ,] VAL1, VAL2, ..., VALn)   VII.1.2

Appendix D
Syntax Errors

These are the syntax errors for Version IV.0.   Syntax errors for
other versions may be somewhat different.

1: Error in simple type
2: Identifier expected
3: unimplemented error
4: ')' expected
5: ': ' expected
6: Illegal symbol (terminator expected)
7: Error in parameter list
8: 'OF' expected
9: '(' expected
10: Error in type
11: '' expected
13: 'END' expected
14: ';' expected
15: Integer expected
16: '= ' expected
17: 'BEGIN' expected
18: Error in declaration part
19: error in <field-list>
20: '.' expected
21: '*' expected
22: 'INTERFACE' expected
23: 'IMPLEMENTATION' expected
24: 'UNIT' expected

50: Error in constant
51: ': = ' expected
52: 'THEN' expected
53: 'UNTIL' expected
54: 'DO' expected
55: 'TO' or 'DOWNTO' expected in for statement
56: 'IF' expected
57: 'FILE' expected
58: Error in <factor> (bad expression)
59: Error in variable

60: Must be of type 'SEMAPHORE'
61: Must be of type 'PROCESSID'
62: Process not allowed at this nesting level
63: Only main task may start processes

101: Identifier declared twice
102: Low bound exceeds high bound
103: Identifier is not of the appropriate class
104: Undeclared identifier
105: sign not allowed
106: Number expected
107: Incompatible subrange types
108: File not allowed here
109: Type must not be real
110: <tagfield> type must be scalar or subrange
111: Incompatible with <tagfield> part
112: Index type must not be real
113: Index type must be a scalar or a subrange
114: Base type must not be real
115: Base type must be a scalar or a subrange
116: Error in type of standard procedure parameter
117: Unsatisified forward reference
118: Forward reference type identifier in var declaration
119: Re-specified params not OK for a forward procedure
120: Function result type must be scalar, subrange or pointer
121: File value parameter not allowed
122: A forward function's result type can't be re-specified
123: Missing result type in function declaration
124: F-format for reals only
125: Error in type of standard procedure parameter
126: Number of parameters does not agree with declaration
127: Illegal parameter substitution
128: Result type does not agree with declaration
129: Type conflict of operands
130: Expression is not of set type
131: Tests on equality allowed only
132: Strict inclusion not allowed
133: File comparison not allowed
134: Illegal type of operand(s)
135: Type of operand must be Boolean
136: Set element type must be scalar or subrange
137: Set element types must be compatible
138: Type of variable is not array
139: Index type is not compatible with the declaration
140: Type of variable is not record
141: Type of variable must be file or pointer
142: Illegal parameter solution
143: Illegal type of loop control variable
144: Illegal type of expression
145: Type conflict

146: Assignment of files not allowed
147: Label type incompatible with selecting expression
148: Subrange bounds must be scalar
149: Index type must be integer

150: Assignment to standard function is not allowed
151: Assignment to formal function is not allowed
152: No such field in this record
153: Type error in read
154: Actual parameter must be a variable
155: Control variable cannot be formal or non-local
156: Multidefined case label
157: Too many cases in case statement
158: No such variant in this record
159: Real or string tagfields not allowed
160: Previous declaration was not forward
161: Again forward declared
162: Parameter size must be constant
163: Missing variant in declaration
164: Substition of standard proc/func not allowed
165: Multidefined label
166: Multideclared label
167: Undeclared label
168: Undefined label
169: Error in base set
170: Value parameter expected
171: Standard file was re-declared
172: Undeclared external file
173: FORTRAN procedure or function expected
174: Pascal function or procedure expected
175: Semaphore value parameter not allowed

182: Nested UNITs not allowed
183: External declaration not allowed at this nesting level
184: External declaration not allowed in INTERFACE section
185: Segment declaration not allowed in INTERFACE section
186: Labels not allowed in INTERFACE section
187: Attempt to open library unsuccessful
188: UNIT not declared in previous uses declaration
189: 'USES' not allowed at this nesting level
190: UNIT not in library
191: Forward declaration was not segment
192: Forward declaration was segment
193: Not enough room for this operation
194: Flag must be declared at top of program
195: Unit not importable

201: Error in real number - digit expected
202: String constant must not exceed source line
203: Integer constant exceeds range
204: 8 or 9 in octal number
250: Too many scopes of nested identifiers
251: Too many nested procedures or functions
252: Too many forward references of procedure entries
253: Procedure too long
254: Too many long constants in this procedure
256: Too many external references
257: Too many externals
258: Too many local files
259: Expression too complicated

300: Division by zero
301: No case provided for this value
302: Index expression out of bounds
303: Value to be assigned is out of bounds
304: Element expression out of range
398: Implementation restriction
399: Implementation restriction

400: Illegal character in text
401: Unexpected end of input
402: Error in writing code file, not enough room
403: Error in reading include file
404: Error in writing list file, not enough room
405: 'PROGRAM' or 'UNIT' expected
406: Include file not legal
407: Include file nesting limit exceeded
408: INTERFACE section not contained in one file
409: Unit name reserved for system
410: disk error

500: Assembler error

Appendix E
ASCII Characters

Dec	Oct	Hex	Char		Dec	Oct	Hex	Char		Dec	Oct	Hex	Char		Dec	Oct	Hex	Char
0	000	00	NUL		32	040	20	SP		64	100	40	@		96	140	60	
1	001	01	SOH		33	041	21	!		65	101	41	A		97	141	61	a
2	002	02	STX		34	042	22	"		66	102	42	B		98	142	62	b
3	003	03	ETX		35	043	23	#		67	103	43	C		99	143	63	c
4	004	04	EOT		36	044	24	$		68	104	44	D		100	144	64	d
5	005	05	ENQ		37	045	25	%		69	105	45	E		101	145	65	e
6	006	06	ACK		38	046	26	&		70	106	46	F		102	146	66	f
7	007	07	BEL		39	047	27	'		71	107	47	G		103	147	67	g
8	010	08	BS		40	050	28	(		72	110	48	H		104	150	68	h
9	011	09	HT		41	051	29	)		73	111	49	I		105	151	69	i
10	012	0A	LF		42	052	2A	*		74	112	4A	J		106	152	6A	j
11	013	0B	VT		43	053	2B	+		75	113	4B	K		107	153	6B	k
12	014	0C	FF		44	054	2C	,		76	114	4C	L		108	154	6C	l
13	015	0D	CR		45	055	2D	-		77	115	4D	M		109	155	6D	m
14	016	0E	SO		46	056	2E	.		78	116	4E	N		110	156	6E	n
15	017	0F	SI		47	057	2F	/		79	117	4F	O		111	157	6F	o
16	020	10	DLE		48	060	30	0		80	120	50	P		112	160	70	p
17	021	11	DC1		49	061	31	1		81	121	51	Q		113	161	71	q
18	022	12	DC2		50	062	32	2		82	122	52	R		114	162	72	r
19	023	13	DC3		51	063	33	3		83	123	53	S		115	163	73	s
20	024	14	DC4		52	064	34	4		84	124	54	T		116	164	74	t
21	025	15	NAK		53	065	35	5		85	125	55	U		117	165	75	u
22	026	16	SYN		54	066	36	6		86	126	56	V		118	166	76	v
23	027	17	ETB		55	067	37	7		87	127	57	W		119	167	77	w
24	030	18	CAN		56	070	38	8		88	130	58	X		120	170	78	x
25	031	19	EM		57	071	39	9		89	131	59	Y		121	171	79	y
26	032	1A	SUB		58	072	3A	:		90	132	5A	Z		122	172	7A	z
27	033	1B	ESC		59	073	3B	;		91	133	5B	[		123	173	7B	{
28	034	1C	FS		60	074	3C	<		92	134	5C	\		124	174	7C		
29	035	1D	GS		61	075	3D	=		93	135	5D	]		125	175	7D	}
30	036	1E	RS		62	076	3E	>		94	136	5E	^		126	176	7E	~
31	037	1F	US		63	077	3F	?		95	137	5F	_		127	177	7F	DEL

Bibliography

Entries with an asterisk are referenced in the text of this book. Entries without an asterisk are books that may be of interest to the Pascal programmer. We have taken the liberty of annotating some of these entries; the opinions given are no more than our personal judgement.

* 1. American National Standards Committee,
     "Specification for the computer programming
     language -- Pascal;"
     ANSI/IEEE Pascal Standard X3J9/81-093 JPC/81-093
     This is expected to supplant Jensen & Wirth as the
     Pascal standard within the United States.

* 2. Bowles, Kenneth L.,
     Beginner's Guide for the UCSD Pascal System;
     Peterborough, New Hampshire: Byte Books, 1980.

* 3. Clark, Randy, editor,
     UCSD p-System and UCSD Pascal Users' Manual;
     San Diego: SofTech Microsystems, 2nd edition, 1981.
     The reference to the p-System for Version IV.0.

* 4. --------, editor,
     UCSD p-System Installation Guide;
     San Diego: SofTech Microsystems, 1981.

* 5. --------, editor,
     UCSD p-System Internal Architecture Guide;
     San Diego: SofTech Microsystems, 1981.

* 6. Dahl, O-J., Dijkstra, E.W., and Hoare, C.A.R.,
     Structured Programming;
     New York: Academic Press, 1972.
     The original work on this subject: recommended for
     all programmers who take their work seriously.

  7. Findlay, William, and Watt, David A.,
     Pascal: an Introduction to Methodical Programming;
     Potomac, Maryland: Computer Science Press, 1978.
     Among the best introductions to programming,
     standard Pascal, and a structured style.

8. Fox, David, and Waite, Mitchell, Pascal Primer;
    Indianapolis: Howard W. Sams & Co., 1981
    A pleasantly chatty introduction aimed at the
    BASIC programmer. Though it uses UCSD Pascal,
    it doesn't cover the entire language.

9. Grogono, Peter, Programming in Pascal;
    Menlo Park, California: Addison Wesley, 1978.
    A thorough introduction. In general, confusing to
    the beginner but too wordy for the expert.

*10. Jensen, Kathleen, and Wirth, Niklaus,
    PASCAL User Manual and Report;
    New York: Springer-Verlag, 1974.
    To date, the standard reference for Pascal.

*11. Johnson, Lee W., and Riess, R. Dean,
    Numerical Analysis;
    Menlo Park: Addison Wesley, 1977.

12. Kieburtz, Richard B., Structured Programming and
    Problem Solving with Pascal;
    Englewood Cliffs, New Jersey: Prentice-Hall, 1978.
    This was, unfortunately, adapted from a textbook
    on another language. It tends to be hazy.

*13. Overgaard, Mark, "UCSD Pascal: a portable software
    environment for small computers;"
    AFIPS - Conference Proceedings, Vol. 49 (1980).
    The hows and whys of the p-System's portability.

*14. Welsh, J., and Bustard, D.W., "Pascal Plus --
    Another Language for Modular Microprogramming;"
    Software -- Practice and Experience,
    Vol. 9, No. 11 (Nov. 1979).

15. Wilson, I.R., and Addyman, A.M.,
    A Practical Introduction to Pascal;
    New York: Springer-Verlag, 1978.
    A concise and well-written introduction.
    Recommended for programmers, but not
    for novices.

*16. Wirth, Niklaus, "The Programming Language PASCAL;"
    Acta Informatica, Vol. 1, No. 1 (1971).

*17.   --------,
        "Program Development by Stepwise Refinement;"
        Communications of the ACM, Vol. 14, No. 4 (1971).

*18.   --------, Systematic Programming;
        Englewood Cliffs, New Jersey: Prentice-Hall, 1973.
        An excellent introduction to programming which
        uses (but doesn't emphasize) Pascal.   Some
        mathematical background is required.

*19.   --------,
        Algorithms + Data Structures = Programs;
        Englewood Cliffs: Prentice-Hall, 1976.
        A superior introduction to program design.
        It uses Pascal and is aimed at programmers with
        intermediate experience.   Contains an exposition of
        the rationale behind the various Pascal data types.

20.   Zaks, Rodnay, Introduction to Pascal
        (including UCSD Pascal);
        Berkeley: SYBEX, 1980.
        A good, swift introduction for the novice.
        The references to UCSD Pascal are not
        always accurate.

A

abs, 44, 49
Adaptive Quadrature, 250-3
American National Standards Institute, see ANSI
American Standard Code for Information Interchange, see ASCII
and, 54
ANSI, 20, 26, 43
arctan, 49-50
array, 11, 65-71, 99, 190-1, 224-6
ASCII, 22, 56, 98, 220, 341
Assignment, 37, 180, 211-2
atan, see arctan
attach, 163-4, 290

B

Backus-Naur Form, see EBNF
Binary tree, 239-41
Block
    I/O, 85, 143-5, 255, 277-9
    in a program, 107-8, 109, 234
    512 bytes, 100, 143-5, 277-9
blockread, 143-4, 279
blockwrite, 144-5
BNF, see EBNF
Boolean, 10, 54-5, 98, 186-7, 202-3, 307
Bootstrap copier, 280
Bowles, Kenneth, 4, 6
Buffer, file, 100, 255

C

Call-by-reference, 119-20
Call-by-value, 119
case
    record, see **record**, variant
    statement, 13, 125-7, 233
    variant, see **record**, variant
char, 10, 56-7, 98-9, 207-8, 220-1

Character set, 22, 309
chr, 60, 98, 221
Clock interrupt, 291
close, 100, 133, 142, 258, 259, 270
Closing files, see close
Code segment, 110, 154-5, 298
Codepool, the, 153-4, 155, 156, 297
Command prompt, 232, 262-3
Comment, 29-30, 185, 311
Compile-time error, see Syntax error
Compiler option, 17, 30, 115, 132, 165-172, 269, 296
Compound statement, 123, 181
concat, 72-3, 228
Concurrency, 16, 159-64, 283-92
Conditional compilation, 170-2
CONSOLE:, 86, 135, 137, 146, 147, 152
const (constant), 190
    declaration, 10, 104-5, 212
Converting data types, 59-60, 301-2
copy, 73-4
Coroutine, 285-8
cos, 49
Critical section, 285
crunch, 142

D

Dahl, Ole-Johan, 1
Data
    storage, see Space allocation and packed
    type, see type
Date, 235-6
Decimal-to-hex conversion, 303
delete, 74
Device handling, see Input/Output, device
Differences from standard Pascal, see Standard Pascal
Dijkstra, Edsger W., 1
Directory (disk), 100, 101
Disk file, see file, external
dispose, 94, 239
div, 42, 43, 44, 52
Double recursion, 251
downto, 130, 191-2
Dynamic types, 84-94, 238-41

E

EBNF, 21
else, 124-5
eof, 87, 139, 259
eoln, 87, 139
Exclusive or, 54, 289, 307
exit, 114, 132-3, 249
exp, 50
Expression, 11, 36, 38, 182, 211
Extended Backus-Naur Form, see EBNF
external, 16, 113, 172

F

Factorial, 177, 215
false, see Boolean
file, 11, 84-9, 100-1
    comparison, 278
    external, 84, 140-3
    interactive, 86, 88, 135, 136, 137, 139, 143
    internal, 84
    record, 84-9
    untyped, 85, 143-5, 277-8
fillchar, 68-9, 301, 306
Flow of control, 12, 123-33, 243-54
for statement, 13, 130-1, 180-1
forward declaration, 103, 109-10, 154
function, 12, 14, 37, 117-21, 200-2, 245-54

G

get, 88, 265-276
Global, see Scope
goto statement, 104, 131-2, 243-4
gotoxy, 152

H

halt, 133
Heap, the, 94, 153-4, 156, 157-8, 161, 297
Hex conversion, 303

Hoare, C.A.R., 1, 2

I

I/O, see Input/Output
Identifier, 25-8, 103, 178-9, 311
idsearch, 28
if statement, 12, 124-5, 187
implementation part, 111, 112-3, 295
in, 77, 231
Include file, 103, 113, 169-70
Indentation, 32-3, 188
Initialization code, 112, 114-5, 295
input, 86, 87, 104, 135, 139, 146
Input, see Input/Output
Input/Output, 15, 135-52, 255-81
    block, 143-5, 255, 257-9
    character, 135-9, 255, 257-61
    device, 146-52, 255, 280-1
    error, 151-2
    record, 84-9, 255, 262-76
    screen, 152, 304-6
insert, 74
integer, 10, 41-5, 97
Integer-to-string conversion
    intrinsic, (str), 60
    sample program, 227
Integration, 250-3
interactive, 86, 88, 135, 136, 137, 139, 143
interface part, 111, 112-3, 295
International Standards Organization, see ISO
Interrupt, 163-4, 290, 291
intrinsic, 115
Intrinsic routine, 3, 12, 44-5, 48-50, 59-60, 63-4, 68-71,
      72-5, 86-9, 93-4, 101, 135-9, 140-5, 147-52, 155-8,
      161-2, 163-4
ioresult, 151-2, 269
ISO, 20

K

keyboard, 86, 146

L

label, 104, 131-2, 243-4
length, 75, 196, 228
Lexical standards, 19-34, 309-314
Linear regression, 260-1
ln, 50
Local, see Scope
lock, 142
log, 50
Long integer, 10, 51-3, 98, 214-6
Lowercase conversion, 257

M

mark, 158
Matrix multiplication, 224-5
maxint, 41, 51, 179, 214
memavail, 156
memlock, 155, 298
Memory management, 153-8, 297-300
memswap, 155, 298
mod, 42, 43
Module, see unit
moveleft, 69, 301-2, 306
moveright, 70, 301, 306

N

Nesting, see Scope and Include file
new, 93, 238
nil, 27, 91, 92, 101, 164
Nim, 286-8
normal, 142
not, 54

O

Object format, see Space allocation
odd, 60, 98, 307
or, 54
ord, 60, 63-4, 220-1, 223, 307
output, 86, 104, 137

Output, see Input/Output

P

P-code, 4, 110, 172

p-System, 5, 6, 17, 86, 87, 100, 133, 140, 146-164, 172, 255, 256, 283, 297

pack, 28, 96

packed, 67, 95-6, 120, 297

packed array of char, 67, 68, 99, 105

page, 139

Palindrome, 195, 198

Parameter, 14, 109-10, 113

    actual, 117-8, 120, 201

    formal, 117-8, 201

    value, 14, 119

    variable, 14, 96, 119-20, 216

Parsing, 245-7

Pascal file, see **file**, internal

Pascal's Triangle, 189

Peripheral device, see Input/Output, device

pmachine, 28

Pointer, 11, 90-4, 101, 238-41, 300, 303-6

pos

    intrinsic, 75

    sample program, 229

Precedence

    declaration, 103

    operator, 38, 43-4, 48

pred, 64, 222

Predeclared identifier, 20, 27-8, 179, 312-3

Prime factor, 184

Print queue, 262-76

procedure, 13, 117-21, 206-7, 245-54

process, 16, 159-64, 283

processid, 160, 161, 283

program

    heading, 103, 104, 178

    termination, 100, 132-3, 142

Prompt, 232, 262-3

Pseudo-comment, see Compiler option

purge, 87-8

put, 87-8, 265-276

pwroften, 50

Q
Quadratic equation, 217-8

R
Railroad diagram, 318-31
Random access, see seek
Range checking, 64, 72, 167
read, 135-6
readln, 136-7, 186, 258
real, 10, 46-50, 97-8, 179, 216-9
record, 11, 79-83, 100, 234-7
    variant, 79, 81-2, 93, 94, 236-7, 264, 302-6
Recursion, 14, 121, 250-4
release, 158
Remote device, see Input/Output, device
repeat statement, 13, 129, 199
Reserved word, 20, 24, 179, 310
reset, 88, 140-1, 258, 269-70
rewrite, 89, 141, 258, 269-70
Roman numerals, 204-5
round, 60, 182
Routine
    declaration, 106, 213
    size limits, 110
Runtime error, 17, 188

S
Scalar, 11, 61-4, 99, 222-3
scan, 70-1
Scope, 107-9, 200-1
Screen handling, see Input/Output, screen
seek, 143
segment routine, 4, 16, 110, 113, 154, 298
Self-paced instruction, 3
semaphore, 58, 162-4, 284, 286-9, 290
seminit, 162, 163, 285
separate, 115
Separate compilation, see **unit**
set, 11, 76-8, 100, 230-3
signal, 162, 163, 284

Simple types, 40-60, 214-21
sin, 49
sizeof, 101
Space allocation, 95-101
sqr, 45, 49
sqrt, 49
Stack, the, 121, 132, 153-4, 156, 250, 297
Standard Pascal, 20, 23, 24, 26, 30, 43, 55, 58, 67, 71,
       84, 85, 86, 88, 89, 91, 96, 101, 103, 104, 110, 120,
       127, 131, 132, 133, 137, 142, 143, 146, 153
start, 160, 161-2, 283
Statement, 317
   assignment, 37, 180, 211-2
   case, 13, 125-7, 233
   compound, 123
   for, 13, 130-1, 180-1
   goto, 104, 131-2, 243-4
   if, 12, 124-5, 187
   null, 123, 317
   procedure call, 117, 206-7
   repeat, 13, 129, 199
   while, 13, 128-9, 186
   with, 82-3, 234, 236
str, 60
string, 3, 10, 71-5, 99-100, 120, 196-7, 227-9
String-to-integer conversion, 227
Structured programming, 1, 9, 200
Structured type, 65-83
Subrange, 11, 62-4, 99, 223
succ, 64, 222
Symbol table, 239-41
Syntax
   diagram, 318-331
   error, 337-340

T

Terminal handling, see Input/Output, screen
Termination code, 112, 114-5
text, 85, 86, 135, 137, 143, 258, 260
time, 150
treesearch, 28
true, see Boolean
trunc, 59-60, 182
type, 36-7

conversion, 59-60, 301-2
declaration, 61, 62, 105, 208-9, 212
Typeless parameter, 68

U

UCSD, see University of California, San Diego
unit, 4, 15, 111-5, 132, 293-6
   intrinsic, 115
   separate, 115
Unit I/O, see Input/Output, device
unitbusy, 147
unitclear, 147
unitread, 147-8, 281
unitstatus, 148-9
unitwait, 149
unitwrite, 149-50, 281
University of California, San Diego, 2
unpack, 28, 96
Untyped file, 85, 143-5, 277-8
Uppercase translation, 220, 231
uses declaration, 111-2, 113-4, 295, 296

V

Value parameter, see Parameter, value
var (variable), 36
   declaration, 10, 106, 178, 212-3
   parameter, see Parameter, variable
varavail, 156, 299-300
vardispose, 158
Variant record, see **record** variant
varnew, 157, 299-300
Version
    I.5,   110, 111, 154-5, 156
    II.0,   110, 111, 115, 154-5, 156
    II.1,   110, 111, 115, 154-5, 156
    III.0,   110, 111, 115, 154-5, 156, 159
    IV.0,   5, 43, 97, 110, 113, 115, 132, 153,
               154-5, 156, 159

W

wait, 162, 163, 284
while statement, 13, 128-9, 186
Wirth, Niklaus, 1, 3, 5, 308
with statement, 82-3, 234, 236
write, 137, 186
writeln, 137-8, 180, 258

X

XOR, see Exclusive or

Y

Yreka Bakery, 199